THE FOUNDATIONS OF NATURAL MORALITY

THE FOUNDATIONS OF NATURAL MORALITY

On the Compatibility of Natural Rights
and the Natural Law

S. ADAM SEAGRAVE

THE UNIVERSITY OF CHICAGO PRESS
CHICAGO AND LONDON

The University of Chicago Press, Chicago 60637
The University of Chicago Press, Ltd., London
© 2014 by The University of Chicago
All rights reserved. Published 2014.
Paperback edition 2016
Printed in the United States of America

25 24 23 22 21 20 19 18 17 16   2 3 4 5 6

ISBN-13: 978-0-226-12343-1 (cloth)
ISBN-13: 978-0-226-38067-4 (paper)
ISBN-13: 978-0-226-12357-8 (e-book)
DOI: 10.7208/chicago/9780226123578.001.0001

Library of Congress Cataloging-in-Publication Data

Seagrave, S. Adam, author.
 The foundations of natural morality : on the compatibility of natural rights and the natural law / S. Adam Seagrave.
      pages cm
 Includes bibliographical references and index.
 ISBN 978-0-226-12343-1 (cloth : alk. paper)—
 ISBN 978-0-226-12357-8 (e-book) 1. Ethics—History. 2. Natural law—History. 3. Locke, John, 1632–1704. I. Title.
 BJ71.S434 2014
 171'.2—DC23
                                                    2013025710

TO ROSIE

Right consisteth in liberty to do or to forbear, whereas Law determineth and bindeth to one of them; so that law and right differ as much as obligation and liberty, which in one and the same matter are inconsistent.
—Hobbes, *Leviathan*

CONTENTS

	Acknowledgments	ix
	Introduction	1
1.	Locke on Natural Rights and the Natural Law	24
2.	Self-Consciousness, Self-Ownership, and Natural Rights	56
3.	From Natural Rights to the Natural Law	83
4.	Natural Morality	120
5.	Practical Applications	141
	Bibliography	163
	Index	171

ACKNOWLEDGMENTS

Earlier versions of material in Chapters 1 and 3 appeared as "Self-Ownership vs. Divine Ownership: A Lockean Solution to a Liberal Democratic Dilemma" (*American Journal of Political Science* 55.3 [July 2011]: 710–23) and "Cicero, Aquinas, and Contemporary Issues in Natural Law Theory" (*Review of Metaphysics* 62 [2009]: 491–523), respectively.

I'd like to thank, first of all, a few formative early influences on my thinking about natural law and related issues in the history of political thought during my graduate career: Walter Nicgorski, Catherine Zuckert, Mary Keys, and John Roos. I was uniquely prepared to receive their wisdom by the faculty at Thomas Aquinas College, and in particular by the guidance and example of Michael McLean. I also owe a very large debt of gratitude to the anonymous readers of earlier versions of this manuscript; this book is much the better for their astute commentary and critiques. Thirdly, I am very grateful to John Tryneski for his faith in this project and for the singular wisdom and prudence with which he guided it to successful completion. The completion of this book was facilitated by a postdoctoral fellowship sponsored by the Jack Miller Center, and for this I am extremely grateful.

The most significant of intellectual debts incurred in the writing of this book is owed to Michael Zuckert, whose interpretations of Locke, natural rights and the history of political thought were absolutely crucial in the formation of the ideas and arguments contained in this book. Without his intellectual guidance, mentorship and friendship, this book would not exist.

I hesitate to hazard an expression of gratitude to my wife, Rosie, since a proper treatment of this topic would fill many books much longer than this one and would require much more eloquence than I could employ. Suffice it to say that without her, books would not be worth writing and life would not be worth living.

INTRODUCTION

The idea of natural law, which has enjoyed one of the longest tenures of any idea in the history of moral and political philosophy, is currently in the midst of one of its periodic resurrections from seeming obsolescence.[1] The origin of this recent revival may be traced to the aftermath of World War II, when philosophers such as Jacques Maritain turned to the natural law as a rational basis for condemning the Holocaust and articulating a moral framework capable of defending human dignity against future violations. Maritain's natural law theory was succeeded by the most widely known version of modern natural law theory, the so-called New Natural Law propounded by Germain Grisez and John Finnis (among others), which has attracted both powerful supporters and vehement critics. The emergence of the New Natural Law theory has, in turn, engendered lively scholarly debates both within natural law theory itself as well as between natural law approaches and modern liberal perspectives.

This renaissance of natural law theory, now reaching maturity at over a half century old, has carried along with it a resurgence of the idea of natural rights, the controversial early modern concept that has served as a conceptual lightning rod of sorts either connecting or disjoining traditional natural law theory and the contemporary idea of human rights. The complex conceptual dynamic between the natural law and natural rights, which had been largely set aside since its initial heyday in the late medieval and early modern periods, was thrust back into the scholarly spotlight in the immediate postwar period by a pair of influential Walgreen Foundation lectures delivered by Jacques Maritain and Leo Strauss. Maritain and Strauss both

---

1. Michael Zuckert, "The Fullness of Being: Thomas Aquinas and the Modern Critique of Natural Law," *Review of Politics* 69 (2007): 28–47.

realized that the time was exceptionally ripe for revisiting natural foundational approaches to moral and political philosophy, including the old but unresolved question of the relation between ancient, medieval and early modern perspectives on such approaches, and each responded to this opportunity in a manner that would become the prototype for opposing sides of a now well-established contemporary quarrel concerning the relationship between natural rights and the natural law.

Maritain argued that natural rights and the natural law were compatible with one another and formed complementary parts of a single natural moral framework, with the modern idea of natural rights being derived directly from and constituting a kind of corollary to the medieval idea of the natural law. The idea of natural rights represented a logical outgrowth of the idea of the natural law, providing a way of expressing certain conditions necessary to living the good life illumined by the natural law.[2] Strauss, on the other hand, argued that "classic natural right," of which the idea of the natural law is a particular variation, is profoundly incompatible with "modern natural right," expressed in terms of subjective natural rights possessed by individuals. Hobbes and Locke, for Strauss, effected a revolution in the history of ideas and marked a sort of "Copernican moment" by inventing a new idea of natural rights that entailed a rejection of preceding expressions of objective natural moral foundations in the medieval and ancient periods.[3] For Maritain the history of moral and political philosophy is a story of gradual and progressive "evolution"; for Strauss, this history is a pitched battle between mutually exclusive alternatives. Each of these positions have only become more entrenched and steadfastly opposed to one another since their initial formulations, as scholars have subsequently marshaled to either side and progressively sharpened each account. As a result we are left both with hopelessly opposed accounts of intellectual history and with profoundly conflicting versions of the natural foundations of moral and political philosophy.

This book represents an attempt to transcend this longstanding debate by offering an entirely new account of natural rights and the natural law in their relation to one another. This account agrees with the Straussian assertion of a historical discontinuity between ancient/medieval and modern versions of natural right while nevertheless denying that this discontinuity

---

2. Jacques Maritain, *Man and the State* (Washington, DC: Catholic University of America Press, 1998), 76–107.

3. Leo Strauss, *Natural Right and History* (Chicago: University of Chicago Press, 1953), 120–251.

is accompanied by an incompatibility or inevitable tension between the two. The modern idea of natural rights is indeed a distinctively modern one, in no way growing out of or deriving from preceding ideas of natural law.[4] Not all new ideas, however, are incompatible with old ones—and such, I argue, is the case with modern natural rights and the ancient/medieval natural law.

Indeed, despite their distinctness in terms of historical origin and logical derivation, the compatibility between the ideas of natural rights and the natural law is so complete as to give rise to a coherent composite concept of natural morality. This idea of natural morality resonates in various ways with rival accounts stretching from Plato and Aristotle to Hobbes and Locke, simultaneously vindicating the truth contained within such disparate accounts and showing their incompleteness when considered in isolation. The discovery of this composite ancient/medieval/modern concept of natural morality constitutes a new attempt to finally redeem the promise of Strauss's and Maritain's influential postwar resurrections of the natural foundational approach to moral and political philosophy, one which both builds upon their insights and unifies the long, distinguished and richly varied history of this approach.

The importance of redeeming this promise extends far beyond the realm of merely academic or intellectual historical debate. Partly—perhaps largely—because of the seemingly insurmountable divisions that have arisen among those concerned with natural moral foundations, popular political discourse has in recent years become increasingly bipolar, segregated into explicitly religious arguments on the one hand and neutralist/antifoundationalist liberal arguments on the other.[5] The former stand on suprarational ground and the latter eschew any sort of grounding in favor of nonrational pragmatic consensus; the ground of natural reason, meanwhile, has been largely abandoned as unfit for habitation.

This bipolarity of political discourse has contributed to serious problems both within the United States and in the international arena. Within the US, religious groups have become increasingly influential in politics as the

---

4. There is an undeniable historical-linguistic continuity connecting the two ideas which is, I argue, insufficient to establish conceptual continuity (S. Adam Seagrave, "Identity and Diversity in the History of Ideas: A Reply to Brian Tierney," *Journal of the History of Ideas* 73, no. 1 [January 2012]: 163–66.)

5. For some of the scholarly sources of this phenomenon see Nicholas Wolterstorff, "An Engagement with Rorty," *Journal of Religious Ethics* 31, no. 1 (Spring 2003): 129–39 and John Rawls, "The Idea of Public Reason Revisited," *University of Chicago Law Review* 64, no. 3 (Summer 1997): 765–807.

sole proponents of timeless moral foundations, and the conflicts between such religious groups and their anti-foundationalist secular liberal counterparts have become increasingly intractable.[6] In the international context, the problems have been even more acute. Since both religious arguments and arguments based on pragmatic consensus are persuasive only among those who already lie within the religious or social group from which such arguments originate, international responses to recent instances of genocide and of radical Islamic violence have conspicuously lacked a unified and coherent justification, resulting in policies that have been either woefully inadequate or hopelessly misguided. Although a myriad of political factors, both domestic and international, have undoubtedly contributed to this problem, the lack of firm and shared intellectual ground on the basis of which to act and persuade in moral matters has been chiefly to blame.[7]

The question of whether such intellectual ground is attainable by human reason, and what it looks like if indeed it does, is precisely the question addressed by philosophers of natural rights and the natural law such as Strauss and Maritain. The failure of such philosophers to sufficiently persuade either each other or the wider academic community of the existence and topography of this ground has significantly contributed to the increasing bipolarity of political discourse, as well as ongoing difficulties in furthering the post–World War II aspiration for a more humane world. If MacIntyre is right that "abstract changes in moral concepts are always embodied in real, particular events,"[8] the persistence of problematic responses to instances of genocide and terrorism since World War II indicates the shortcomings of the changes in moral concepts hazarded in its aftermath. The time is, then,

---

6. Clear examples of this include the same-sex marriage debate and the debate over the Health and Human Services mandate regarding the provision of contraceptives to employees. See "Our First, Most Cherished Liberty: A Statement on Religious Liberty" (United States Conference of Catholic Bishops, Ad Hoc Committee for Religious Liberty, 2012). For a landmark overview of recent trends in religion and politics in the US, see Robert D. Putnam and David E. Campbell, *American Grace: How Religion Divides and Unites Us* (New York: Simon and Schuster, 2010).

7. The issue of international responses to genocide in the post–World War II world is succinctly reviewed and analyzed in Dale C. Tatum, *Genocide at the Dawn of the 21st Century* (New York: Palgrave Macmillan, 2010). Tatum acknowledges the erosion of shared moral "values" as a source of the problematic character of these responses (6), but emphasizes political factors much more heavily throughout. For an earlier and somewhat more sanguine assessment of the postwar experience of shared moral principles—as embodied in the *Universal Declaration of Human Rights*—see Mary Ann Glendon, *A World Made New: Eleanor Roosevelt and the Universal Declaration of Human Rights* (New York: Random House, 2001).

8. Alasdair MacIntyre, *After Virtue*, 2nd ed. (Notre Dame: University of Notre Dame Press, 1984), 61.

once again ripe to revisit the task of Strauss and Maritain and renew the attempt to discern the foundations of natural morality.[9]

CONTINUITY-COMPATIBILITY

Maritain's account established what may be termed the continuity-compatibility position concerning the relationship between natural rights and the natural law. This position consists broadly in the simultaneous affirmation of a continuity between the two concepts, whether this continuity is historical, logical, or both, and a compatibility between them. The affirmation of compatibility is normally cast as a direct conclusion from the continuity between the two concepts; because the idea of natural rights emerged historically from the idea of natural law, or because natural rights are logically derivative from the natural law, the two must be compatible with one another. The continuity-compatibility position has been elaborated in a variety of ways since Maritain by New Natural Law theorists including John Finnis, historians such as Brian Tierney, and political theorists such as Christopher Wolfe. Despite their engagement in otherwise very different projects, each of these scholars takes a position generically similar to Maritain's continuity-compatibility one with respect to the relationship between natural rights and the natural law.

In an important chapter of *Man and the State*, which grew out of his 1949 Walgreen Foundation lectures, Maritain crafts a complex account of the relationship between natural rights and the natural law that subtly blends the historical and logical versions of the continuity position in a cogent argument for compatibility. Written soon after the UN's adoption of the *Universal Declaration of Human Rights (UDHR)*, of which Maritain was a principle drafter, Maritain's discussion is clearly directed toward this political context and explicitly focused on "The Rights of Man." Maritain's aim in this chapter is to set forth his own understanding of the philosophical justification for natural or human rights, or the reasoning behind his own contribution to and endorsement of the *UDHR*.

This understanding turns out to rely heavily on the idea of the natural law; in Maritain's own remarkably clear phrasing, "The philosophical

---

9. This "ripeness" is signaled also by a pair of excellent recent symposia in prominent academic journals on the topic of the natural law and natural rights: *Good Society* 12, no. 3 (2003), which includes contributions from Randy Barnett, Herman Belz, Larry Arnhart, Robert George and others; and *Review of Politics* 64 (2002), which includes contributions from Brian Tierney, John Finnis, and Michael Zuckert, among others.

foundation of the Rights of Man is Natural Law."¹⁰ The idea of natural rights is, in other words, derived from and dependent upon the idea of natural law. Maritain proceeds, accordingly, to elaborate upon his understanding of the natural law before explaining natural rights. Maritain's natural law possesses two distinct aspects: an "ontological" aspect and a "gnoseological" one. The ontological aspect of Maritain's natural law reflects an eternal and unchanging human nature or essence which has a particular "normality of functioning" and a definite set of ends or *telos*.¹¹ The gnoseological aspect of the natural law is the "natural law *as known*" through inclination or "connaturality," developing "in proportion to the degree of moral experience and self-reflection, and of social experience also, of which man is capable in the various ages of his history."¹² While the ontological aspect of the natural law is properly philosophical, the gnoseological aspect is more properly historical.

Maritain derives natural rights from the natural law in its ontological aspect as follows:

> It is because we are enmeshed in the universal order, in the laws and regulations of the cosmos and of the immense family of created natures (and finally in the order of creative wisdom), and it is because we have at the same time the privilege of sharing in spiritual nature, that we possess rights vis-à-vis other men and all the assemblage of creatures.¹³

What Maritain means by this rather vague statement is, as he later attempts to specify, that we human beings possess certain characteristics (particularly a spiritual soul and free will) that set us apart from the rest of nature, bestowing upon us a dignity that transcends the mere fact of our particular existence. Since the natural law in its ontological aspect is simply the normality of functioning of human nature, these rights-bestowing characteristics themselves belong to the natural law. In this way natural rights logically follow from certain natural features of human beings, which are in turn grounded in and belong to the ontological aspect of the natural law.

The derivation of natural rights from the natural law may also be seen clearly in considering natural law's gnoseological aspect. Where the derivation in the case of the ontological aspect was logical—the existence of natu-

---

10. Maritain, *Man and the State*, 80.
11. Ibid., 86.
12. Ibid., 94.
13. Ibid., 95–96.

ral rights is taken to follow from certain characteristics which themselves arise out of the natural law—the derivation in the case of the gnoseological aspect is historical. As Maritain explains,

> Thus it is that in ancient and mediaeval times attention was paid, in natural law, to the *obligations* of man more than to his *rights*. The proper achievement—a great achievement indeed—of the XVIIIth Century has been to bring out in full light the *rights* of man as also required by natural law. That discovery was essentially due to a progress in moral and social experience, through which the root *inclinations* of human nature as regards the rights of the human person were set free[14]

In other words, insofar as natural rights are logically derived from the natural law in its ontological aspect, these rights are eternal and have always existed; insofar, however, as natural rights are actually known to exist, they are a historical by-product of the progressive awareness of the natural law by human beings in history. The derivation from the ontological aspect of natural law establishes logical continuity, while the derivation from the gnoseological aspect establishes historical continuity. Since, for Maritain, moral knowledge is discovered in a roughly Hegelian manner by the necessary progress through history of "man's moral conscience," the logical derivation of natural rights from the natural law ensures the historical derivation.[15] The logical continuity between natural rights and the natural law is, in other words, bound to issue in historical continuity as well.

Maritain's account of the relationship between natural rights and the natural law is still widely regarded as the most important and enduring product of his Walgreen lectures, and it remains perhaps the most complete and profound account of this relationship from the continuity-compatibility perspective. Maritain combines, in concise fashion, an original and seminal natural law theory with an original and seminal account of natural rights. Maritain's two-pronged approach toward the question of continuity between the natural law and natural rights, including both the logical and historical modes, established the two main lines of argumentation for such a continuity that have been pursued since his time. Moreover, Maritain addressed each in a more general and profound manner than has been accomplished by his successors. Whether or not Maritain's account of the compatibility of natural law and natural rights is ultimately persuasive,

14. Ibid., 94.
15. Ibid., 90.

his crucial role in inspiring subsequent theorizing about the relationship between these two concepts should not be overlooked.

Beginning in *Natural Law and Natural Rights* and continuing in more recent writings, John Finnis has constructed an influential argument for the continuity-compatibility position from the perspective of analytic jurisprudence and philosophy. Although Finnis does not explicitly acknowledge an intellectual debt to Maritain, his natural law theory possesses a few striking similarities to Maritain's, and his understanding of the relationship between the natural law and natural rights largely builds upon Maritain's argument for compatibility stemming from logical continuity. Finnis's chapter on rights in *Natural Law and Natural Rights* deals at length, in fact, with an interpretation and discussion of the *UDHR* while curiously neglecting any mention of Maritain's explanation of his own reasoning in helping to draft the document.[16] Whether or not Finnis himself is aware of the ways in which his account of the natural law and natural rights relates to Maritain's, viewing the former in light of the latter provides the most illuminating context for understanding Finnis's own continuity-compatibility arguments.

While Finnis's arguments regarding the relation between the natural law and natural rights are less "ontological" and more analytical than Maritain's, these arguments nevertheless overlap with Maritain's in crucial areas. The modern language of natural rights, for Finnis, is essentially an "instrument for reporting and asserting the requirements or other implications of a relationship of justice *from the point of view of the person(s) who benefit(s) from* that relationship."[17] Finnis's natural rights are "strictly correlative to duties entailed by the requirements of practical reasonableness," i.e., by the natural law.[18] One of these "requirements of practical reasonableness," or duties commanded by natural law, is that "it is always unreasonable to choose directly against any basic value, whether in oneself or in one's fellow human beings."[19] Since one has an absolute duty to refrain from acting directly against any basic value (life, knowledge, friendship, etc.), and since individual human beings are loci for such basic values, one has an absolute duty to refrain from acting directly against a basic-value-in-another. The individual to whom such a duty is owed may, according to Finnis's account, be said to possess a natural right.

16. John Finnis, *Natural Law and Natural Rights* (Oxford: Clarendon Press, 1980), 198–226.
17. Ibid., 205.
18. Ibid., 225.
19. Ibid.

This rather circuitous derivation of natural rights from the natural law becomes more intelligible once its similarities to Maritain's account are recognized. For Finnis as for Maritain, human beings possess a certain dignity that is derivative logically from the natural law. On Maritain's account, this dignity stems from the possession of certain characteristics that belong to human nature, or the natural law in its ontological aspect. On Finnis's account, this dignity stems from the individual's instantiation of basic values and the corresponding natural law duty to respect these values. On both accounts, the natural law establishes a certain status or dignity for human beings, and this status or dignity is in turn expressed in terms of natural rights. Finnis and Maritain thus share a fundamental concern to derive natural rights from the natural law, and to establish the compatibility of the one with the other by means of a logical continuity between them.

Finnis appears to part ways with Maritain with respect to the issue of historical continuity in *Natural Law and Natural Rights* by indicating that a "watershed" exists between Aquinas's exclusively objective use of the term *ius* ("right") and Suarez's subjective use of the same term, and thus that the logical continuity Finnis perceives between the natural law and natural rights does not project onto history in the way it does for Maritain.[20] In his later work on Aquinas, however, Finnis argues that Aquinas did in fact speak of rights in the subjective sense frequently associated with the modern usage, indicating that no "watershed" needed to be crossed after all in traveling from Aquinas to modern natural rights.[21] While Finnis thus ends up endorsing some version of historical continuity as well, the centerpiece of his account of the natural law and natural rights remains his argument for a logical continuity between them.

The case for historical continuity is, however, the centerpiece of Brian Tierney's continuity-compatibility account.[22] As a medieval historian, Tierney is interested to establish the ongoing relevance of medieval moral and political philosophy to contemporary debates, focusing his efforts on arguing for a historical continuity between the medieval idea of the natural law and modern ideas of natural rights. If modern natural rights represent a development of, rather than a departure from, medieval understandings of natural law, then a proper understanding of modern natural rights requires some understanding of the medieval natural law. Tierney argues for his

---

20. Ibid., 207.
21. John Finnis, *Aquinas: Moral, Political, and Legal Theory* (Oxford: Oxford University Press, 1998), 133–36, 170, 176.
22. Brian Tierney, *The Idea of Natural Rights* (Atlanta: Scholars Press, 1997).

historical continuity thesis by providing detailed treatments of numerous lesser-known medieval and early modern philosophers and jurists, suggesting that those who argue for historical discontinuity between the concepts of the natural law and natural rights simply miss the trees for the forest.

According to Tierney the idea of natural rights grew organically together with and out of the idea of the natural law beginning in the twelfth century. Although Tierney acknowledges the importance of late medieval and early modern developments in the concept of natural rights, he maintains that the essential components of these later developments were already present in some form in its early medieval iterations. He identifies these enduring components as the ideas of self-dominion and a permissive natural law, building a convincing body of textual historical evidence for their presence in writings dating to the early medieval period.[23] In identifying these two essential components of the idea of natural rights, Tierney ends up also constructing an argument for logical continuity in support of his primary argument for historical continuity. This, of course, makes sense—since the way in which natural rights emerge historically from the natural law is through the presumably logical thinking of philosophers and jurists, historical continuity of the type advocated by Tierney would be expected to entail logical continuity as well.

Tierney's predominantly historical argument for continuity between the ideas of the natural law and natural rights constitutes a thorough and concrete working out of the more general and theoretical historical continuity argument outlined by Maritain. Maritain had already argued that the idea of natural rights was essentially a potential part of the natural law that required only the gradual progress of history and, with it, "man's moral conscience," in order to come more fully to light. While Tierney's historical evidence for the premodern traces of modern natural rights thinking may have surprised many, his discoveries were in effect predicted by Maritain's general account. While Maritain himself refrained from engaging in the historical research necessary to substantiate his theory of the historical dynamism of the natural law in its progressive and gradual march toward modern natural rights, Tierney's work may be viewed as elaborating upon and providing support for precisely this position. In this way Tierney contributed to the complex continuity-compatibility position originated by Maritain through

---

23. Brian Tierney, "Natural Law and Natural Rights: Old Problems and Recent Approaches," *Review of Politics* 64 (Summer 2002): 389–406; "Historical Roots of Modern Rights: Before Locke and After," *Ave Maria Law Review* 3 (Spring 2005): 23–43; "Dominion of Self and Natural Rights Before Locke and After," in *Transformations in Medieval and Early-Modern Rights Discourse*.

his pursuit of the historical continuity line of argument in much the same way as Finnis did with respect to the argument for logical continuity.

While Tierney's historical continuity argument is generally typical of that embraced by historians of ideas,[24] there is considerable variation among such historians regarding the precise description and depth of this continuity. Richard Tuck, in his *Natural Rights Theories: Their Origin and Development*, provides a particularly ambiguous case.[25] Tuck frames his historical exploration of the history of natural rights thinking as a way of explaining the unprecedented centrality of rights to modern political discourse, a centrality associated with the independence of such rights from the idea of natural law.[26] Tuck introduces a distinction between "passive rights," which are merely the secondary correlates of the natural law duties of others, and "active rights," which imply the broader sort of individual moral sovereignty described in H. L. A. Hart's well-known article.[27] While this distinction and framing would seem to place Tuck at odds with the continuity-compatibility position, Tuck goes on to argue that "It is among the men who rediscovered the Digest and created the medieval science of Roman law in the twelfth century that we must look to find the first modern rights theory, one built round the notion of a passive right."[28] In other words, Tuck proceeds to trace "modern" rights back to the twelfth century—as Tierney will later—and to identify the sort of "passive" rights that are the mere correlates of the natural law with a modern rights theory. Thus, while Tuck's straightforward acknowledgment of the distinction between "modern" rights theories and premodern ones, as well that between "active" and "passive" rights, appears to lead him away from the continuity-compatibility position, the historical arguments that occupy the remainder of the work quickly draw him back into a version of this position.

Francis Oakley presents a similarly ambiguous case, but his ambivalence emerges in the reverse order: after spending an entire book arguing for a strong version of the continuity-compatibility position reminiscent of Tierney's, Oakley adds "a final, somewhat more tentative and diffident

24. See, for example, Janet Coleman, "*Dominium* in Thirteenth- and Fourteenth-Century Heirs: John of Paris and Locske," *Political Studies* 33 (1985): 73–100; and Scott Swanson, "The Medieval Foundations of John Locke's Theory of Natural Rights: Rights of Subsistence and the Principle of Extreme Necessity," *History of Political Thought* 18 (1997): 399–458.

25. Richard Tuck, *Natural Rights Theories: Their Origin and Development* (New York: Cambridge University Press, 1979).

26. Ibid., 1.

27. Tuck, 5–7; H. L. A. Hart, "Are There Any Natural Rights?" *Philosophical Review* 64 (1955): 175–91.

28. Tuck, 13.

reflection" in the closing pages of his work that undermines this position.[29] While Oakley holds fast to the conclusion that "No dramatic breaks are evident" in the intellectual history of natural law and natural rights, he nevertheless admits that "a new modality of ethical thinking had definitively emerged" by the eighteenth century whereby natural rights were perceived to be "morally foundational" and independent of the natural law.[30] Although Oakley ultimately endorses Tierney's historical argument for continuity, he isn't entirely comfortable with this argument.[31]

Christopher Wolfe's account in *Natural Law Liberalism* differs from these intellectual historical arguments by focusing primarily on the issue of compatibility and only incidentally on the issue of continuity.[32] The reasons for this difference may be found first in Wolfe's unique focus on constructing a public philosophy from the union of the two concepts, and secondly in Wolfe's treatment of the somewhat more general and vague idea of "liberalism" in place of the idea of natural rights. Wolfe is thus concerned with showing a more practical sort of compatibility between natural law theory and liberalism rather than with arguing for a theoretical compatibility between the ideas of the natural law and natural rights. This concern with establishing practical compatibility leads Wolfe to treat the issue of continuity, which is of paramount importance for Maritain, Finnis and Tierney, in a relatively brief and passing fashion.

Even this brief and incidental treatment of the continuity issue is enough, however, to establish Wolfe's account as an important instance of the type of continuity-compatibility position originated by Maritain. In a chapter devoted to arguing directly for the compatibility between liberalism and natural law, Wolfe addresses the potential difficulty involving the "centrality of rights" within liberalism and the apparent absence of rights within the natural law tradition.[33] According to Wolfe, "any proponent of classical natural law" should acknowledge the existence and importance of

---

29. Francis Oakley, *Natural Law, Laws of Nature, Natural Rights: Continuity and Discontinuity in the History of Ideas* (New York: Continuum, 2005), 106.

30. Ibid., 109.

31. Cary Nederman similarly embraces a more ambiguous or qualified version of the historical continuity-compatibility position epitomized by Tierney ("Review of Brian Tierney, *The Idea of Natural Rights* and *Rights, Law and Infallibility in Medieval Thought*," *American Journal of Legal History* 42 (1998): 217–19; "Empire and the Historiography of European Political Thought: Marsiglio of Padua, Nicholas of Cusa, and the Medieval/Modern Divide," *Journal of the History of Ideas* 66 (2005).

32. Christopher Wolfe, *Natural Law Liberalism* (Cambridge: Cambridge University Press, 2006).

33. Ibid., 188.

rights for the following reason: "If it is *wrong* for A to hit B, then B can be said to have a *right* not to be hit by A. If it is a principle of justice that A *ought to* give x to B, then B can be said to have a *right* to x from A."[34] This is, of course, precisely the same sort of logical continuity argument elaborated by Finnis and unearthed by Tierney in his treatment of the Spanish Neo-Thomists and their reinterpretation of Aquinas. On this argument, natural rights are simply, in Finnis's terms, linguistic "instruments" for sorting out the particular implications of the natural law, and are thus entirely derivative from and logically dependent on the natural law.[35]

Wolfe does, unlike most of the other continuity-compatibility thinkers since Maritain, seriously consider an objection from the discontinuity-incompatibility side; namely, that the understanding of natural rights indicated by his logical continuity argument ignores the disputed question of the relative priority of natural rights and natural law.[36] Wolfe's response to this objection is twofold: first, the priority issue doesn't pose a problem so much as a choice between two alternatives—one may simply assert the priority of the natural law and deny the priority of natural rights; and secondly, "the need to recognize a larger context for rights [such as, for example, the natural law] is nothing more or less than what many an intelligent liberal would say."[37] In other words, a natural law theorist can circumvent the thorny theoretical issue of relative priority and simply assert the priority of the natural law to natural rights in the manner suggested by the logical continuity argument Wolfe presents. In doing so, moreover, one need not fear that one is alienating at least the more moderate or right-thinking element of the modern liberal tradition.

If Finnis and Tierney (along with Tuck, Oakley and others) primarily elaborate upon the logical and historical continuity part of Maritain's position, Wolfe primarily elaborates upon the compatibility part of this position. Finnis attempts to show that natural rights are logically dependent upon and derivative from the natural law, Tierney provides arguments purporting to illustrate how natural rights are historically dependent upon and derivative from the natural law, and Wolfe focuses on how these two forms of continuity issue in actual practical compatibility. While this is admittedly a substantial simplification of each of these thinkers' overall aims and concerns, even with respect to the single issue of the relationship between

---

34. Ibid., 189.
35. Finnis, *Natural Law and Natural Rights*, 205.
36. Wolfe, *Natural Law Liberalism*, 189.
37. Ibid., 189–90.

the natural law and natural rights, it nevertheless constitutes a defensible distillation of these aims and concerns with respect to Maritain's original continuity-compatibility argument. Considered in this way as a single coherent line of argument, the continuity-compatibility position provides a cogent and compelling portrayal of how our modern idea of natural rights relates to the medieval idea of the natural law.

DISCONTINUITY-INCOMPATIBILITY

Strauss's position, in contradistinction to Maritain's, may be termed the discontinuity-incompatibility position. This position simultaneously affirms a discontinuity between the concepts of natural law and natural rights, whether this discontinuity is historical, logical, or both, and an incompatibility between them. The two components of this position do not stand in quite the same relation to each other as the components of the continuity-compatibility position do; while the affirmation of discontinuity contradicts the primary argument for compatibility, it does not normally provide sufficient support for the affirmation of incompatibility. Rather, the discontinuity-incompatibility position generally works the other way around: since natural rights and the natural law are incompatible concepts in themselves, they cannot blend into one another logically or historically in the way the continuity position argues.

In *Natural Right and History*, which, like Maritain's *Man and the State*, grew out of his Walgreen Foundation lectures, Strauss frames the discontinuity-incompatibility position not in terms of natural law and natural rights, but rather with respect to two versions of what he terms "natural right." Where Maritain sees the subjective "rights of man" in the modern period as an organic outgrowth of the medieval natural law, Strauss sees in "modern natural right" a decisive rejection of and explicit departure from the ancient and medieval "classic natural right."[38] According to Strauss's interpretation, "classic natural right," which was originated by Socrates and includes Plato, Aristotle, Cicero and Aquinas among its proponents, affirms a "natural articulation of the whole" whose exploration is the task of philosophy.[39] Classic natural right emphasizes the "whole" over the individual, as well as the obligations of the individual to conform to the stan-

---

38. Strauss, *Natural Right and History*, 166–202. Michel Villey should also be mentioned as an important contemporary proponent of a similar position on the character of modern natural rights (*La formation de la pensee juridique modern*, 4th ed. [Paris, 1975]).
39. Ibid., 123.

dards of virtue or the natural law over the freedom or rights of the individual considered in isolation. "Modern natural right," on the other hand, involves a "deliberate lowering of the ultimate goal" of human life from wisdom and virtue to mere self-preservation and self-gratification.[40] For the proponents of modern natural right, which especially include Hobbes and Locke, "the fundamental moral fact is not a duty but a right; all duties are derivative from the fundamental and inalienable right of self-preservation."[41] According to Strauss's account, modern natural right arises in explicit reaction to classic natural right and constitutes a clear rejection of it. In this way the incompatibility between the two answers the question of continuity—since modern natural right is profoundly different from, and even in direct contradiction with, classic natural right, the one could not have arisen either logically or historically from the other.

Although Strauss frames his account in terms of classic and modern natural right rather than the natural law and natural rights, these two pairings are interchangeable with one another when considered with respect to the question of the relationship between the concepts within each pair. While the question of how the idea of natural law relates to Strauss's classic natural right is a difficult and meaningful one which has since been the subject of some debate, it is at least clear that Strauss includes the idea of natural law within classic natural right throughout *Natural Right and History*.[42] Strauss's modern natural right is, moreover, essentially identical with the idea of subjective natural rights. The permissibility of treating these two pairings as equivalent for the purposes of this debate is further underscored by the fact that those on the continuity-compatibility side tend to identify Strauss's account as the inspiration for their opposition. More recent scholars who have taken discontinuity-incompatibility positions on the question of the relationship between the natural law and natural rights have also clearly built upon Strauss's original account in constructing their own arguments. Therefore, while Strauss's terminology is somewhat different from that employed by Maritain, he has nevertheless served as the progenitor for a definite discontinuity-incompatibility answer to the question of the relationship between the natural law and natural rights in much the same way as Maritain inspired subsequent continuity-compatibility answers.

The manner in which Strauss's account has served as the inspiration for the discontinuity-incompatibility position since his time may be seen most

---

40. Ibid., 178.
41. Ibid., 181.
42. Ibid., 120, 163.

clearly in the writings of Ernest Fortin. In a review essay of Finnis's *Natural Law and Natural Rights*, Fortin opens his critique of Finnis's continuity-compatibility account by suggesting that Finnis is insufficiently aware of the degree of difficulty of the task he has set himself, since "Defending the synonymity or the fundamental harmony of these two originally antithetical doctrines is unfortunately not always as easy as one would like it to be."[43] Fortin proceeds to elaborate upon this difficulty, arguing that

> In contrast to the natural law theory, the natural rights theory proceeds on the assumption that these same human beings exist first of all as complete and independent wholes, endowed with prepolitical "rights" for the protection of which they "enter" into a society that is entirely of their own making.[44]

The directly contradictory assumptions, or "radically different premises," regarding human nature with which the two theories or doctrines begin ensures that one must choose between them when setting up moral and political foundations.[45] Fortin states this point in Strauss's terms of "rights" vs. "duties": "Rights and duties are said [by Finnis] to be correlative, as indeed they are . . . but this still leaves open the question as to which of the two is the fundamental moral fact."[46] According to Fortin, Finnis fails to recognize that the natural law and natural rights represent distinct, profoundly opposed concepts that stand in competition with one another for foundational status in moral and political philosophy.

Fortin's critique of Finnis's argument provides an exceptionally clear illustration of the contours of this debate by applying Strauss's account in *Natural Right and History* to the question of the relationship between the natural law and natural rights, and directly employing this Straussian discontinuity-incompatibility account in opposition to Finnis's continuity-compatibility account. Although Fortin doesn't directly cite Strauss as the inspiration behind his critique of Finnis, Strauss's influence is obvious throughout. Like Strauss, Fortin frames the interplay between ancient/medieval and modern perspectives in terms of duties vs. rights, and similarly emphasizes the status of each as mutually exclusive candidates for being

---

43. Ernest Fortin, "The New Rights Theory and the Natural Law," *Review of Politics* 44 (October 1982): 590–612, 594.
44. Ibid., 595.
45. Ibid., 597.
46. Ibid., 599.

the "fundamental moral fact."⁴⁷ Underscoring the interchangeability of Strauss's classic natural right/modern natural right pairing with the natural law/natural rights pairing, Fortin locates the logical and historical discontinuity within each pairing at precisely the same point Strauss had three decades earlier, stating that the "watershed" mentioned by Finnis

> is not to be located somewhere between Thomas and Suarez; it occurs with Hobbes, who set the stage for all subsequent discussions of this matter by denying that human beings are political by nature . . . and by proclaiming the absolute priority of rights to duties.⁴⁸

Fortin thus provides considerable clarity to this debate by showing how Strauss's Walgreen lectures provide a cogent and ready answer to Finnis's updated and transformed version of the continuity-compatibility position originated by Maritain in his own lectures.

Fortin's trenchant critique of Finnis's attempted assimilation of natural rights with the natural law overlaps in significant ways, moreover, with the simultaneously raging communitarian-liberal debate. Just as Fortin, following Strauss, perceives a decisive—and regrettable—break in the transition from ancient and medieval modes of thinking about natural morality to modern ones, so broadly communitarian thinkers such as Michael Sandel, Alasdair MacIntyre, Charles Taylor and Mary Ann Glendon attempt to illuminate the novelty and problematic character of the "distinctively modern," "atomistic," "dispossessed" or "punctual" self in comparison with premodern conceptions of the individual in community.⁴⁹ As each of these thinkers notice, this problematic modern "self" originated along with, and is nourished by, modern ideas of subjective natural rights; while the premodern, community-oriented "self" flourished under premodern ideas of classic natural right or natural law. In this way, "communitarian" scholars

---

47. Strauss, *Natural Right and History*, 181.
48. Fortin, "The New Rights Theory and the Natural Law," 602.
49. Michael Sandel, *Liberalism and the Limits of Justice*, 2nd ed. (New York: Cambridge University Press, 1998), 85, 92–93; Alasdair MacIntyre, *After Virtue*, 2nd ed. (Notre Dame: University of Notre Dame Press, 1984), 58–61, 68–70; Charles Taylor, "Atomism," in *Powers, Possessions and Freedom*, ed. Alkis Kontos (Toronto: University of Toronto Press, 1979), 39–61; Charles Taylor, *Sources of the Self: The Making of the Modern Identity* (Cambridge: Harvard University Press, 1989), 25–52, 159–76; Mary Ann Glendon, *Rights Talk: The Impoverishment of Political Discourse* (New York: The Free Press, 1991).

may be discerned on the periphery of the discontinuity-incompatibility position originated by Strauss.[50]

This Straussian position carried on by Fortin and echoed by the communitarians has received further clarification, updating and strengthening at the hands of Michael Zuckert. In a chapter of *Launching Liberalism* entitled "Do Natural Rights Derive From Natural Law? Aquinas, Hobbes, and Locke on Natural Rights," Zuckert pinpoints two issues that appropriately frame the debate between the successors of Maritain and Strauss with respect to the question of the relationship between the natural law and natural rights: the "priority problem" and the "foundational problem."[51] These problems overlap somewhat, with the priority problem referring to the question of which of the two concepts is taken to be more fundamental with respect to the other, and the foundational problem including also the question of even more fundamental foundations such as the disparity between teleological and deontological approaches to moral and political philosophy. In framing the debate in this way, Zuckert clearly echoes Strauss's and Fortin's foregrounding of the issues of priority and fundamentality.

Zuckert also echoes Strauss and Fortin in his approach to these problems, carefully considering the question of compatibility as a basis for answering the questions of both logical and historical continuity. After first discussing Aquinas's natural law theory in itself, Zuckert argues that this theory serves as "unpromising raw material" for deriving the modern idea of natural rights since "there are important elements of Thomistic theory that resist this translation" into natural rights.[52] Zuckert formulates the significant difficulties involved in attempting to fit the idea of natural rights into the idea of the natural law in this way:

> A rights version focuses on self-assertion of agents; the genuine natural law version focuses on the moral command or address to each. The rights version misrepresents, or at least encourages a misunderstanding,

---

50. This doesn't mean that liberal scholars are necessarily associated with the continuity-compatibility position. Michael Zuckert, for example, argues vigorously against MacIntyre's critique of natural rights in *Launching Liberalism* (Lawrence: University Press of Kansas, 2002, 331–63), but is nevertheless clearly on the discontinuity-incompatibility side, as is discussed in what follows. Other liberal scholars such as Dworkin (*Taking Rights Seriously* [Cambridge: Harvard University Press, 1977]; *Justice for Hedgehogs* [Cambridge: Harvard University Press, 2011]) don't clearly address the debate about natural rights and the natural law at all.

51. Michael Zuckert, *Launching Liberalism*, 174–75.

52. Ibid., 187, 185.

of the nature of morality: conscientiousness, not self-assertion, is the proper moral attitude.[53]

The modern idea of natural rights implies the existence of "a realm of personal sovereignty or of free choice," while natural law doctrines only admit of rights "to adhere to the natural law mandate in a truly human way, that is, through the use of the agent's reason and will."[54] The idea of natural rights emphasizes the freedom of the individual considered as an individual, while the idea of the natural law emphasizes the duties of the individual when considered as a part of some larger context. Thus, while continuity-compatibility theorists such as Finnis, whom Zuckert explicitly addresses, may attempt to draw a line of logical and historical continuity between the ideas of natural law and natural rights, they can only hope to do so by dramatically altering either one or the other concept from its typical understanding. In their genuine or definitive forms, the idea of the natural law and that of natural rights have independent philosophical and historical origins and stand in inevitable tension with one another.

Although Zuckert stands generally on the side of discontinuity-incompatibility along with Strauss and Fortin, he significantly parts ways with both in his interpretation of one of the central historical figures in the history of the idea of natural rights: John Locke. While Strauss's Locke does not substantially differ from Hobbes in his understanding of natural rights, Zuckert's Locke elaborates an original and decidedly un-Hobbesian account of natural rights on the basis of an original theory of self-ownership. According to Zuckert's interpretation, Locke's natural rights are "moral" in a way that Hobbesian rights are not since they imply correlative duties of forbearance on the part of others. As a result of this crucial difference, Locke is cast by Zuckert as a constructive thinker, not only rejecting the preceding natural law or classic natural right tradition as Hobbes did, but also providing something that Hobbes did not: a viable new foundation to replace the old. It is for this reason that Zuckert's Locke is said to "launch liberalism" rather than simply to negate natural law.

Zuckert's interpretation of Locke is an unusual and compelling one, differing significantly from more common interpretations of Locke as a traditional Christian natural law theorist, a more cautious Hobbesian, or simply a hopelessly confused combination of the two. While this Locke is undoubtedly on the "modern" side of an intellectual historical divide, he

---

53. Ibid., 185.
54. Ibid.

renders this modern side somehow more palatable than Hobbes and many other moderns do. Although Zuckert agrees with Strauss and Fortin on the incompatibility of the natural law and natural rights as well as on their historical and logical discontinuity with one another, he doesn't think, with Strauss, Fortin and most others on the discontinuity-incompatibility side, that modern natural rights are inferior to or less persuasive than their premodern counterparts. With Locke's distinctive contribution, modern natural rights become at least as theoretically viable as the ancient idea of classic natural right or the medieval one of the natural law.

DISCONTINUITY-COMPATIBILITY: A NEW ANSWER TO A VERY OLD QUESTION

Zuckert is correct to look to Locke for new and persuasive ways to understand the idea of natural rights both in itself and in its relation to that of the natural law, and in what follows I will elaborate upon his recovery of Locke's insight with respect to the grounding of natural rights in self-ownership. I will also argue, however, that Locke's thought illuminates the possibility of a third position with respect to the ongoing debate over the relationship between the natural law and natural rights. While Locke has been generally recognized as the single most important intellectual historical figure for this debate by both sides, or perhaps rather because he has been so recognized, he has hitherto been placed firmly on either the continuity-compatibility or the discontinuity-incompatibility side. The fact that Locke's placement on either side of this debate, as well as his related placement on either side of the transition from the medieval to the modern periods, may be supported with cogent interpretations of his thought evidences the very point that will be argued herein: namely, that Locke provides the key to transcending this debate entirely by indicating a new and more persuasive position than either of the existing ones.

The outlines of this Lockean key emerge by attending to the most persuasive claims of the two major schools of Lockean interpretation, which align closely with the two sides of the broader continuity-compatibility/ discontinuity-incompatibility debate. According to one school of interpretation, Locke is a traditional natural law thinker in the line of Aquinas and Hooker who rejects Hobbes's radical reinterpretation of natural rights. According to the other, Locke's allegiance to the traditional natural law doctrine is only ink-deep; the overall thrust of Locke's thought is, rather, firmly within the trail blazed by Hobbes. The former school of interpretation is, I argue, generally correct in its former point: namely, that Locke subscribes to the idea of natural law, even if it is perhaps not quite the traditional natural law of Aquinas. The latter school, on the other hand, is generally correct in its latter point: Locke's natural rights doctrine, while importantly different from Hobbes's, stands on the Hobbesian side of a watershed in natural rights thinking.

Locke's simultaneous attachment to a version of the ancient/medieval natural law and to a genuinely "modern" version of natural rights jars badly with both the continuity-compatibility and the discontinuity-incompatibility accounts. According to the former account, Locke's genuinely modern natural rights doctrine can't exist; according to the latter account, such a doctrine can't coexist with an ancient/medieval idea of natural law. This unexpected confluence brings us to the following crossroads: either Locke's moral and political thought is simply incoherent, or Locke illumines a third position with respect to the relationship between natural rights and the natural law. My argument that Locke does, in fact, bring to light a viable third position hinges upon his analysis of the individual human being into his objective humanity on the one hand and his subjective unique selfhood on the other, an analysis that is explicitly elaborated in the *Essay* and that runs consistently, though more subtly, through Locke's other writings as well.

This new position suggested by my interpretation of Locke may be termed the discontinuity-compatibility position. As the name indicates, this position, in good academic fashion, simultaneously agrees with and contradicts both of the existing positions in the debate. According to this position, the continuity-compatibility theorists are ultimately correct in their conclusion of compatibility but entirely incorrect in their continuity premises; natural rights are compatible with the natural law despite having their own independent philosophical and historical origins. This new position begins in agreement with Strauss and his successors on the point of logical and historical discontinuity, but ends in agreement with Maritain and his successors on the point of ultimate harmony. Since this ultimate compatibility doesn't arise automatically from continuity, however, and since Locke himself provides only an intimation of this position, elaborating the discontinuity-compatibility position will primarily involve original constructive argumentation rather than creative exegesis of existing texts or thinkers.

Since the discontinuity-compatibility position affirms neither the incompatibility of two different concepts nor the compatibility of two aspects of or variations upon the same concept, but rather the compatibility of two different concepts, this position also issues in a new composite concept which I will call simply "natural morality." Since the ideas of the natural law and natural rights may each be viewed as expressions of the single notion of morality, the composite idea of natural morality that results from the discontinuity-compatibility position combines, I argue, some of the central insights uncovered during the course of intellectual history on this subject. In addition to making sense of intellectual history when looking backward, this idea of natural morality also contains the forward-looking potential to make more sense of contemporary moral and political issues than is currently possible.

If this new position on the natural foundations of moral and political philosophy is persuasive, it may also have significant implications for the more fundamental contemporary debate between "foundationalist" and "anti-foundationalist" approaches to such questions. While the natural law and natural rights define the two most influential foundationalist perspectives on morality and politics, the long-standing debate regarding the relationship between them has given credence to the anti-foundationalist claim that the ultimate truth about such matters either doesn't exist or is entirely beyond our collective grasp. Foundationalist approaches are sharply divided among themselves, while anti-foundationalists are relatively unified largely because they have fewer and shallower grounds for disagreement. The discontinuity-compatibility position would, however, simultaneously combine the independent persuasive force of natural law and natural rights doctrines while cutting across and providing a potential escape from the rigid debate within the foundationalist camp as it currently stands. In this way the new position outlined herein, if persuasive, may constitute an important step toward ultimately restoring foundationalist approaches within moral and political philosophy to their previously dominant status.

I will begin my elaboration of the discontinuity-compatibility position and the new conception of natural morality it makes possible with a detailed analysis and discussion of John Locke's thought. Locke, I will argue, possesses an innovative, sophisticated and coherent understanding of the relationship between the concepts of Divine ownership and self-ownership which underpins, in turn, an innovative and coherent understanding of the relationship between the natural law and natural rights. Contrary to common interpretations, Locke does not simply reject either Hobbes on the one hand or the Christian natural law tradition on the other, but rather embraces central elements of both and combines them in an intriguing and original manner. In addition to this reconciliation of the natural law with natural rights, Locke also intimates a justification for natural rights themselves which is independent from the idea of natural law, relying solely on the concept of self-ownership through self-consciousness. In Chapter 2, I elaborate upon this Lockean insight and construct an original account of and justification for the idea of natural rights stemming ultimately from the descriptive phenomenon of self-consciousness. I argue that this phenomenon logically entails the idea of self-ownership, which in turn entails the normative concept of natural rights by means of what I call an "ordering fact."

Chapter 3 shows how the justification for natural rights in the preceding chapter necessarily entails a justification for the idea of natural law. This is because the idea of self-ownership, which grounds natural rights through one ordering fact, also includes a second ordering fact whose normative implications constitute the natural law. The idea of the natural law that results from this second ordering fact is, I proceed to argue, congruent with the natural law tradition as contained in the writings of Cicero and Aquinas. The way in which this congruence works is set forth through detailed exegeses of Cicero's and Aquinas's texts. These first three chapters present the core arguments for the discontinuity-compatibility position and the idea of natural morality in a symmetrical manner by beginning and ending with detailed textual arguments which are connected by an original account of natural rights and the natural law in their relation to one another.

After presenting these core arguments, I proceed in Chapter 4 to explain how they join to form a coherent account of natural morality that combines the ideas of natural law and natural rights in a way that differs from and is superior to existing arguments from logical or historical continuity. I then explain how this account might be applied to a few issues of contemporary political relevance, suggesting that this application would render the debates regarding these issues more dialogical and constructive while persuasively indicating certain directions for public policy. Finally, I conclude with a brief summary of the manner in which my account broadly relates to intellectual history, attempting to recover and combine both ancient/medieval and modern perspectives on natural morality.

CHAPTER ONE

Locke on Natural Rights and the Natural Law

It is fitting to begin our task with an interpretation of John Locke's writings, since Locke in many ways uniquely bestrides the medieval and modern eras, including crucial features of both intellectual periods in his thought. According to the assessment of Brian Tierney, for example, Locke was simultaneously "an important influence in the formation of modern liberal ideas, including ideas concerning rights," and also a traditional medieval natural law theorist in the mold of Saint Thomas Aquinas or Richard Hooker.[1] Influential and persuasive interpretations placing Locke firmly on either side of the medieval-modern transition abound. For Strauss and Macpherson, Locke clearly stands on the "modern" side of this transition along with Hobbes; for Dunn, Tierney and many others Locke stands just as clearly on the "medieval" side along with Hooker and Aquinas.[2]

This persistent disagreement is indicative of the particular difficulty of intellectual history in comparison to ordinary history—the task of determining the chronology of events is a much more straightforward one than

---

1. Brian Tierney, "Historical Roots of Modern Rights: Before Locke and After," *Ave Maria Law Review* 3 (2005): 23–43, 25.

2. Strauss (1951); Macpherson (1962); Dunn (1969); Tierney (2005). Lee Ward provides an excellent recent example of the "modern" interpretation of Locke in *John Locke and Modern Life* (New York: Cambridge University Press, 2010). Other interpretations along the lines traced by Strauss and Macpherson include Harvey Mansfield, "On the Political Character of Property in Locke," in *Powers, Possessions and Freedom: Essays in Honor of C. B. Macpherson*, ed. A. Kontos (Toronto: Toronto University Press, 1979) and Thomas Pangle, *The Spirit of Modern Republicanism: The Moral Vision of the American Founders and the Philosophy of Locke* (Chicago: University of Chicago Press, 1988), 129–275. For surveys of other overlapping debates in the recent Lockean literature, see Paul E. Sigmund, "Jeremy Waldron and the Religious Turn in Locke Scholarship," *Review of Politics* 67 (2005): 407–18, as well as Zuckert, *Launching Liberalism*, 25–56.

that of determining the chronology of ideas, since events generally exist in a discrete and readily distinguishable form while ideas do not. Persons and events are concrete; ideas are abstract. Any attempt to clearly describe or locate this medieval-modern transition, as well as to place Locke with respect to it, is thus bound to embroil one in a series of overlapping intellectual historical debates, including especially the one already surveyed between continuity-compatibility positions and discontinuity-incompatibility ones. It is, nevertheless, necessary to hazard an overview of the immediate intellectual historical context of thinking about the natural law and natural rights from which Locke emerges in order to fully appreciate the potential fruitfulness of Locke's own doctrine in blazing a new discontinuity-compatibility path of inquiry concerning the relationship between natural rights and the natural law.[3]

Locke's doctrine of natural rights and the natural law may indeed be viewed as the tip of an intellectual iceberg that stretches from Locke back to Francisco Suarez and the Spanish Thomists of the sixteenth century, including intermediate thinkers such as Pufendorf, Hobbes, Grotius and Hooker, among others. In the years, decades and centuries preceding Locke's writings, the concepts of right (*ius*), law (*lex*) and property ownership (*dominium*) gradually developed in a manner that helped to prepare the ground for Locke's own understanding. Along with this gradual conceptual development that connects Locke to a tradition extending ultimately to the twelfth-century jurists, Hobbes's radical outlying departure from this tradition simultaneously separates Locke from it. In terms of his intellectual historical context, then, Locke's own doctrine of natural rights and the natural law may most profitably be seen as the complex and novel product of constructive innovations by fundamentally traditional thinkers and the destructive rejection of the tradition by Hobbes. Pufendorf, Grotius, Hooker and Suarez trace a continuous pathway, however circuitous at points, between Locke's doctrine and the medievals; Hobbes, on the other hand, opens the door to a radically new understanding that turns the medieval doctrine on its head.

The Spanish Thomists, including Suarez along with others such as Las Casas and Vitoria, attempted to build a concept of subjective natural rights into Aquinas's natural law, defining *ius* to mean a "faculty" or "power" inhering in a subject in a manner clearly reminiscent of later ideas of

---

3. For a more extended argument regarding the distinctiveness of Locke's doctrine, see S. Adam Seagrave, "How Old Are Modern Rights? On the Lockean Roots of Contemporary Human Rights Discourse," *Journal of the History of Ideas* 72, no. 2 (April 2011): 305–27.

natural rights.[4] They also spoke of the related concept of one's ownership (*dominium*) over oneself, again bringing to mind later ideas of individual self-ownership.[5] In these ways the Spanish Thomists elaborated upon the preceding natural law tradition in a manner that pointed toward recognizably modern understandings of subjective natural rights. These innovations are, however, exceedingly modest when considered in light of the overarching similarities between the Spanish Thomists and the traditional medieval natural law doctrine. Despite the shift in focus toward the individual manifested by the relatively new significations of *ius* and *dominium*, the Spanish Thomists still conceived of this individual as existing within a thick objective context of natural law, along with the associated contexts of natural human community and God's supreme governance of the world. For Vitoria, for example, the phrase "I have a right" was simply equivalent to "it is permitted" by natural law; the realm of subjective natural rights remained strictly circumscribed within a much more extensive and fundamental context of objective natural law.[6] The Spanish Thomists merely clarified and devoted more explicit attention to the subjective implications of objective moral contexts that were already implicitly recognized by traditional natural lawyers from Aquinas to Cicero and the Stoics.

Hooker, who is now most well-known for Locke's quotation of his writings in the *Second Treatise*, occupies a place somewhat similar to the Spanish Thomists, introducing a few modest elaborations upon the traditional medieval natural law doctrine while remaining firmly within its fundamental orientation by the objective moral contexts within which the individual exists. Hooker's minor departures from the Thomistic natural law doctrine stem largely from his post-Reformation emphasis upon an Augustinian understanding of the Fall and its consequences.[7] While the traditional natural law doctrine views political society as entirely natural, following Aristotle's assertion that human beings are "by nature political animals" in Book I of the *Politics*,[8] Hooker puts an Augustinian twist on Aristotle's develop-

---

4. Francisco Suarez, *Selections from Three Works: De Legibus, ac Deo legislatore* (1612); *Defensio Fidei Catholicae et Apostolicae Adversus Anglicanae Sectae Erores* (1613); *Opus de Triplici Virtute Theologico: Fide, Spe, et Charitate* (1621). Classics of International Law, 20, James Brown Scott, ed. Vol. 1, Latin text, facsimiles from original eds.; vol. 2, English texts, trans. by Gwladys L. Williams, Ammi Brown and John Waldron (Oxford, 1944), *De Legibus*, I.ii.5. See also Tierney, *The Idea of Natural Rights*, 301–15; "Historical Roots," 39; Zuckert, *Natural Rights and the New Republicanism*, 141.
5. Tierney, "Dominion of Self and Natural Rights."
6. Tierney, "Historical Roots," 39.
7. See Zuckert, *Natural Rights and the New Republicanism*, 222–30.
8. Aristotle, *Politics*, 1253a.

mental account of political society. While political society may be natural to human beings as they were originally created, the situation becomes complicated by the effects of the Fall: a pre-political condition of the sort Aristotle describes is not simply part of an argument for the naturalness of political society, but rather a reflection of the consequences of fallen human nature. For Hooker, it is the "defects and imperfections" of fallen human nature—and not human nature simply—that lead to the necessity of political society, introducing the possibility of a state of nature-like situation which Locke seizes upon and significantly extends in Chapter II of the *Second Treatise*.[9] Despite the use to which Locke puts Hooker's innovation upon the traditional Thomistic natural law doctrine, however, this innovation itself is a very modest one. Hooker doesn't so much depart from or alter the received natural law doctrine regarding the naturalness of political society as he reinterprets this naturalness to include a coordinate emphasis upon fallen human nature.

Grotius's innovations upon medieval understandings of the natural law and natural rights are more significant and transformative than Hooker's or Suarez's, so much so in fact that he has been singled out by some scholars as "a last, indispensable arch of the bridge" connecting the medieval and modern periods.[10] Tierney concludes his account of the development of the modern idea of natural rights with a chapter entitled "Grotius: From Medieval to Modern,"[11] Tuck sees Grotius as in many ways the single most pivotal figure in the history of natural rights theories,[12] and even Zuckert, in arguing ultimately for the crucial role played by Locke, admits that Grotius "contributed to the ultimate triumph of the natural rights philosophy" because he "accustomed political men to thinking about politics in terms that the natural rights philosophy would later adopt."[13]

The elements of Grotius's thought that scholars tend to focus upon in highlighting his modern innovations upon traditional medieval thinking about natural rights and the natural law are his well-known "*etiamsi*,"[14] his narrowing of the idea of natural law to predominantly include only respect

---

9. Locke, *Two Treatises*, II.ii.15.
10. Tierney, *The Idea of Natural Rights*, 316.
11. Ibid.
12. Tuck, *Natural Rights Theories*, 58–81.
13. Zuckert, *Natural Rights and the New Republicanism*, 149.
14. That is, the idea that "even if" God did not exist, there would be some place for the idea of natural law. Hugo Grotius, *De Jure Belli ac Pacis Libri Tres* (1625). Classics of International Law 3, James Brown Scott, ed. 2 vols. Vol. 1, Latin text, facsimile of 1646 ed.; vol. 2, English text, trans. by Francis W. Kelsey et al. Washington, DC, 1913 (vol. 1); Oxford, 1925 (vol. 2), Prolegomena.

for natural rights,[15] and his inclusion of an individual power of punishment for offenses against the natural law reminiscent, in a general way, of Locke's later executive power of the law of nature.[16] In each of these ways Grotius does indeed offer significant innovations upon the traditional framework for understanding natural rights and the natural law, innovations that distance him further from the medieval Thomistic doctrine than either Suarez or Hooker. Despite these innovations, however, Grotius does not in fact break with preceding doctrines and inaugurate a distinctively modern mode of thinking about natural rights and the natural law in the way suggested by scholars such as Tuck and Haakonssen.[17] As Tierney and Zuckert effectively show, Grotius's innovations upon the traditional natural law remain fundamentally within the broad orientation of that tradition, with the natural law and its correlative emphasis on the naturalness of human community retaining their primacy over natural rights and the importance of the individual considered in isolation.[18]

In the *De jure belli*, for example, though Grotius does indeed include and emphasize a subjective understanding of *ius*, this particular understanding is derived from the traditional objective understanding in a manner parallel to that traced by the Spanish Thomists.[19] Grotius's objective natural law remains fundamental and his subjective natural rights secondary, even if the former is narrowed to include little more than the latter. And while Grotius does espouse the idea of an individual power of punishment for offenses against the natural law, this power plays a very different and less radical role in Grotius's thought than it does in Locke's.[20] Even Grotius's "*etiamsi*" is not, carefully considered, fundamentally different from the traditional natural law doctrine of Aquinas—just as Aquinas distinguishes the natural law from the eternal law and the divine law, rendering the natural law itself epistemologically independent of belief in the existence of God,

---

15. Tierney, *The Idea of Natural Rights*, 317; Tuck, *Natural Rights Theories*, 67; Zuckert, *Natural Rights and the New Republicanism*, 142–43.

16. Zuckert, *Natural Rights and the New Republicanism*, 230–40; Tuck, *Natural Rights Theories*, 62–63.

17. Haakonssen, "From Natural Law to the Rights of Man: A European Perspective on American Debates," in *A Culture of Rights*, ed. M. J. Lacey and K. Haakonssen (Cambridge University Press, 1991), 19–51, at 25; "Hugo Grotius and the History of Political Thought," *Political Theory* 13 (1985): 239–65; Tuck, "Grotius, Carneades and Hobbes," *Grotiana*, n.s. 4 (1983): 43–62.

18. Tierney, *The Idea of Natural Rights*, 316–42; Zuckert, *Natural Rights and the New Republicanism*, 119–49.

19. Grotius, *De jure belli*, 1,1.3, 2; 1.1.4, 2.

20. Zuckert, *Natural Rights and the New Republicanism*, 230–40.

Grotius grants "a certain place" to the idea of natural law even considered apart from God's existence.[21]

While Grotius thus alters the traditional natural law doctrine in ways that render it more amenable to modern concepts of natural rights, it is Hobbes who first opens the door to a genuine and distinctively modern doctrine of natural rights. Hobbes accomplishes this by entirely detaching natural rights from the idea of natural law, establishing the former as primary and the latter as derived. In perhaps the most frequently quoted passage in all of his writings, and rightfully so, Hobbes asserts that "Right [*ius*] consisteth in liberty to do or to forbear, whereas Law [*lex*] determineth and bindeth to one of them; so that law and right differ as much as obligation and liberty, which in one and the same matter are inconsistent."[22] Where Grotius, Hooker and Suarez all sought to derive a subjective concept of natural rights from the idea of natural law, or to carve out a space within the natural law for such rights,[23] Hobbes begins with a subjective concept of natural rights divorced from the idea of the natural law and proceeds to build a new concept of natural law upon it. Where the preceding tradition conceived of the individual human being as necessarily existing within a thick objective context of the natural law, natural community and God's supreme governance of the world, Hobbes conceives of the individual as an isolated subject. Hobbes's radical break with the preceding tradition of thinking about natural rights and the natural law is so clear that even Tierney is compelled to admit that Hobbes's thought represents a simple "aberration."[24] Although Tuck points out some important elements of continuity between the absolutism of Hobbes's political thought and that of some of his predecessors,[25] with respect to his doctrine of natural rights and the natural law Hobbes presents a clear contrast with preceding thought. It is only with Hobbes that the possibility of conceiving of natural rights independently from the idea of natural law comes into view.

Following upon the heels of Grotius's significant innovations and Hobbes's radical break, Pufendorf reflects some of the uncertainty and even confusion reigning at this transitional point in intellectual history. Like Locke, Pufendorf is difficult to place with respect to Hobbes's modern aberration on the one hand and the innovative traditionalism of those such as

---

21. S. Adam Seagrave, "Cicero, Aquinas, and Contemporary Issues in Natural Law Theory," *Review of Metaphysics* 62 (2009): 491–523.
22. Hobbes. *Leviathan*, I.xiv.3.
23. In the manner ably outlined by Tierney in "Natural Law and Natural Rights."
24. Tierney, "Historical Roots," 25.
25. Tuck, *Natural Rights Theories*.

Grotius on the other. Indeed, Pufendorf's first major work was an attempt to synthesize these two strands of thought, including clear Hobbesian echoes both in his characterization of the natural law as well as in his separation of natural rights from this natural law.[26] The difficulties Pufendorf encountered in this attempt are reflected in his later shift away from both Hobbes's and Grotius's ideas of natural rights. Convinced that Hobbes's natural rights could not be genuine rights since they didn't include correlative duties in others, and believing that the only way to introduce such duties would be through convention or agreement, Pufendorf extended and deepened Grotian conventionalism to the point of denying the existence of genuine natural rights altogether.[27] While Pufendorf's voluntarist concept of natural law appears to have influenced Locke's, especially as Locke presents this concept in his early *Questions Concerning the Law of Nature*, Pufendorf's conventionalist account of rights—and the associated idea of ownership or *dominium*—is precisely what Locke argues against in Chapter V of the *Second Treatise*.[28] Pufendorf may thus be seen as a reflection of the profound difficulty introduced by Hobbes for thinking about natural rights and the natural law; beset on either side by Hobbes's upending of the tradition and the transformed remnants of that tradition itself, Pufendorf found himself unable to finally construct a coherent and persuasive account of natural rights and the natural law in their relation to one another.

If Hobbes's thought represents the unruly youth, and Pufendorf's perhaps the awkward adolescence, of a new modern understanding of the relationship between natural rights and the natural law, Locke's doctrine represents its full maturity. Locke was the first, and also in fact the last, thinker to successfully pass through the Hobbesian doorway to independent natural rights without first unburdening himself of the medieval tradition of natural law. While Locke's concept of natural rights is itself very different from Hobbes's, and his concept of natural law is far from readily identifiable with the traditional medieval natural law, he nevertheless coherently combines

---

26. Samuel Pufendorf, *Elementorum Jurisprudentiae Universalis Libri Duo* (1660). Classics of International Law, 15, James Brown Scott, general ed. Vol. 1, Latin text, facsimile of 1672 ed.; vol. 2, English text, trans. by W. A. Oldfater (Oxford, 1931). See Tuck, *Natural Rights Theories*, 156–58; Zuckert, *Natural Rights and the New Republicanism*, 191–93.

27. Samuel Pufendorf, *De Jure Naturae et Gentium Libri Octo* (1672). Classics of International Law, 17, James Brown Scott, general ed., 2 vols. Vol. 1, Latin text, facsimile of 1688 ed.; vol. 2, English text, trans. by C. H. and W. A. Oldfather (Oxford, 1934), III.v.3. See Zuckert, *Natural Rights and the New Republicanism*, 275; Tuck, *Natural Rights Theories*, 159–60.

28. For a fuller discussion of these issues, see Zuckert, *Natural Rights and the New Republicanism*, 188–204, 248–52; cf. James Tully, *An Approach to Political Philosophy: Locke in Contexts* (New York: Cambridge University Press, 1993), 281.

core aspects of both in a manner that illumines an entirely new understanding of the relationship between the two. The key to understanding Locke's new understanding of the relationship between natural rights and the natural law lies in attending to his reconciliation of what he perceives to be the respective bases of each concept: self-ownership and Divine ownership.

THE NR LOCKE VS. THE NL LOCKE

One of the more controversial issues in recent Lockean scholarship concerns the meaning of Locke's repeated assertions in the *Second Treatise* to the effect that "every man has a *property* in his own *person*."[29] Locke's meaning is obscured by the apparent contradiction this assertion introduces when considered in conjunction with his famous "workmanship argument" in Chapter II.[30] In this earlier passage, Locke declares human beings to be the property of "one omnipotent, and infinitely wise maker . . . whose workmanship they are." The manner in which these two statements are reconciled within Locke's thought goes very far toward determining the relationship between Locke and the natural law tradition on the one hand (especially St. Thomas Aquinas and Hooker) and the Hobbesian natural rights doctrine on the other. Indeed, the most widespread and influential interpretations of Locke's political thought may be broadly defined by their attempts to make sense of this apparent contradiction.

Insofar as Locke is interpreted to privilege the Divine workmanship model of property in human beings, he appears to be a natural law thinker following generally in the footsteps of Aquinas and Hooker.[31] Locke's natural rights, on this account, are derived from this traditional natural law in the manner indicated by the Spanish Thomists.[32] Just as Locke's understanding of self-ownership is equivalent to a "liberty to use" God's property, so "natural rights" are a shorthand expression for indicating the permissions of the natural law.[33] For Locke, since "The world belongs to God and its right disposal is determinable solely by his authority," it follows that "all human values were to be elicited from [the] inexhaustible matrix" of the

---

29. John Locke, *Two Treatises of Government*, II.v.27.
30. Ibid., II.ii.6.
31. Jeremy Waldron (*God, Locke, and Equality*) doesn't fit this characterization quite as well as Dunn, Tully and Tierney, since his emphasis on the Divine workmanship model takes him in a different and less traditional interpretive direction.
32. Tully, *A Discourse on Property*, 64–65; Tierney, "Dominion of Self," 185–92.
33. Tierney, "Dominion of Self," 185–94; "Historical Roots," 36–40.

Creator-created relation.[34] With respect to his historical context, Locke's purpose is to counter the various absolutist theories of Hobbes, Grotius, Pufendorf, and Filmer by showing how "a convincing resistance theory" could be derived from a theory of the natural law.[35]

Insofar as Locke is taken to privilege the self-ownership model of property in human beings, on the other hand, he appears to be a modern natural rights theorist who continues the Hobbesian "aberration"[36] from the medieval tradition in important ways. This Locke follows Hobbes's rigid distinction between "right" and "law," placing the former at the center and foundation of his political theory in contradistinction to and at the expense of the latter.[37] Far from deriving natural rights from the natural law in a benign neo-Thomistic manner, Locke in fact reverses the order of priority by grafting a novel understanding of natural law onto a natural rights-based framework.[38] The "core" of Locke's political philosophy is not the fact of God's ownership of the world and His government by natural law, but rather "the notion of human beings as rights bearers by nature because they are self-owners."[39] Whether he is portrayed as a more cautious Hobbesian, a proponent of "possessive individualism,"[40] or the innovative founder of a new and persuasive doctrine of liberalism, this Locke's historical significance lies not in reestablishing the medieval understanding of natural law as a basis for political philosophy but rather in "launching" a modern political philosophy based upon natural rights and self-ownership.

Each of these conflicting interpretations, like the models of property with which they are intimately connected, possesses a substantial basis in Locke's writings. In support of the first Locke (the traditional natural law theorist, or "NL Locke"), one may cite Locke's early work on the law of nature, his commitment to and frequent arguments for natural theology, his reliance on Hooker and the notion of natural law in the *Second Treatise*, and his Christian convictions. Considering these points, it is indeed plausible to assert with Tully that Locke's purpose in the *Second Treatise* is to "reestablish natural law as a basis for his rights theory."[41] While Hobbes asserted that in the state of nature "every man has a right to everything,

---

34. Dunn, *The Political Thought of John Locke*, 24–26.
35. Tully, *A Discourse on Property*, 54–55.
36. Tierney, "Historical Roots," 25.
37. Strauss, *Natural Right and History*, 226–27.
38. Zuckert, *Natural Rights and the New Republicanism*, 272–75; *Launching Liberalism*, 190–97; Strauss, *Natural Right and History*, 226–27.
39. Zuckert, *Launching Liberalism*, 193.
40. C. B. Macpherson, *The Political Theory of Possessive Individualism: Hobbes to Locke*.
41. Tully, *A Discourse on Property*, 55.

even to one another's body,"[42] Locke's state of nature "has a law of nature to govern it, which obliges every one," teaching that "no one ought to harm another in his life, health, liberty, or possessions. . . ."[43] It is only after establishing that every one is *"bound to preserve himself"* as an implication of God's workmanship and the command of the law of nature that Locke speaks of the Hobbesian-sounding *"right of self-preservation."*[44] Moreover, the *"state of perfect freedom"* which characterizes Locke's state of nature exists only "within the bounds of the law of nature."[45] Lockean natural rights, it seems, follow as a consequence from the prior duties and permissions of the natural law.

Proponents of the second Locke (the modern natural rights theorist, or "NR Locke"), however, may claim a similarly plausible basis in Locke's texts for their interpretation. Despite Locke's frequent invocations of the law of nature throughout the *Second Treatise*, it was nevertheless, as Laslett remarks, "always 'beside his present purpose' for Locke to demonstrate the existence and content of natural law."[46] Although Locke devoted his early *Questions Concerning the Law of Nature* to precisely this task, he declined to publish it even at the persistent urging of his friend Tyrrell.[47] Moreover, Locke's treatment of the natural law in the *Questions* falls far short of either adequately addressing Laslett's complaint or establishing the continuity of his thought with Aquinas and the Spanish neo-Thomists.[48] Locke's *Questions* may, in fact, rather indicate his rejection of the traditional natural law framework and a closer affinity to Hobbes.[49] In Question VI, Locke considers the Thomistic contention that the natural law may be known "from the natural inclination of mankind," and answers simply, *Negatur*.[50] Locke also denies Aquinas's assertion that certain basic precepts of the natural law are "known to all," frequently insisting that the natural law is known only to "the sounder and more perceptive part" of mankind and only with the application of considerable industry and self-control.[51] Further, Locke asserts in the *Questions* that the immortality of the human

---

42. Hobbes, *Leviathan*, I.xiv.4.
43. Locke, *Two Treatises*, II.ii.6.
44. Ibid., II.ii.6–11.
45. Ibid., II.ii.4; cf. II.v.30; II.vi.59.
46. Peter Laslett, "Introduction" to *Two Treatises*, 82.
47. Locke, *Questions*, 44–45.
48. Horwitz, "John Locke's *Questions Concerning the Law of Nature*: A Commentary."
49. Zuckert, *Natural Rights and the New Republicanism*, 187–215, 272–75; *Launching Liberalism*, 187–93.
50. Locke, *Questions*, fol. 61. cf. St. Thomas Aquinas, *Summa Theologica*, I-II.94.2.
51. Locke, *Questions*, fol. 16–17. cf. Aquinas, *Summa Theologica*, I-II.93.2.

soul "must . . . be necessarily assumed for the existence of the law of nature," since "law will have no force if there is no punishment."[52] In the *Essay*, however, Locke carefully avoids the task of establishing the "certainty, or probability of a future State," affirming only that such a state "is at least possible."[53] In *The Reasonableness of Christianity*, Locke further states that "Before our Saviour's time, the Doctrine of a future State, though it were not wholly hid, yet it was not clearly known in the World. 'Twas an imperfect view of Reason. . . ."[54]

On the basis of these and other considerations adduced by advocates for "NR Locke," one may conclude that Locke's early work on the law of nature, which represents his fullest and most systematic treatment of this law, only raises more questions regarding the character and status of his natural law doctrine than it answers. Locke's commitment to a doctrine of natural rights, on the other hand, is abundantly clear from the political philosophy of the *Second Treatise*. Locke's stated purpose in the *Second Treatise* is, after all, precisely to show how "*Political power*," or a "*right* of making laws,"[55] arises from the consent of natural rights-bearing individuals and to establish its proper end in the protection of these rights. Since Locke identifies "the *Idea* of *Property*" with "a right to any thing,"[56] his many statements regarding "property" throughout the *Second Treatise* may be readily translated into rights-language without altering Locke's meaning. Thus, in concluding his detailed discussion of property (i.e., rights) in Chapter V, Locke in effect states that "man, by being master of himself, and *having a right to his own person (proprietor of his own person), and the actions or labour of it, had still in himself the great foundation of rights (property)*."[57] Locke's frequently recurring formulation of the primary end or purpose of political society may also be accurately restated in terms of rights: "The great and *chief end*, therefore, of men's uniting into commonwealths, and putting themselves under government, *is the protection of their rights (preservation of their property)*."[58]

The failure of a government to pursue this end, according to Locke, constitutes a justification for revolution. Since this point represents the most

---

52. Locke, *Questions*, fol. 76. cf. *Essay*, II.xxi.55; II.xxviii.5.
53. Locke, *Essay*, II.xxi.70.
54. Locke, *Reasonableness*, 203.
55. Locke, *Two Treatises*, II.i.3.
56. Locke, *Essay*, IV.iii.18.
57. Locke, *Two Treatises*, II.v.44.
58. Ibid., II.ix.124.

important and far-reaching practical-political consequence of the *Second Treatise*, it merits quotation at length:

> Whensoever therefore the *legislative* shall transgress this fundamental rule of society; and either by ambition, fear, folly or corruption, *endeavour to grasp* themselves, *or put into the hands of any other, an absolute power* over the lives, liberties, and estates [i.e., the property or rights] of the people; by this breach of trust they *forfeit the power* the people had put into their hands for quite contrary ends, and it devolves to the people, who have a right to resume their original liberty, and, by the establishment of a new legislative, (such as they shall think fit) provide for their own safety and security, which is the end for which they are in society.[59]

It is only because "the people" possess the rights to life, liberty, and external property both before and after the formation of political society and its government that they also possess a right to revolt. Locke noticeably refrains from invoking some variation of the traditional resistance doctrine associated with the natural law, that "an unjust law is no law"; natural rights, not the natural law, appear to form the core of Locke's resistance theory.

The fundamental disagreement between these two interpretations is a consequence of the shared assumption that a coherent Locke cannot travel both directions on a one-way street; he must either derive natural rights from the natural law, or the natural law from natural rights. Locke must be either "NL Locke" or "NR Locke," traditional or modern; an "NLNR Locke" is an inconsistent or incoherent Locke.[60] This assumption is precisely parallel to that of the incompatibility of Divine ownership and self-ownership of the individual human being. Locke, however, did not perceive, and need not have perceived, an insurmountable difficulty in reconciling the fact of God's property in His workmanship with human beings' property in themselves. However undeveloped and implicit it may be in Locke's writings, the means of such a reconciliation is discernible throughout these writings. In drawing out and clarifying a Lockean solution to the troublesome notions of ownership and property with respect to individual human

---

59. Ibid., II.xix.222.
60. Simmons (*The Lockean Theory of Rights*, 68–79) is a notable exception to this characterization, though his attempt to stake out a middle position within this debate is very different from the one that follows. Simmons' Locke is a kind of moral "pluralist" (79), while the Locke depicted in what follows might more accurately be described as a dual-foundationalist.

beings, a resolution of the conflict between the "NL Locke" and the "NR Locke" comes into view.

WORKMANSHIP, PROPERTY AND LOCKE'S "POTTER-GOD"

It is appropriate to begin the development of this Lockean solution with an examination of Locke's *Questions Concerning the Law of Nature*, since this early work contains the germs of many of Locke's later and more familiar writings. Locke's *Questions* is, as Robert Horwitz accurately notes, "uncommonly complex and perplexing, even when measured by the standards set by his other works."[61] As a result of such difficulties in interpretation, this early text provides pliable material which may be molded in support of a variety of interpretations of Locke's more mature works. On the one hand Locke's *Questions* may be plausibly cited as evidence for the fundamental place of the traditional natural law and Divine workmanship in Locke's political thought.[62] On the other it may in fact lend support to arguments which depict a more distinctively "modern" Locke who abandons the traditional natural law framework and the Divine workmanship model in favor of the natural rights framework and the self-ownership model which prominently emerge in his later writings.[63] Alternatively, the complexity and interpretive difficulties present in Locke's *Questions* may simply reflect Locke's ultimate confusion regarding the status of a natural law framework which he stubbornly holds despite the insuperable difficulties of rationally establishing its existence.[64]

The most plausible interpretation of Locke's *Questions* possesses elements of each approach. In his *Questions* Locke sets forth a particular version of the natural law/Divine workmanship framework which he finds more persuasive than preceding versions (i.e., those of Grotius and Aquinas). Locke's own version, however, is undoubtedly heterodox in its retreat to a minimalist conception of the Creator as little more than a necessary supposition for human existence and the ordered regularities of nature. This conception of the Creator in Locke's preferred version of the natural law, besides introducing potential difficulties in establishing the natural law as

---

61. Robert Horwitz, "John Locke's *Questions Concerning the Law of Nature*: A Commentary," 252.
62. Cf. James Tully, *A Discourse on Property*, 38–50, 63.
63. Cf. Robert Horwitz, "John Locke's *Questions*: A Commentary;" Michael Zuckert, *Launching Liberalism*, 169–97.
64. Cf. John Dunn, *The Political Thought of John Locke*, 25.

a *law*,⁶⁵ leaves sufficient philosophical "room" for the robust doctrine of natural rights and self-ownership that emerges in his later works. Thus, while the *Questions* does evidence the importance of the natural law/Divine workmanship framework to Locke's political philosophy, it is a relatively controversial, minimalist and undeveloped conception that does not preclude the emergence of a strong natural rights/self-ownership framework alongside it.

Throughout the *Questions*, Locke almost entirely avoids any reference to Revelation or the distinctively Christian conception of God in exploring the central elements of the natural law. Indeed, Locke explicitly removes Revelation from his discussion of the natural law as a possible "means of knowledge which . . . does not concern our present argument."⁶⁶ Locke's God in the *Questions* is, in fact, little more than a "potter-God" who effects the original formation of "clay" into a distinctive shape and possesses the power to destroy His vessel.⁶⁷ In Question V, Locke presents his strongest argument for the existence of God, whose "superior will" is required for the existence of the natural law,⁶⁸ by asserting simply that "all the multitude of inanimate beings or animals other than man cannot produce man, who is far more perfect than they; nor can man produce himself."⁶⁹ Therefore, according to Locke, "there exists some creator other than ourselves, more powerful and wiser, who at his pleasure can bring us into being, preserve, and destroy us."⁷⁰ Within Locke's account, this creator is not identifiable as the God of the Old or New Testaments; it is simply "some superior power," or "some powerful and wise being who has jurisdiction and power over men themselves."⁷¹ Although Locke explicitly invokes the analogy of the "potter" and "clay" at the conclusion of the argument, he does not quote or provide any reference to its biblical source.⁷² The important point, for Locke's purposes, is that the "potter-God" possesses a "will" and the power to enforce obedience to this will.⁷³

This argument possesses remarkable similarities both with Locke's argument for the existence of God in the *Essay Concerning Human Understanding* and with the "workmanship" argument in the *Two Treatises*. In

---

65. See Zuckert, *Launching Liberalism*, 188–91.
66. John Locke, *Questions*, fol. 23.
67. The reference here is drawn from Romans 9:21, Isaiah 29:16, and Isaiah 30:14.
68. John Locke, *Questions*, fol. 12.
69. Ibid., fol. 54.
70. Ibid., fol. 55–56.
71. Ibid., fol. 58.
72. Ibid.
73. Cf. fol. 87.

the *Essay*, Locke grounds his argument for God's existence in the proposition that "Non-entity cannot produce any real Being," or that "what had a Beginning, must be produced by something else."[74] Locke goes on to argue that the necessary eternal Being *"must be also the most powerful"* since "what had its Being and Beginning from another, must also have all that which is in, and belongs to its Being from another too. All the Powers it has, must be owing to, and received from the same Source."[75] These statements closely parallel Locke's assertions in the *Questions* that (1) "nothing might be the cause of itself"[76] and that (2) "we owe to him (the creator) and to him alone our body, soul, life, whatever we are, whatever we possess, and also whatever we can be."[77] The *Essay* and the *Questions* present a remarkably similar conception of the natural (i.e., abstracting from a consideration of superadded grace) relationship between God and humankind: (1) God is the necessary supposition for the fact that human beings are something rather than nothing, and (2) His will is the only explanation for why human beings possess the particular arrangement of powers, abilities and characteristics which distinguish them from other created beings.

In the "workmanship" argument of the *Second Treatise*, Locke states that since human beings are "all the workmanship of one omnipotent, and infinitely wise maker . . . they are his property, whose workmanship they are, made to last during his, not one another's pleasure . . ."[78] Locke's use of the term "workmanship" and the particular phrase "made to last" when speaking of the relationship between God and humankind evokes an image strikingly similar to that of the "potter-God" presented in the *Questions*. The God of the "workmanship" argument makes human beings to last "during his . . . pleasure," just as the "potter-God" of the *Questions* "at his pleasure can bring us into being, preserve, and destroy us."[79] The God of the *Questions*, the *Essay*, and the "workmanship" argument of the *Second Treatise* does little beyond giving existence to human beings and furnishing them with a particular arrangement of powers or "like faculties."[80] In fact, the "workmanship" argument itself, viewed within its context, is as much an argument for the limits of God's relationship to humankind as it is for the existence of such a relationship. Although it is important for Locke that

---

74. John Locke, *An Essay Concerning Human Understanding*, IV.x.3.
75. Ibid., IV.x.4.
76. Locke, *Questions*, fol. 54.
77. Ibid., fol. 88.
78. Locke, *Two Treatises*, II.ii.6.
79. Locke, *Questions*, fol. 56.
80. Locke, *Two Treatises*, II.ii.6.

human beings receive their existence and powers from God, it is equally important for his purposes that human beings do *not* receive "an undoubted right to dominion and sovereignty" from God.[81] In the "workmanship" argument, therefore, we appear to be presented with the same "potter-God" who plays a prominent role in the *Questions*.

CONCURRENT UNIVOCAL PROPERTY

In addition to providing the clearest account of Locke's conception of the proprietary relationship between humankind and their Creator, an account which recurs in both the *Essay* and the *Second Treatise*, the *Questions* also intimates the manner in which God's property in humankind may coexist with human beings' property in themselves and external objects. In an important passage within Question VIII, Locke asserts that

> Since god is superior to all things, and he holds as much right and authority [*jus et imperium*] over us as we cannot hold over ourselves ... it is right that we live according to the prescription of his will. God has created us out of nothing and, if it is his pleasure, he will return us to nothing again. We are, therefore, subject to him by supreme right [*summo jure*] and absolute necessity [*summa necessitate*].[82]

Although Locke is attempting to describe God's "right and authority" over humankind, he begins by defining it negatively in terms of human beings' right and authority over themselves. God's right and authority over humankind is simply what is left over after the limit of human beings' right and authority over themselves is reached; or, alternatively, it is the difference between the total "amount" of right and authority under which human beings exist and that portion which they hold over themselves. As circuitous and odd as this description appears, Locke's phrasing (*tantum ... quantum*) clearly indicates such an understanding. The sentence which follows clarifies this understanding by restating in concise form the central attribute of the "potter-God:" the ability to create *ex nihilo* and to preserve or destroy created beings at "his pleasure." This unique ability is the source of God's portion of right and authority over human beings, and introduces a relation of dependence in addition to the independence which follows from human beings' right and authority over themselves. Locke concludes by

---

81. Ibid., II.ii.4.
82. Locke, *Questions*, fol. 88–89.

characterizing God's right and authority over humankind, which has been described in both negative and positive terms in the preceding two sentences, as "highest," "supreme" or "absolute" (*summum*).

Later in the *Questions*, Locke returns to the problematic issue of the coexistence of Divine and human ownership or property with respect to the same object in refuting an objection drawn from the Bible. The argument Locke opposes claims that the obligation of the law of nature "can be suspended by the command of god," and therefore that this law is not binding in a "perpetual and universal" manner.[83] In the particular biblical example provided, Locke's objector claims that God may suspend the law of nature which prescribes that "to each should be given what belongs to him or that no one should seize what belongs to another . . ."[84] Locke answers this objection by asserting that "were god to command a person not to return a thing he has received as a loan, the obligation of the law of nature would not cease, but the ownership [*dominium*] of the thing itself." Locke goes on to explain how this is possible: "For the goods of fortune are never ours in such a way that they cease to belong to god. He is the supreme master [*supremus dominus*] over all things . . ."[85]

This passage indicates two important features of Locke's understanding of the coexistence of Divine and human ownership of particular objects. First, the "thing . . . received as a loan" is not in any way conceived to be owned by the receiver prior to God's special command; the receiver's mere *use* of the thing loaned does not give him a property right in it. The lender possesses exclusive ownership (vis-à-vis other human beings) of the thing prior to God's command, and the receiver possesses exclusive ownership of it after God's command. Secondly, Locke's depiction of the concurrent ownership of God and human beings in particular objects significantly differs from the lender/receiver structure of ownership. While the user of a thing loaned does not in any way own the thing, the lender himself *does* despite the "supreme" ownership of God.

It is clear from both of these passages in the *Questions* that when Divine and human ownership coexist with respect to the same object, the object is God's property to a higher degree than or in a superior sense to that in which it is the property of the human being. What is not immediately clear, however, is precisely how this hierarchical structure of ownership ought to be understood or described. Perhaps the most widely accepted in-

---

83. Ibid., fol. 102.
84. Locke, *Questions*.
85. Locke, *Questions*.

terpretation is encapsulated by Tully: "Man's property is the right to use and preserve what is essentially God's property, similar to a tenant's property."[86] Arguing in a similar manner, Tierney characterizes Locke's doctrine of concurrent Divine and human property rights as the "standard medieval doctrine" which distinguishes between *dominium directum* (ultimate ownership) and *dominium utile* (ownership of use).[87]

The interpretation of Locke's "property" given by Tully, Tierney and others in a similar vein does indeed accurately represent the relationship between God's property and that of humankind as a whole in creation considered also as a whole. The text which the proponents of this interpretation are wont to cite is Locke's statement in the *First Treatise* that "In respect of God, the Maker of Heaven and Earth, who is sole Lord and Proprietor of the whole World Man's Propriety in the Creatures is nothing but a *Liberty to use them*, which God has permitted . . ."[88] The terms of Locke's statement are (1) God, the Maker of Heaven and Earth; (2) the whole World; (3) Man in general, or humankind; and (4) Creatures in general, or Creation. The complex proprietary relationship which arises out of the interaction of these four terms in Locke's statement may be derived, according to Locke, both from "natural *reason*" and from "*revelation*." Natural reason indicates that "men, being once born, have a right to their preservation, and consequently to meat and drink, and such other things as nature affords for their subsistence," while Revelation indicates that, as a result of the "grants God made of the world to *Adam*, and to *Noah*, and his sons, it is very clear, that God . . . *has given the earth to the children of men;* given it to mankind in common."[89] The conventional interpretation of Lockean property expounded by Tully and Tierney adequately handles the proprietary relationship between the four terms identified within Locke's quotation above; this proprietary relationship is Locke's primary concern throughout the *First Treatise* within the context of his critique of Filmer. The conventional interpretation noticeably falters, however, once the terms of the proprietary relationship are altered to reflect other aspects of Locke's doctrine of property which emerge in the *Second Treatise*.

How, for instance, does this relationship look once the four terms are expressed as (1) God, the Maker of Heaven and Earth; (2) the whole World; (3) *a particular human being;* and (4) *himself*? This is, of course, another

86. James Tully, *A Discourse on Property*, 114.
87. Brian Tierney, "Dominion of Self and Natural Rights Before Locke and After," 177.
88. Locke, *Two Treatises*, I, 39. Quoted in Tully, *A Discourse on Property*, 62, and Tierney, "Dominion of Self," 177.
89. Locke, *Two Treatises*, II.v.25.

way of asking how the property right of Locke's "potter-God" of the *Questions* or the "workmanship" argument coheres with Locke's assertion of a particular human being's property right in or ownership of a particular object, such as himself or his "person." Many scholars, including Tully and Tierney, simply apply Locke's characterization of the "inclusive" or general proprietary relation to the "exclusive" or particular case.[90] Just as the property of humankind in creation as a whole ("inclusive" property) is nothing but a "liberty to use" creation in an inclusive manner, so the property of a particular human being in a particular object ("exclusive" property) is nothing but a "liberty to use" the particular object in an exclusive manner. This simple application of the general to the particular case, however, leads to conclusions that are both at variance with much of Locke's texts and lack the moral implications of exclusive property or private rights.

First, the application of a distinction between *dominium directum* and *dominium utile*, or ultimate ownership and use-ownership, to particular or exclusive property is nowhere indicated by Locke himself. Indeed, even the term "exclusive property" is redundant in the context of Locke's doctrine; Locke's "property," which remains undifferentiated and univocal throughout his writings, consistently implies exclusivity. In discussing proprietary claims in particular objects, Locke distinguishes between the relative nobility of the ownership attributed to God and to human beings as well as the object of the ownership of each. These are distinctions of accidental quality and relation; neither occurs at the level of the *kind* of ownership. The distinctions between "ultimate" ownership and "tenant" ownership, or "inclusive" and "exclusive" property, on the other hand, do occur at this higher-order level. Locke's distinction with respect to the relative nobility of ownership emerges most clearly in the *Questions*, while his distinction with respect to the object of ownership is primarily treated in the *Essay* and the *Two Treatises*.

In the *Questions*, Locke divides the "right and authority" under which human beings exist into two portions: God's, or that portion which we "cannot hold over ourselves," and ours (that portion which we *can* hold over ourselves).[91] He then designates God's portion as the higher or more noble one by attributing the "supreme right" over human beings to God. Locke could, at this juncture, have introduced the standard distinction between ultimate ownership and use-ownership, or essential ownership and

---

90. The terminology of "exclusive" and "inclusive" rights or property is taken from Tully, *A Discourse on Property*, 60–61.
91. Locke, *Questions*, fol. 88–89.

derivative ownership. Instead of utilizing these more rigid distinctions and marking out God's ownership as the "essential" or "real" *kind*, however, Locke describes God's ownership as somehow different *in degree*, or "the highest." Similarly with respect to particular objects other than human beings themselves, Locke designates God as the "supreme master over all things" without either denying the concurrent dominion of a human being or invoking a clear essential/derivative or owner/user distinction.[92] In these passages, Locke affirms the simultaneous or concurrent ownership by God and human beings of particular objects, including human beings themselves, and distinguishes between higher and lower (or more and less noble) forms of ownership. Far from drawing a distinction in kind between the ownership attributed to each, Locke's text indicates that the concurrent ownership of God and human beings ought to be understood univocally.

The proprietary claims of two distinct entities, such as God and a human being, can only be both concurrent (in the same object) and univocal (identical in *kind* or meaning) if there is a way in which the object owned may be understood to be *two* within one. In other words, if an object may be divided into two by the understanding while remaining unified in its concrete existence, each object distinguished by the understanding may have a different owner. It is in this way that concurrent univocal ownership becomes possible. In the present case, if a particular human being may be divided into two by the understanding, the concurrent univocal ownership of a human being by God and the human being himself is possible. Such a division is, in fact, implied throughout Locke's texts, and especially within the *Essay* and the *Second Treatise*. Locke consistently employs a twofold consideration of human beings, in terms of (1) the particular arrangement of powers or faculties that distinguishes humankind from other creatures (and simple nonbeing), and (2) the self-consciousness and personhood that distinguishes one human being from another. Considering the human being in light of (1), he is owned by God; considering the human being in light of (2), he owns himself.[93]

In the *Second Treatise*, the "workmanship" argument presents a clear instance of Locke's consideration of human beings in light of the powers that distinguish humankind in general from other creatures. Locke begins the argument by identifying the "law of nature" with "reason," i.e., a power

---

92. Ibid., fol. 102.

93. Tully in fact affirms a similar-sounding interpretation of Lockean property in *A Discourse on Property*, 105–110, but maintains that Locke held a fundamentally Thomistic, or pre-Grotian, understanding of ownership, property and rights. This interpretation of Locke's understanding of property and rights is challenged in what follows.

or faculty specific to humankind but not unique to any particular human being. Immediately after the assertion that human beings are "his property, whose workmanship they are," Locke refers to the "like faculties" with which human beings are similarly "furnished."[94] The "workmanship" argument speaks only of human beings *as* particular members of a species or kind and endowed with the powers or faculties proper to this kind. Considered in this way, and leaving aside the ways in which one particular human being is distinguished from another, human beings are clearly owned by the "potter-God" of the *Questions* who originally fashioned them out of nothing.

In Chapter V of the *Second Treatise*, Locke moves away from the common and toward the particular. Locke first reiterates that "the earth, and all inferior creatures, [are] common to all men,"[95] i.e., humankind in general has been given dominion over the earth and inferior creatures by the grant of God and the duty of self-preservation.[96] Thus far, humankind is the property and workmanship of God and human ownership is, if it exists at all, a simple use-ownership (the standard medieval *dominium utile*). "Yet," Locke continues, "every man has a *property* in his own *person*: this no body has any right to but himself. The *labour* of his body, and *work* of his hands, we may say, are properly his." This brief passage speaks strongly, and even definitively, against applying the interpretations of Tully and Tierney to Locke's arguments in the *Second Treatise*.

First, Locke draws a clear distinction between what is "common" and what he describes as the *"property"* of human beings; the earth, and all inferior creatures, are evidently *not* the property of humankind in general. If Locke had intended to distinguish between two kinds of property, or two instances of the same kind of property, his use of the locution "though . . . yet" is simply inexplicable. If the earth, and all inferior creatures, are to be understood as the property of humankind in the standard mode of use-ownership or "inclusive" property, there is no reason why the fact that "every man has a *property*" in something would seem to be excluded by Locke's initial statement about what is "common." Similarly, if Locke understands the exclusive property every man has in his "own *person*" as a *"Liberty to use"* his own person in a manner similar to his liberty to use "the earth, and

---

94. Locke, *Two Treatises*, II.ii.6.
95. Ibid., II.v.27.
96. See II.v.25. This passage gives a kind of recapitulation of Locke's arguments throughout the *First Treatise*, in which he is concerned to refute Filmer's conception of private property rights by arguing for the existence of an original commons.

all inferior creatures," one would expect the two statements to be conjoined rather than sharply contrasted.

The sharp contrast drawn in this key passage between what is "common" and "property" is, in fact, the organizing theme of Chapter V of the *Second Treatise* as a whole. Locke begins the chapter by introducing "a very great difficulty," namely, "how any one should ever come to have a *property* in any thing" on the supposition that the earth has been "given ... to mankind in common."[97] In effect, Locke here questions whether his refutation of Filmer's doctrine of property in the *First Treatise* on the basis of what is "common" has actually ruled out the only possible means by which property may be acquired. At the conclusion of the chapter, Locke recapitulates his answer to this difficulty as an explanation of "*how labour could at first begin a title of property* in the common things of nature ..."[98] In other words, Locke agrees with Filmer's contention that an individual may possess a "*title of property* in the common things of nature." Locke disagrees, however, with the mechanism by which particular property comes into being within Filmer's account; it is not a combination of God's private grant and successive inheritance, but "*labour*" which gives a title of property. Although Locke speaks of the "joint property of this country, or this parish," even this quasi-common property is clearly distinguished from that which is "common ... to all mankind."[99] At no point during this discussion does Locke invoke an understanding of "common" or "inclusive" property;[100] Locke's "unquestionable property" is definitively particular and exclusive in contradistinction to the inclusive commons.[101]

Neither, moreover, is Locke's property differentiated into "ultimate" or "essential" and "tenant" or "use" kinds. The very passage from the *First Treatise* which Tierney and others chiefly rely upon in locating such a distinction does, in fact, speak strongly against reading this distinction into Locke's doctrine. A more careful interpretation of this passage serves both to connect the mistaken interpretations of Tully and Tierney with one another, and to more clearly illuminate Locke's unique doctrine itself. The passage, whose latter section is widely quoted in isolation, reads as follows:

---

97. Ibid., II.v.25.
98. Ibid., II.v.51.
99. Ibid., II.v.35.
100. Tully, *A Discourse on Property*, 53–65.
101. Locke, *Two Treatises*, II.v.27; see also II.v.28, 29, 32.

however, in respect of one another, Men may be allowed to have propriety in their distinct Portions of the Creatures; yet in respect of God the Maker of Heaven and Earth, who is sole Lord and Proprietor of the whole World, Mans Propriety in the Creatures is nothing but that Liberty to use them, which God has permitted[102]

The second section of this passage corresponds to the first section of the passage in Chapter V of the *Second Treatise*;[103] although Locke appears to be defining "Mans Propriety" as a *"Liberty to use,"* he is in fact rejecting human property in favor of the property of "God the Maker of Heaven and Earth." This second section, "in respect of God," expresses the relationship (as noted above) between God and humankind in general with regard to "the whole World." Considering this relation, God is *"sole* Lord and Proprietor" (emphasis added), and humankind's *supposed* property in other creatures is "nothing but" a liberty to use in accordance with God's permission.

The first section of the passage from the *First Treatise* similarly corresponds to the second section of the passage in Chapter V of the *Second Treatise*. Locke indicates that human beings in fact do "have propriety in their distinct Portions of the Creatures" when they are considered *as individuals*, i.e., "in respect of one another. . . ." Thus, with respect to one another as individuals and with regard to "distinct Portions of the Creatures" rather than "the whole World," a human being may have property which "no body has any right to but himself."[104] It is in this manner that Locke speaks of human property and natural rights throughout Chapter V of the *Second Treatise*, in explicit contradistinction to the "liberty to use" of the *First Treatise* which humankind in general enjoys with respect to creation as a whole.

From the *Second Treatise* it is clear that a human being's relationship to "himself," "his own *person*," and *"the actions or labour of it,"*[105] is an instance of human *property* as opposed to "nothing but that *Liberty to use"* them. Just as Locke introduces the discussion of Chapter V by distinguishing every man's property "in his own *person*" from what is "common," so he concludes by reiterating that the particular external property founded upon one's property in himself, his own person, and his actions or labor

---

102. Ibid., I.iv.39.
103. Ibid., II.v.27.
104. Locke, *Second Treatise*.
105. Ibid., II.v.44.

is "perfectly his own, and did not belong in common to others."[106] Thus *"labour,* in the beginning, *gave a right of property"* prior to and independent of any compact or agreement.[107] Throughout Chapter V, Locke treats of human beings "in respect of one another" and as individuals; considered in this way, human beings clearly have a property in themselves, their "persons," and their actions as opposed to a mere "liberty to use" them.

The "workmanship" argument, on the other hand, treats of human beings "in respect of God the Maker of Heaven and Earth." Considered in this way, human beings are not individuals possessing property and rights but, rather, parts of a community of beings who are "furnished with like faculties," are under a "law of nature," are the property of God rather than themselves, and are given a "liberty to use" the earth and inferior creatures. This argument, like those in the *Questions*, does not ground Locke's doctrine of natural rights or the exclusive property of an individual in himself; it does, however, ground Locke's version of the natural law. Moreover, the workmanship model provides the key to understanding how human beings, considered as individuals, may acquire a property in their persons and actions similar to the manner in which God's workmanship engenders His property in humankind in general.[108]

DIVINE VS. HUMAN WORKMANSHIP AND SELF-OWNERSHIP

The source of God's title to property in humankind and creation as a whole is not difficult to surmise in Locke's texts; God's "workmanship" has caused their very existence. A more difficult question to answer is how Locke understands the source of individual human beings' title to property in their "persons" or selves. Since (1) Locke appears to affirm a univocal meaning of property in both instances, and (2) differences in the justificatory source of property constitute differences in the meaning of the term,[109] it would

---

106. Ibid. II.v.28, 29, 32.
107. Ibid., II.v.45.
108. On the significance of the analogy Locke draws between God's workmanship or labor and that of human beings, see Tully, *Discourse on Property*, 35-38 and 116-24; cf. Richard Ashcraft, *Revolutionary Politics and Locke's "Two Treatises of Government"* (Princeton: Princeton University Press, 1986), 259.
109. This premise is derived from the distinction between property and mere possession. The latter is an empirical fact, while the former includes, in addition, a moral component that relies on some justification. Thus this justification enters into the very definition of the term "property."

seem that human beings could only possess a property in their persons or selves if they somehow caused the very existence of these entities. From the conception of the "potter-God" developed throughout Locke's texts, God only directly or immediately causes the existence of the various powers or faculties which distinguish humankind from other creatures. He does not, however, immediately cause the full individuation of human beings into distinct persons with distinct consciousnesses of themselves. This task is directly accomplished by a form of human "workmanship" that grounds the exclusive title of individual human beings to property in themselves.[110]

By marking out the object of the property described in Chapter V of the *Second Treatise* as the "person" or the "self,"[111] Locke directs the reader to his developed discussion of these particular terms in the *Essay Concerning Human Understanding*. In Book II of the *Essay*, in his treatment "*Of Identity and Diversity*," Locke carefully distinguishes between the terms "*Substance*," "*Man*," "*Person*," and "*Self*." Substance, according to Locke, is that which "we take to be the *substratum*, or support, of those *Ideas* we do know."[112] "Substance" establishes the most basic level of distinction between something and nothing, being and non-being. Man, by Locke's definition, is "an Animal of such a certain Form," or a particular "Shape and Make."[113] "Man," therefore, establishes the distinction between beings of a certain kind or type and other creatures of different "shapes and makes." Person, according to Locke, is "a thinking intelligent Being, that has reason and reflection, and can consider it self as it self, the same thinking thing in different times and places; which it does only by that consciousness, which is inseparable from thinking, and as it seems to me essential to it."[114] "Person" establishes the distinction between particular individuals, or "thinking things," of a common "shape and make." Self, finally, is defined as "that conscious thinking thing, which is sensible, or conscious of Pleasure and Pain, capable of Happiness or Misery, and so is concern'd for it *self*, as far as that consciousness extends."[115] "Self" is thus Locke's term for a "person" (a

---

110. This point is in direct disagreement with Waldron's attempted refutation of the analogy between God's workmanship and human labor in *God, Locke, and Equality: Christian Foundations of John Locke's Political Thought* (New York: Cambridge University Press, 2002), 162–64. Waldron's argument addresses an overly strict interpretation of the analogy as a near identity, while the interpretation that follows is far more nuanced and complex than this.

111. Ibid., II.v.27, 44.

112. Locke, *An Essay Concerning Human Understanding*, I.iv.18.

113. Ibid., II.xxvii.8.

114. Ibid., II.xxvii.9.

115. Ibid., II.xxvii.17.

"thinking thing" which *can* "consider it self as it self") which actually *does* "consider it self as it self . . . by consciousness."[116]

The first two of these entities, "substance" and "man," are the products of God's workmanship and are thus His exclusive property. These in fact correspond closely to the two characteristic activities of Locke's "potter-God" which appear in the *Questions*, the *Essay*, and the *Two Treatises*: original creation *ex nihilo* and the determination of a particular arrangement of powers or faculties which distinguishes one kind of being from another. The latter two, however, "person" and "self," are the immediate products of human workmanship and are thus the exclusive property of individual human beings. These entities come into being as a direct result of "that consciousness, which is inseparable from thinking, and . . . essential to it."[117] According to Locke, this consciousness is that which "makes every one to be, what he calls *self*; and thereby distinguishes himself from all other thinking things." Therefore, it is the individual human activity of "thinking," and the state of self-consciousness that necessarily accompanies this activity, which actually *makes* the "self" and "person" and fully individuates particular human beings.[118]

During the course of this discussion in the *Essay*, Locke clearly establishes the direct relevance of the notions of "person," "self," and "consciousness" to his discussion of particular human property in the *Second Treatise* by explaining how the interrelationship of these ideas establishes individual ownership of one's actions. In a passage which is remarkably similar to those found in sections 27 and 44 of Chapter V in the *Second Treatise*, Locke states:

> That with which the *consciousness* of this present thinking thing can join it self, makes the same *Person*, and is one *self* with it, and with nothing else; and so attributes to it *self*, and owns all the Actions of that

---

116. Locke also describes the relation between "person" and "self" in the following manner in II.xxvii.26: "*Person*, as I take it, is the name for this *self*. Where-ever a Man finds, what he calls *himself*, there I think another may say is the same *Person*. It is a Forensick Term appropriating Actions and their Merit . . ." These two formulations are related and consistent, though this consistency will not be fully explored here.

117. Ibid., II.xxvii.9.

118. According to Tully, "Although ownership of one's intentional actions is a paradigmatic case of maker's rights, property in one's person is less clearly explicable in the same terms" (109). While Tully accurately notes the difficulty in such an explication, it is my contention that property in one's person or self *is* explicable in the same terms, in a manner to be explained more fully in the following chapter.

thing, as its own, as far as that consciousness reaches, and no farther; as every one who reflects will perceive.[119]

In this passage, Locke argues for the ownership of one's external actions or labor on the basis of a prior or more fundamental act of "labor," i.e., workmanship or "making," accomplished by consciousness.[120] In the *Second Treatise* Locke asserts that labor is "the unquestionable property of the labourer" because "every man has a *property* in his own *person*."[121] One's property in his own person or self stems, in turn, from the appropriating or "joining" ability of self-consciousness described in the *Essay*. The appropriating, extending, and joining activity or "labor" of self-consciousness thus makes the individual human being "master of himself, and *proprietor of his own person, and the actions or labour of it*,"[122] in a manner analogous to that in which God is "sole Lord and Proprietor" of creation as a whole.[123]

CONCURRENT UNIVOCAL OWNERSHIP AND "NESTING" PROPERTY

Locke thus intimates a persuasive account of the concurrent univocal property of God and the human being in the particular human being himself. The particular human being is the property of God and herself in the very same sense of the word "property," i.e., the product of workmanship or labor. The conflict or contradiction which this situation appears to present is circumvented by Locke's division of the particular human being into two distinct objects by the understanding: the human being and the unique self. Insofar as the individual is a human being, she is the exclusive property of God whose workmanship she is; insofar as the individual is a unique self, she is the exclusive property of herself in virtue of the activity of her self-consciousness. When Locke speaks of human beings as the workmanship or property of God, he is speaking of human beings as substances and as members of a kind or type of creature. When he speaks of human beings as the

---

119. Locke, *Essay*, II.xxvii.17.

120. This more abstract understanding of Locke's "labor" possesses some important similarities with Simmons' insightful description of Lockean labor as "purposive activity" in *The Lockean Theory of Rights* (Princeton: Princeton University Press, 1992), 273–74.

121. Ibid., II.v.27.

122. Ibid., II.v.44.

123. See Locke's statement in *Two Treatises*, I.iv.30: "God makes him *in his own Image after his own Likeness*, makes him an intellectual Creature, and so capable of *Dominion*."

workmanship or property of themselves, he is speaking of them as persons and as reflective or conscious selves.

Although the particular human being is concurrently and univocally owned by God and the human being himself, there is nevertheless an order of nobility and ultimate causality between the two "workmen" of the human being. Within the particular human being, humanity is prior to and a necessary precondition for the production of unique selfhood. Without first existing, and possessing the powers of "reason and reflection,"[124] the unique self cannot be produced by the individual activity of consciousness. Moreover, the human being is originally produced by Locke's "potter-God" *ex nihilo*, whereas the unique self is fashioned out of the preexisting materials furnished by the senses and reflective experience. Therefore, although the unique self is immediately and directly produced by the individual activity of self-consciousness, it is mediately and indirectly produced by God as a first or ultimate cause. As a result of these considerations, Locke affirms the "supreme right" of God over human beings and His supreme ownership over all existing things.

The supremacy of God's proprietary claim or right in the human being does not, however, render self-ownership merely derivative or insignificant. Self-ownership does not thereby become a matter of God's (or the natural law's) permission or of Divine Grace considered in the narrow sense. On a Lockean understanding, God creates the humanity of the individual in such a way that the human individual shares in His creative activity by making, in turn, the unique self. God does not *allow* human beings to own themselves, but creates them *as* potential self-owners. An intriguing corollary of such an account is that this understanding of self-ownership cannot come into conflict with Divine ownership in the case of the individual human being. The unique self cannot be disjoined from the human being; every human being exists as a human being-unique self complex. Although the *actions of* a unique self may be in tension or conflict with God's ownership of the human being (in the case of suicide, for example), the distinction between one's self and one's particular actions is an integral aspect of the very consciousness that engenders self-ownership.

The picture of property in the particular human being that emerges from Locke's complex treatment is thus a kind of "nesting" property. The property which the human being possesses in himself is identical in kind with the property which God possesses in the human being. God's property in the human being, however, is more noble or higher than the human being's

---

124. Locke, *Essay*, II.xxvii.9.

property in himself. Both rights of property, moreover, coexist in a single human being. Although this understanding of the compatibility of Divine and self-ownership of the human being is implicit and undeveloped within Locke's texts, the idea of "nesting" property rights both makes sense of Locke's apparently contradictory assertions and establishes the possibility of concurrent univocal property in particular human beings.

NATURAL LAW AND NATURAL RIGHTS

By applying the Lockean notion of concurrent and univocal "nesting" property to the relationship between the natural law and natural rights in Locke's political philosophy, the possibility of a coherent "NLNR Locke" begins to come into focus. If the natural law and natural rights may be derived in a manner parallel to that of Divine ownership and self-ownership, i.e., according to the twofold structure of the individual as a human being and a unique self, they similarly need not be rigidly ordered as primary and derived.

Such a parallel is, in fact, suggested by the frequent association or conjunction of Divine ownership with the natural law, and self-ownership with natural rights, in many of Locke's texts. Perhaps the clearest single example of the association between Divine ownership and the natural law occurs in the "workmanship" argument of the *Second Treatise*.[125] In this passage, Locke first affirms a proposition: "The *state of nature* has a law of nature to govern it, which obliges every one: and reason, which is that law, teaches all mankind" that "no one ought to harm another in his life, health, liberty, or possessions." This affirmation is substantiated by the "workmanship" argument which follows: "for men being all the workmanship of one omnipotent, and infinitely wise maker. . . ." Why would one be inclined to affirm the existence of a law of nature? *Because* humankind is "his (God's) property, whose workmanship they are. . . ." Human beings are under a natural law insofar as the "workman" God exercises his proprietary claim over them. This right of property possessed by God is immediately in *humankind*,[126] i.e., human beings considered as a "community of nature" sharing in "like faculties," or as a species rather than as individuals. Throughout this passage Locke refers to human beings in the plural and in terms of what is common: "mankind," "all," "they," "we," and "us" are

---

125. Ibid., II.ii.6.
126. I say "immediately" here in order to allow for the "mediated" ownership of the individual *as* an individual by God.

the primary terms of Locke's argument. Insofar as the individual is a being with membership in a particular species, he is dependent on or exists under the cause of his being and humanity. He is therefore obligated by a moral rule or "law of nature" to act in accordance with the given hierarchical arrangement of his natural powers or faculties, i.e., in accordance with the superiority of "reason."

A clear example of the association of self-ownership and natural rights, on the other hand, occurs in Chapter V of the *Second Treatise*. The term "law of nature" is, remarkably, almost entirely absent from this chapter, which is concerned with the mechanisms by which "any particular man" acquires "a *property* in several parts of that which God gave to mankind in common."[127] This particular property is, moreover, described as a "private right."[128] Such a private right is possessed by an individual human being in his *"person," "self," "labour," "work," "actions,"* and the external objects with which *"labour"* is "joined" or "mixed."[129] Each of these private rights find their *"great foundation"* in the fact that the individual is *"proprietor of his own person."*[130] In this discussion of natural rights, it is the individual human being who is explicitly marked out as the "workman,"[131] indicating the similar or analogous basis of Divine and self-ownership of the individual human being.[132] Whereas the natural law stems from the humanity of the individual, in respect of which he is God's "workmanship," natural rights stem from the unique selfhood of the individual, in respect of which the individual is himself a "workman."

Although Locke's natural law and natural rights need not be derived one from the other, the natural law nevertheless represents a higher or nobler source of morality than natural rights, standing above rights-based morality as Divine ownership stands above self-ownership. Locke's political philosophy in the *Second Treatise*, however, appears to begin and end with natural rights rather than the natural law. While the *"fundamental law of nature"* is *"the preservation of mankind,"* or God's property, the "great and *chief end"* of political society and government is *"the preservation of their* (i.e., human individuals') *property* (i.e., rights)."[133] What could explain this apparent disparity? First, as is evidenced from the analysis of Locke's

---

127. Locke, *Two Treatises*, II.v.25–26.
128. Ibid., II.v.28.
129. Ibid., II.v.27, 44.
130. Ibid., II.v.44.
131. Ibid., II.v.43.
132. Compare with Locke's statement in the *First Treatise* regarding this analogy, I.iv.30.
133. Locke, *Two Treatises*, II.ix.124; II.xi.135.

Questions Concerning the Law of Nature ventured above as well as other considerations adduced by proponents of the "NR Locke," it is not clear that Locke was ever convinced of the existence of a natural law in what Strauss calls "the proper sense."[134] Moreover, political societies and human governments are formed in order to regulate the relations of individuals with one another and to effectively and harmoniously unite the individuals composing a community. They are thus primarily concerned with individual human beings "in respect of one another"[135] or *as* individuals rather than as members of a species or kind of being. And finally, the security of natural rights is a prerequisite for discharging the duties of the natural law; a slave is restrained from acting in accordance with his rational nature or humanity. The protection of natural rights is thus a more urgent task for political society than that of enforcing the natural law.

CONCLUSION

Locke's "nesting" account of self-ownership and Divine ownership, as well as natural rights and the natural law, provides an ingenious and promising inspiration for achieving a genuine and coherent reconciliation of ancient/medieval and modern conceptions of morality. Locke is undoubtedly concerned with distinctively "modern" conceptions of natural rights derived from considerations of the individual as a unique self, or with moral and political "individualism" in a certain sense. This concern is tempered and balanced, however, by a simultaneous attachment to premodern perspectives regarding the importance of an objective context within which the individual is situated. Locke thus follows Hobbes' natural rights orientation while rejecting Hobbes' radical departure from the natural law tradition.

Locke's account itself is, however, problematically vague and incomplete; the precise manner in which Locke's natural rights are grounded in his conception of the unique self in the *Essay* is extraordinarily difficult to determine, and Locke's doctrine of natural law remains on an exceedingly general level throughout his writings. The original accounts of the concepts of natural rights and the natural law to follow may, then, be viewed as filling in the details of the framework suggested first by Locke. While Locke may thus be credited with illuminating the contours of the account that

---

134. Strauss, *Natural Right*, 226. The proper or strict sense of the natural law here indicates that this law is "knowable to the unassisted human mind, to the human mind which is not illumined by divine revelation" (163), and thus is "promulgated in the state of nature" (226).

135. Locke, *Two Treatises*, I.iv.39.

follows, this account will nevertheless often proceed along non- or perhaps even un-Lockean paths.

The account of natural rights that immediately follows in Chapter 2, for example, already leaves the definitively Lockean realm and becomes more vaguely "Locke-ish." While the idea of the unique self that is actively formed from individual self-consciousness is indeed a Lockean one, the manner in which this formation and its consequences are explained occurs almost entirely apart from interpretations of Locke's writings themselves. The account of the natural law in Chapter 3 leaves even the "Locke-ish" realm—excepting only its general fit within the Lockean framework of the twofold human being/unique self structure—and is indeed non-Lockean (though not, on my interpretation, anti-Lockean). As indicated above, Locke consistently shied away from endorsing the traditional natural law doctrine, largely, I believe, due to its entanglement with epistemological issues surrounding ideas of human nature that Locke attacks in the *Essay*. Chapter 4 is similarly not intended to be an interpretation of Locke's thought, but only an extensive elaboration upon the basic Lockean insight of the twofold structure of the individual outlined above. Thus, while my interpretation of Locke provides a starting point for the arguments that follow, these arguments themselves are intended to stand independently of Locke's thought. Though Locke provides an indispensable flashlight, he won't serve as our guide along the way.

CHAPTER TWO

Self-Consciousness, Self-Ownership, and Natural Rights

In searching for a persuasive justification for the modern conception of natural rights, the most fruitful starting point lies in the Lockean idea of self-ownership through self-consciousness intimated in the preceding chapter's interpretation of Locke's thought. Locke's unique self is the product of the phenomenon of self-consciousness, and the natural rights attaching to the unique self result from the idea of self-ownership that necessarily accompanies this self-consciousness. Although these connections were left underdeveloped by Locke himself, when adequately explained they join to form a stronger and more persuasive justification for natural rights than any existing ones.

The discussion that follows is, to reiterate a point made at the conclusion of the preceding chapter, not intended to be an interpretation of Locke's thought, but rather an argument for the connections between self-consciousness, self-ownership and natural rights, connections drawn in an implicit manner by Locke himself. In attempting to make these connections explicit, I have occasionally drawn on concepts and modes of argumentation that may legitimately be argued to be contrary to, or at least very different from, Locke's thought itself. There are, for instance, Aristotelian elements within the following discussion that one might argue would be resisted by Locke. For this reason the argument that follows is not quite Lockean (except where otherwise explicitly indicated), but only "Locke-ish."

NATURAL RIGHTS IN CONTEMPORARY DISCOURSE

The pervasiveness of "rights talk" in both popular discourse and contemporary scholarly debates is a well-attested fact.[1] As rights are increasingly claimed by individuals, deployed in political rhetoric, and adjudicated in the courts, scholarly debates regarding the meaning, scope and content of human rights have struggled to keep pace. One class of rights, which may be termed "positive" or "artificial," is determined by positive laws and judicial decisions. Arguments regarding these rights concern the interpretation of such laws and decisions and seek to answer the question of whether X has a right to Y as a consequence of these governmental acts. Another, much more controversial, class of rights, which may be termed "human" or "natural," is determined prior to positive laws and judicial decisions. Arguments regarding these rights concern not whether X has a positive right to Y, but rather whether X *should* have a positive right to Y on the basis of X's human or natural rights. Positive rights follow from governmental acts, while natural rights are understood to guide and limit such acts.

Positive rights are the primary concern of lawyers and judges; natural rights, on the other hand, are the primary concern of moral, legal, and political philosophers. The meaning, content, and scope of natural rights has been a subject of continuous and contentious debate from the time of Hobbes and Locke to the present. Among the most pressing questions within contemporary debates regarding natural rights are whether natural rights are prior to the natural law;[2] whether there are positive or "benefit" natural rights as well as negative or "liberty" ones;[3] and, most basically, what it means to "have a right" at all.[4] Amidst the swirl of discussion concerning these and other important questions, one question has been curiously neglected or, perhaps, avoided: what *is* a right? The reason for this avoidance appears to be twofold. First, it is often asserted and widely assumed that a right is a type of claim made by individuals; the question of "what is a right" has thus

---

1. Mary Ann Glendon, *Rights Talk: The Impoverishment of Political Discourse* (New York: The Free Press, 1991).

2. Michael Zuckert, *Launching Liberalism: On Lockean Political Philosophy* (Kansas, 2002), 175.

3. Sotirios A. Barber, "Liberalism and the Constitution," and Michael P. Zuckert, "On Constitutional Welfare Liberalism: An Old-Liberal Perspective," in *Liberalism: Old and New*, ed. Ellen Frankel Paul, Fred D. Miller, Jr. and Jeffrey Paul (Cambridge: Cambridge University Press, 2007), 234–88.

4. Michael Zuckert, *Launching Liberalism*; Alan Gewirth, *Reason and Morality*; John Finnis, *Natural Law and Natural Rights*.

been answered to general satisfaction at least in a vague or general manner.[5] Secondly, the question itself cannot be pressed too far due to the assumption, whether conscious or unconscious, of the "naturalistic fallacy;" a right, as a moral principle like "the good," does not possess any objective ontological status and is thus similarly indefinable.[6]

The characterization of a right as a kind of claim is plausible due to the close association between possessing a right and claiming to possess a right. One doesn't generally "see" a right unless it is attached to an actual or potential right-claim. Thus Feinberg, Gewirth and many others loosely define a particular right as a moral claim, or a claim of immunity from interference by others. Gewirth begins with particular right-claims, as a loose equivalent of particularized rights, and ends with a system of universal rights.[7] The problem involved in beginning with a right-claim and ending with a system of rights, or in identifying a particular right with a particular right-claim, is that it sidesteps the question of what a right is. In the first place, a right-claim is not a simple entity. It is composed of two elements: a right and a claim to possess a right. Not all claims are claims to possess a right, and the very act of claiming the possession of a right implies the possession of this right prior to the act of claiming. In the second place, this method implicitly asserts that rights exist only in the plural; rights emerge from the multiplication of a right-claim rather than a right. Why is the plural of a right-claim not simply many right-claims? How can the existence of many rights be logically or epistemologically prior to the existence of a single right?

By critiquing the identification of a right with a right-claim, however, one runs afoul of the second reason for avoiding the question of what a right is, consisting in the argument that a right is, in principle, inextricable from the normative right-claim which includes it. Just as "the good" does not exist in some objective, descriptive realm apart from individual desiring and willing, so a right does not exist apart from individual right-claiming. Something is not desired because it is good, but rather it is good because it is desired; similarly, a right is not claimed because it is possessed, but rather it is possessed because it is claimed. A right does not have an objective, definable existence. It only comes into being through a generalizable or universalizable intersubjectivity; an individual right exists after a right-claim becomes a wider system of rights which is then applied back to the

---

5. Zuckert, *Launching Liberalism*; Gewirth "Moral Rationality," 20; Joel Feinberg, "The Nature and Value of Rights," *Journal of Value Inquiry* 4, no. 4 (Winter 1970): 243–57, 249; Rex Martin, *A System of Rights* (Oxford: Clarendon Press, 1993), 51–72.

6. G. E. Moore, *Principia Ethica*, Chapter I, Section 10.

7. Gewirth, "Moral Rationality," 19–29; *Reason and Morality*, 42–47.

individual right-claimant. In this way, rights have thoroughly normative beginnings which preclude the descriptive question of what a right "is."

This discussion leads to a distinction between what one might call the strict and loose understandings of a possessed right. According to the strict understanding, the expression "X has a right to Y" means that in a manner similar to that in which X has a house, a car, an idea or a personality, X possesses something called a right with respect to some object Y. The strict understanding both clearly distinguishes between a right and a right-claim (i.e., a right is something that exists prior to being actually claimed to exist), and does not take the naturalistic fallacy or "is-ought" problem as a preliminary assumption. In short, the strict understanding ascribes a clear and determinate meaning to the words in the expression "X has a right to Y," while taking the literal meaning of the words themselves seriously. According to the loose understanding, the expression "X has a right to Y" is a kind of shorthand, or a "linguistic expression,"[8] normally signifying much more than the simple possession of an object. It may mean that X has made a moral claim to Y which is then universalized and applied back to X in the form of a right, that X has a desire for some object Y, that X has some characteristic which is deemed worth of respect, that others have a duty to refrain from interfering with X, or that the natural law commands (or permits) X to do something. On the loose understanding, the expression "X has a right to Y" is extraordinarily flexible and vague, potentially signifying an indeterminate range of situations or relationships involving X and Y. The loose understanding allows for the identification of a right and a right-claim, and is much more compatible with the assumption of the "is-ought" problem. The loose understanding, in short, is not particularly concerned with ascribing a clear and determinate meaning to rights language, nor with taking the literal signification of the words themselves seriously.

The contemporary predominance of the loose understanding of rights is far from a novel development; indeed, the language of subjective rights found its historical origin in precisely such a loose understanding. As Tierney's thorough historical studies of the development of rights language indicates, the subjective expression of rights grew almost imperceptibly out of their objective function associated with the natural law. The Spanish Thomists, who played a prominent role in this development, equated the phrase "I have a right" with "it is permitted" according to the natural law.[9] As subjective rights came to be conceived as morally and politically foundational

---

8. Finnis, *Natural Law and Natural Rights*.
9. Tierney, "Historical Roots," 39.

rather than as derivative from the natural law, however, the loose understanding became increasingly problematic. While it may be acceptable to hold a loose understanding of concepts derivative from more determinate foundations, it is as undesirable to hold such a loose understanding of foundational concepts as it is to build a castle upon sand. Although two especially notable attempts were made during the early modern period to set forth a strict understanding of subjective rights, one of these abandoned the indispensable moral element of rights language while the other was insufficiently developed and problematically underdetermined.[10] Thus the loose understanding of rights has survived, and indeed thrived, in the absence of a determinate grounding context such as the natural law.[11]

The persistence of the loose understanding of rights into the contemporary period has had a number of significant disadvantages. The most important of these consists in the pliability such an understanding introduces with respect to the meaning, content and scope of natural rights. The continuous and rapid increase in the number of widely recognized natural rights throughout the modern and contemporary periods, as well as the persistent difficulty in reaching any agreement with respect to the justification for and meaning of these rights, are evident symptoms of the loose understanding. When an expression, such as "X has a right to Y," becomes progressively detached from any strict or determinate understanding of the words themselves, it becomes quite easy to adapt this expression to a variety of loosely related circumstances or settings. In the case of the expression of a subjective right in particular, the loose understanding lends itself to the ad-hoc adaptation of rights language to a variety of particular agendas, passions and goals. Rights language becomes a protean tool to be used by political actors and ordinary individuals alike to serve a wide range of disparate ends, never holding still long enough to be apprehended by scholarly reflection.

Proceeding according to a strict understanding, on the other hand, restrains the problematic excesses of "right talk" and brings the meaning, content and scope of natural rights into focus. By setting aside the issue of the "is-ought" problem or "naturalistic fallacy" as an assumption that will be shown to be mistaken in what follows, such a strict understanding becomes possible. The question, then, may be broached: what is a natural right, and how can it be possessed by individuals? An adequate answer to

---

10. Hobbes and Locke.

11. Such a loose understanding has resulted in the dilution of rights-language from "natural rights" to "human rights."

this question must begin with the uniquely human phenomenon of self-consciousness.

SELF-CONSCIOUSNESS

Self-consciousness refers to the state which characterizes and constitutes the self. The self is defined by self-consciousness, such that the self does not exist without or prior to a consciousness of the self. Whether "situated" or "unencumbered," thick or thin, the self is that which accompanies the state of self-consciousness.[12] This definition of the self solely in terms of self-consciousness closely follows Locke's conception of what Charles Taylor calls the "punctual" or "neutral" self, a conception that comes under heavy fire from Taylor in his *Sources of the Self*.[13] According to Taylor, to speak of someone as a self is to speak of him as a "being of the requisite depth and complexity to have an identity" in the sense described by Taylor.[14] Taylor's conception of "identity" consists in the possession of some orientation with respect to questions concerning the good, or some moral "horizon" or "framework," that contributes to one's "self-interpretation" or location within "moral space." Each of these interrelated aspects of identity, moreover, can only come to be within an already existing network of "webs of interlocution" with other human beings. Taylor's self is thus defined as already situated within a shared moral space, and as thickly endowed with self-interpretations, relationships and interactions with others, and definite orientations with respect to the good.

In so defining the self, however, Taylor has put the self-interpreting and self-defining cart before the simply self-conscious horse, or rather neglected the latter altogether in his preoccupation with the former. Taylor's aim in defining the self in terms of a rich identity, orientation towards the good, and interactions with others is clearly to combat what he perceives to be the radically individualistic trend of Western moral and political philosophy. Michael Sandel, in a similar vein, delivered a powerful critique of John Rawls's *A Theory of Justice* as premised on a false portrayal of the "unencumbered self."[15] Sandel, like Taylor, argued that the self does not exist prior

---

12. Michael Sandel, *Liberalism and the Limits of Justice* (Cambridge: Cambridge University Press, 1998); John Rawls, *A Theory of Justice*. Original Edition (Cambridge: Harvard University Press, 1971); Charles Taylor, *Sources of the Self: The Making of the Modern Identity* (Cambridge: Harvard University Press, 1989).
13. Taylor, *Sources of the Self*, 159–77.
14. Ibid., 32.
15. Sandel, *Liberalism and the Limits of Justice*, 82–95.

to or in abstraction from webs of relationships, notions of the good, linguistic frameworks, and so on. While Taylor's broad communitarian point is well taken, his analysis neglects the distinction between individuals that is necessarily presupposed by the process of identity formation and self-interpretation upon which he focuses his attention. A basic consciousness of the self must clearly preexist, at least logically, the more complex processes of self-interpretation or self-definition Taylor emphasizes.[16] The simple formation of the first-person or "I" perspective is clearly a prerequisite for engaging in any reflective activity.[17] Otherwise, there would be no way of distinguishing *my* identity from *yours* or anyone else's; we would all lose ourselves, rather than find ourselves, in Taylor's "webs of interlocution."

Taylor's fundamental mistake lies in his conception of the transition from Locke's basic reflective awareness, or self-consciousness, to identity-formation and self-interpretation as a qualitative change rather than a change in degree. Although Taylor may agree that his conception of identity presupposes a more basic, Lockean form of self-consciousness, he affirms the existence of the self only after the transition from Lockean self-consciousness to participation in complex webs of linguistic relationships with others. If, however, this transition represents a continuous change among varying degrees of self-consciousness rather than a sharp break marking the creation of the self, as I will argue, the self would in fact exist from the first appearance of self-consciousness, as Locke affirms. This is not to deny the validity of Taylor's broader point regarding the importance of relationships, language, and orientations towards the good in the ongoing construction of the self. It is only to notice that individual capacities and operations, such as those relating to the self, are necessarily presupposed by, and serve as the ontological foundation for, the moral spaces we create in our interactions with others.

Although the self that I, with Locke, take to be defined by self-consciousness is often conceived as a static entity or fixed object, self-consciousness is in fact a state of continuous activity rather than a static one insofar as it is a species of reflective activity in a broad sense of the term.[18] As a reflective activity, self-consciousness also admits of degrees, ranging from the basic reflective awareness of oneself which accompanies all waking activity to more acute consciousness of oneself and voluntary introspec-

---

16. For an excellent discussion of this topic see Bermudez, *The Paradox of Self-Consciousness* (Cambridge: The MIT Press, 1998).

17. Bermudez, *The Paradox of Self-Consciousness*, 2–5.

18. This point is similar to Taylor's regarding the dynamic constitution of the self during his discussion of the self as an object of study in *Sources of the Self*, 33–34.

tion. On the more basic end of this spectrum, self-consciousness does not produce any idea of the self or its characteristics and is both involuntary and continuous. On the other end of the spectrum, self-consciousness does result in the formation of ideas regarding the self and is discontinuous.[19] Self-consciousness in general specifically distinguishes human beings from other animals; only human beings appear to possess even a basic reflective awareness of themselves and therefore only human beings are selves at all. Only human beings cannot perceive without also perceiving that they perceive,[20] or act without also perceiving that they are acting.

Reflection, in a broad sense, may be described in terms of the simultaneous coexistence of and interplay between sameness and difference, unity and multiplicity. When an object is placed in front of a mirror, for example, the image in the mirror does not actually multiply the object; there remains one object and one mirror. The image of the object, however, is doubled; there are now two images, (1) that associated with the actual object, and (2) that associated with the mirror. Since, moreover, the image in the mirror is simply a projection or reproduction of the object itself onto the reflective surface, the image in the mirror is also identical with or the same as the object itself. The mirror has not doubled the object but has rather made the object itself "double." In an analogous manner, human beings are constituted as selves by the simultaneous presence of two distinct perspectives or "images": (1) an "embedded" or concrete perspective and (2) an "I" or detached perspective. The human being, like the object, becomes "doubled" by reflection without losing her ultimate unity and singularity.

Self-consciousness as basic reflective awareness involves the possession of the "I" perspective and the attachment of this perspective to all of one's actions. This means simply that human beings invariably associate their actions with an awareness that it is "I" who perform them. Thinking, perceiving and acting become "I think," "I perceive" and "I act." Human actions are distinguished from other events, or the actions of other animals, by their association with such an "I" perspective. While the "I" perspective is attached to all human actions, it is at the same time detached or separable from each of these actions. The "I" which performed an action yesterday or last year is not different from the "I" which acts today or the "I" which will act in the future. This "I" even performs multiple actions simultaneously without compromising its identity and unity. To say that the "I" perspective

---

19. This degree of self-consciousness consists in something like Taylor's "self-interpretation."
20. John Locke, *Essay Concerning Human Understanding*, II.xxvii.9.

is a partially detached one is merely to indicate that while this particular action is inseparably linked with the "I," the "I" is linked not only with this action but innumerable others in the past, present and future. Yesterday's actions, today's actions and tomorrow's actions are distinct, while the "I" which is associated with all of them is identical.

The "I" perspective does not, however, achieve such a degree of separability or distance from particular actions that the "I" becomes an external observer of these actions. Even when past actions are surveyed or considered, the "I" perspective is recognized to have accompanied these actions and to be the same "I" perspective which is now associated with the action of considering them. The "I" is necessarily combined with a perspective which is "embedded" in concrete and particular actions, such that the "I" cannot arise in the absence of particular action and a perspective which accompanies the particularity of the action. Just as thinking, perceiving and acting do not occur without the accompaniment of the "I" perspective, so the "I" itself does not exist in isolation from these particular actions. The "embedded" perspective, like the physical object placed in front of a mirror, constitutes a necessary component of reflective activity and rules out the possibility of a wholly detached or external "I" which merely observes concrete and particular actions.[21]

It is the simultaneous coexistence of these two perspectives, that of the "I" and that which is concretely "embedded," which constitutes self-consciousness as basic reflective awareness. Insofar as self-consciousness defines the self, the "I" perspective and the "embedded" perspective may be described as complementary elements or ingredients of the self. By attending to other forms of reflection, such as deliberate introspection, it becomes evident that even self-consciousness as basic reflective awareness is not merely a static condition but rather an activity or operation. Examining these other, more obviously "reflective," forms of activity illuminates aspects of basic reflective awareness which are not otherwise clearly discernible. Such an examination both (1) confirms the propriety of understanding basic reflective awareness analytically in terms of the two perspectives outlined above, and (2) reveals that, contrary to immediate experience, the two perspectives which constitute self-consciousness as basic reflective awareness are not simply given but rather arise out of a continuous and specifically human activity.

---

21. So this does not imply the sort of mind-body dualism often associated with Descartes' thought.

Deliberate introspection, or more acute forms of self-consciousness such as embarrassment, are characterized by a pronounced distinction or separation between the "I" perspective and the "embedded" one. These reflective activities involve the cultivation, whether wholly voluntary or partially involuntary, of a perspective which is detached from one's particular "embedded" circumstances. Thus in the case of introspection, one views certain aspects or features of oneself as objects somehow independent of the abstract observational perspective adopted. The possibility of self-development or self-improvement is premised on the possibility of such a reflective activity, in which one divides oneself into two somehow distinct entities: (1) an object constituted by particular features, actions and circumstances; and (2) a subject constituted by a partially external perspective. The first entity is "embedded" in concrete circumstances, while the second is the "I" which stands over and above the "embedded" aspect of oneself. Thus "I" recall, analyze and evaluate particular ideas, actions and their circumstances almost as objective data which, though they occurred in a manner that included both perspectives of self-consciousness, are treated primarily in terms of their "embeddedness," i.e., as distinct from the "I" perspective which views them.

The cultivation of the detached "I" perspective characteristic of such reflective activities falls far short, however, of complete abstraction from all "embeddedness." The "I" does not look upon the embedded self as wholly other or alien to its perspective; indeed, the "I" perspective recognizes its inextricable association with the embedded self it observes. The case of deliberate introspection involves, however, a sharpening of the distinction between the "I" perspective and the "embedded" one and a stretching of the distance between the two to its limit. While engaging in such an activity one is more clearly "double" than while engaging in other, less reflective activities. Instances of heightened reflection are, moreover, not characteristics or conditions but operations or activities. The "I" perspective is cultivated and more completely assumed, and the "embedded" perspective is abandoned as far as possible. Such instances of reflection may be begun and concluded at will, and consist in a motion from ordinary self-awareness to more focused or heightened reflective awareness.

This motion, moreover, is not from an unreflective state to a reflective one, but rather from a basic reflective state to a more developed one. The "I" perspective which is cultivated and focused in the reflective activity of introspection is not spontaneously conjured by human beings when engaging in such activity, but rather highlighted to a greater degree than in ordinary basic reflective awareness. Although it is more closely joined to the "embedded" perspective in the basic awareness accompanying other activities, the "I" perspective is already present in this basic awareness. Since (1) instances of heightened reflection, such as deliberate introspection, are operations or activities rather than static conditions, and (2) the difference between instances of heightened reflection and ordinary basic reflective awareness is better understood in terms of a difference in degree or focus rather than a difference between an operation and a static condition or one between different kinds of operation, it follows that (3) basic reflective awareness, or ordinary self-consciousness, is, like introspection, a reflective activity or operation.

If self-consciousness as basic reflective awareness and instances of heightened reflection such as deliberate introspection are both reflective operations differing only in degree of intensity, they must both proceed from a single human capacity. Just as any activity implies and presupposes the ability to perform the activity, so too reflective operations presuppose a capacity for reflection. The operation of this capacity which is the most basic, continuous and involuntary is self-consciousness; other reflective operations, such as introspection, are more developed, discontinuous and voluntary. Self-consciousness as basic reflective awareness is, indeed, discontinuous and voluntary to a degree; one may temporarily suspend the reflective activity of self-consciousness by sleeping or taking certain drugs and medications. This limited ability to suspend self-consciousness, in fact, counts as an important additional piece of evidence for its status as an operation or activity as opposed to a given static condition. Borrowing Aristotle's terminology,[22] one may characterize the relationship between self-consciousness as basic reflective awareness and more developed reflective activities as the first and second actualities, respectively, of the power or capacity for reflection.

SELF-OWNERSHIP AND "ORDERING FACTS"

Since self-consciousness characterizes and constitutes the self, and since this self-consciousness is an operation of the reflective capacity of the individual, it follows that the reflective capacity of the individual in fact produces or makes the self.[23] Thus the individual may be viewed as either a

---

22. Aristotle, *De Anima*, II.1.412a-13a.
23. The "reflective capacity" or "capacity for reflection" ought to be understood as referring to "the individual in virtue of the reflective capacity" whenever actions such as production, or relations such as ownership, are ascribed to it as to a subject.

potential self or an actual self depending upon whether one attends to the individual's reflective capacity or to the operation of this capacity.[24] The individual is a potential self in virtue of his possession of the reflective capacity, and an actual self in virtue of the most basic operation of this capacity in self-consciousness as basic reflective awareness. Thus dividing the individual according to the understanding, while continuing to acknowledge his ontological unity, we may assert that the potential self produces or makes the actual self through the operation of the reflective capacity.

If the individual in fact makes her self, this would seem to imply *prima facie* the absurdity that the individual human being exists before she exists, or that the individual's existence presupposes the individual's existence. The self, however, is not identical with the individual human being, but rather refers to a consideration of the human being in light of a particular aspect or characteristic, i.e., self-consciousness. The selfhood of the individual is only one aspect, albeit a centrally important one, of the individual's existence. The production of the actual self by the potential self already presupposes as given the existence of the "substance" and "man" aspects of the individual, to use the terms of Locke's analysis in the *Essay*. That an individual has substantial being, and that he has a particular supply and arrangement of powers specific to the kind of being he is, are given prior to any activity of the individual. No notion of self-creation or self-production reaches these fundamental aspects of the individual human being. In a manner similar, but far more basic and unnoticed, to that in which an individual makes herself an athlete, a musician, or a professor, an individual makes herself a "self" to begin with. This specific limitation in the meaning of "self" mitigates the apparent absurdity or radicalism of the assertion that the individual, in virtue of his reflective capacity, produces or creates himself.

Understanding the production of the self by the potential self illuminates the proper understanding of the common but confusing term "myself," and the self-ownership which this term reflects and implies. The term "myself" implies the following important propositions: (1) each particular human being may be considered (and considers himself) as two distinct entities, a "self" and an entity distinguishable from the "self;" (2) the latter entity owns or has a property in the "self." While this may seem to constitute an overly analytical and literal treatment of language, which develops organically and in a nonanalytical manner, such an analysis is supported by

---

24. This is an instance in which I am utilizing Aristotelian concepts and language that are not found in Locke's account.

an understanding of more developed reflective activities and the manner in which these are spoken of. In the reflective activity of introspection, for instance, the partially detached "I" perspective is cultivated and assumed in a manner which distinguishes this perspective from the more "embedded" self which is observed and evaluated. As a result of this activity, an individual may say things such as "I am proud of myself," or "I have room for self-improvement." In these cases the "self" is treated more like an object than a subject; it is something which may be viewed, considered and altered as from without. As the term "myself" implies, in other words, the self is not coextensive with the individual but is rather an aspect of the individual which may be observed, altered and, in fact, owned.

The question of "what is the entity which is supposed to own the self?" thus constitutes a legitimate object of inquiry. This question may be reframed in the following way: from what vantage point does the "I" claim the self as "mine?" Any vantage point within the actual self must be ruled out of consideration, since the actual self is the object of "my" ownership. The individual as a "substance" would not be inclined to claim ownership of the self, since most substances are not associated with selves and it is not in virtue of the individual's distinctness from nonbeing that he is or has a self. The "man" aspect of the individual appears more promising, since all human beings are or have selves, and being a self specifically differentiates human beings from other animals. It is not, however, in virtue of every element, characteristic or power of the human being that one would be inclined to claim ownership of the self. It is not, for example, on account of any of the elements of "man" which are shared in common with other animals, such as embodiment, sensation or natural appetites that the human being would be inclined to claim ownership of the self. It is not simply, then, the vantage point of the "man" aspect of the individual from which the "I" claims the self as "mine."

The appropriate vantage point must be that in virtue of which the "man" aspect, or one's human nature, becomes associated with the "self" aspect. This consists in the human capacity which is responsible for the production of the "I" perspective and its combination with the "embedded" perspective in constituting the self, i.e., the reflective capacity. The individual considered in light of the reflective capacity is, moreover, what has been identified as the "potential self." It is thus the potential self, or the "man" aspect of the individual considered with reference to a particular capacity or power, with which the "I" perspective identifies when it claims the "self" as "mine" in the term "myself." The entity which is somehow different from and owns the actual self is nothing other than the potential self. The term "myself" thus implicitly includes the claim that the potential self, with which "I" am identifying, owns the actual self.

The next task becomes, then, that of evaluating the implicit claim of the potential self to own the actual self. Does the potential self in fact own the actual self, such that the actual self is the exclusive property of the potential self with respect to other individuals? Just as to have a property in the sense of characteristic or feature implies that this characteristic is "proper" to oneself, so to have property in something implies that this other thing is in some related manner also "proper" to or an extended part of oneself. The concept of ownership reflects the exclusivity of property, such that the relationship between the property holder and his property includes a legitimate basis for the exclusion of others with respect to whom the object is not "proper."[25] Thus the concept of property ownership involves a relationship between the owner and the property owned which both establishes a connection between the two sufficient to render the property a virtual part of or "proper" to the owner, and supplies the owner with a legitimate basis for excluding others from his property. Each of these criteria of property ownership are, in fact, met by the relationship between the potential self and the actual self.

This relationship is one of making or, in Locke's terms, "workmanship." Although the workmanship of the potential self in making the actual self is certainly not creation *ex nihilo*, it is a stronger form of workmanship than other instances of human art such as the making of a house or a chair. Like the making of a house or chair, the making of the actual self involves the use of preexisting materials in fashioning an entity which did not exist before the activity of the workman. Thus while the entity made, be it a house or an actual self, depends upon preexisting material causes, it also depends upon the efficient causality of the workman. The making of the actual self, however, differs from other common instances of human making in its continuity. A chair is made once and for all, but the actual self is made and remade continually since its existence is coextensive with the operation of the reflective capacity. Insofar as this perpetual or continual dependence establishes a stronger and more intimate relationship than the simple dependence of the chair on the carpenter, the workmanship of the potential self in making the actual self is a more radical or stronger form of workmanship than other ordinary instances of human workmanship.

---

25. This point resonates with the analysis of Martin in *A System of Rights* as well as Tully's distinction between "inclusive" and "exclusive" property rights in *A Discourse on Property*.

In the case of the carpenter's chair, the dependence of the chair on the workmanship, or labor, of the carpenter for its existence makes the chair a kind of extended part of the carpenter and "proper" to him in a particular way. The idea of the chair as a virtual part of the carpenter is reflected in the common expression that one can "see" the workman in his workmanship, i.e., that the carpenter produced the chair not simply as *a* carpenter, but as *this* one. The carpenter is, further, concerned for his chair in a way that he is not concerned for other chairs; he has labored to bring it into existence and he has done so for some conscious purpose which links the chair's existence to his own. In Lockean terms, the carpenter has "mixed his labor" with the chair, and done so in a purposive, self-conscious manner.[26] The carpenter also possesses a legitimate basis for the exclusion of others from the destruction or use of the chair in virtue of these aspects of the carpenter-chair relationship. This basis lies in both the efficient cause-effect relationship between the two as well as the virtual whole-part relationship thereby established. These two aspects of the carpenter-chair relationship are absent from any relationship subsisting between this chair and others. It is this initial basis for exclusion which underlies and is presupposed by subsequent forms of ownership.

The case of the workmanship or labor of the potential self in making the actual self includes each aspect of the carpenter-chair relationship, and thus fulfills the criteria of ownership, to a greater degree. The actual self is "proper" to the potential self, or a virtual part of the potential self, in a much more intimate sense than the chair is proper to the carpenter. This is evidenced by the difficulty one encounters in distinguishing the potential self from the actual self at all; since the actual self is the first actuality of the potential self, or the first product of the operation of the potential self, the two entities often appear identical. While the potential self is of wider extension than the actual self, since the potential self admits of further actualities as well as a purely potential state, the potential self is first and foremost defined by its relationship to the actual self as its primary product. It is for this reason that the term "potential self" is appropriate to the human being considered in light of the reflective capacity. The actual self may also be said to be a "part" of the potential self, in the sense that it is that part of the potential self which has reached its most basic level of actuality. The analogue here is the carpenter who is compelled to make a chair whenever he works; while he may go on to make tables and shelves, he often only makes chairs and is incapable of making anything else before

---

26. Locke, *Two Treatises*, II.v.

making a chair. One might plausibly call this carpenter a "chair maker," and would view chairs as even more "proper" to this carpenter than his other products.

The potential self also possesses a legitimate basis for excluding others from the destruction or use of the actual self both in virtue of this whole-part relationship and in virtue of the dependence of the actual self upon the potential self as an effect on its efficient cause. Since the actual self is "proper" to and a part of the potential self, and since the potential self produces or makes the actual self through its operation, the actual self and the potential self are intimately related to one another. Moreover, and in contradistinction to the carpenter-chair example, the actual self is dependent upon the potential self in a continuous manner. The potential self does not produce the actual self once and for all; rather, the existence of the actual self is coextensive with the operation or activity of the potential self. When the operation of the potential self is suspended, as in the case of sleep, the actual self ceases to be. The reason for this continual dependence lies in the characterization of basic self-consciousness as an activity rather than a static condition, and in the inseparability of the self and self-consciousness. Thus the efficient cause-effect relationship between the potential self and the actual self is stronger than many instances of this relationship, such as the carpenter-chair example, in which the continued existence of the effect does not depend upon the continued operation of the efficient cause.

This relationship between the potential self and the actual self is unique; it does not subsist between the actual self and other individuals. Whatever legitimate bases other individuals might have for controlling, using or destroying the actual self, the potential self retains a basis for excluding such interference through the unique aspects of its relationship to the actual self. This relationship invariably enters the balance on the side of exclusion (i.e., it stands as a basis for exclusion) since the actual self is an inextricable part of the potential self, and since the continued existence of the actual self depends upon the continued existence of the potential self. The relationship between the potential self and the actual self thus fulfills the criteria of ownership, and the potential self is indeed justified in claiming the actual self as "mine."

It may be objected that the foregoing account of self-ownership includes contestable "ought" premises at its foundation which are let in, as it were, through the back door. Doesn't the argument for self-ownership as presented ultimately rely on an assertion of "maker's rights,"[27] or the premise

---

27. Tully, *A Discourse on Property*, 136.

that others "ought not" use or destroy what one has caused to exist? In order to understand why it does not, it is necessary to distinguish between (1) "ought" propositions and (2) propositions which are both based upon "factual" or descriptive ones and possess normative implications. These latter types of propositions are difficult to analyze on the basis of the "is-ought" dichotomy; they stand on descriptive bases but cast a normative shadow. "Ought" propositions, on the other hand, are thoroughly normative. They may not be analyzed into descriptive components or squarely placed on descriptive bases; their normativity is not implied but already fully present.

The descriptive propositions or facts upon which propositions of type (2) depend are facts regarding a given order, or "ordering facts." These ordering facts reflect fixed, ordered relationships between two entities. Such facts are, considered in themselves, simple descriptive propositions: X stands to Y in a fixed, ordered relationship. The normative or "ought" implications to which ordering facts give rise result from the possibility of contravening action, i.e., action against or in contradiction with the ordering fact. In the particular case of self-ownership, the operative ordering fact consists in the production of the actual self by the potential self. Since the potential self produces the actual self, a cause-effect relationship subsists between them which is both fixed and ordered. It is fixed because the actual self exists only as the effect of the operation of the potential self, and it is ordered in terms of priority and posteriority, independence and dependence, as a consequence of the general relationship between causes and effects. The normative implications of the self-ownership based upon this ordering fact result, in turn, from the possibility of others acting in a manner inconsistent with the potential self-actual self relationship. Such contravening actions do not, of course, alter the ordering fact, which is assumed to be fixed beyond the reach of human activity. Contravening action is, rather, action *in spite of* the ordering fact, or *as if* the contrary of the ordering fact were actually true. While the concrete determination of whether a certain action is in contravention of a given ordering fact is a matter of particular judgment, the possibility of contravening action is at least fairly obvious. For example, it is not difficult to see how various forms of coercion, such as the extreme case of enslavement, contravene the ordering fact of self-ownership. Acts of coercion are clearly actions *in spite of* the self-ownership of the coerced, or *as if* the individual did not in fact own himself.

In this way the derivation of the concept of self-ownership avoids both the charge of contestable foundational normativity and that of the illicit is-ought inference. The concept of ordering facts which give rise to propositions with normative implications enables the derivation of self-ownership, with its normative implications, from the wholly descriptive concept of self-consciousness. According to Locke, moreover, it is precisely "by being master of himself, and *proprietor of his own person*" that a human being possesses natural rights.[28] A natural right, properly understood, rests on the basis of this self-ownership, and constitutes a normative implication following from the possibility of acting contrary to the ordering fact present in self-consciousness.

NATURAL RIGHTS

Taking the possession of a natural right in the strict sense, a natural right may be defined as *a basis for moral claims residing within or deriving from the individual*. This definition constitutes the most plausible equivalent for the variety of assertions of natural rights abounding in contemporary moral and political discourse. When one asserts a natural right "to X," or that one *ought* to have a recognized legal right "to X," a claim "to X" is undoubtedly included in this assertion. This claim is assumed to be a moral one, or one that imposes a duty of action or forbearance on the part of others; otherwise, there would be no reason for asserting the claim at all. Since the act of asserting a natural right must be distinguished from the possession of a natural right if the claiming is to make literal sense, the natural right itself must be the underlying basis for the moral claim which renders this claim justified, reasonable, or persuasive. Finally, this basis for moral claims can only be literally possessed by the individual if it is located within or arises from the individual himself. If the basis for the moral claim were the natural law, the divine law or some other external moral framework, one could not literally possess or "have" the basis for one's moral claim any more than one could possess these external moral frameworks. It is thus reasonable to treat the phrase "I have a right to X" as equivalent to the phrase "I have a basis for a moral claim to X which resides within or is derived from myself as an individual."

Taking natural rights in this strict sense, self-ownership constitutes the foundational natural right. It has been argued that the concept of property ownership includes, as a normative implication, a basis for excluding others from the use or destruction of the property owned. In the case of self-ownership, this basis lies in the ordering fact of the potential self-actual self relationship, or the potential self's role as efficient cause of the actual

---

28. Locke, *Two Treatises*, II.v.44.

self. This ordering fact may be contravened by the actions of others; others may use or destroy the actual self in spite of the potential self-actual self relationship. In the face of this possibility of contravening action, self-ownership acquires its normative implications, and the basis for the exclusion of others becomes a basis for moral claims raised against others. Self-ownership as a basis for moral claims, moreover, resides within and derives from the individual rather than from some other moral framework. The potential self, the actual self and the ordering fact of the relationship between them are all contained within each individual and arise from diverse considerations of the individual. Self-ownership derives from self-consciousness, which, though it is profoundly influenced, shaped and given content by an individual's environment and relationships with others, nevertheless remains an activity performed by the individual *as* an individual. Even a thoroughly situated or "encumbered" self is directly produced by the activity of the potential self, or the individual considered in light of his reflective capacity. Self-ownership thus constitutes a basis for moral claims residing within or deriving from the individual, i.e., a natural right.

Locke's famous triad of primary natural rights (life, liberty and property) are not, strictly speaking, natural rights themselves but rather objects to which human beings have a natural right. Each of these objects represent that to which, not that on the basis of which, moral claims are made. Life, liberty and property (as well as the pursuit of happiness) are the primary objects of natural right because they follow most immediately from self-ownership and are the most general in scope. Most, if not all, other objects of natural right may be included under the head of one of these primary objects. The next question becomes, then, that of showing whether and how the primary moral claims to life, liberty, and property follow from the basis of self-ownership.

LIFE

The natural right to life, or to "self-preservation," is given particular emphasis by early modern natural rights thinkers such as Hobbes and Locke. Hobbes includes self-preservation within the very definition of "the right of nature," as the fundamental object of "the liberty each man hath to use his own power."[29] The right to self-preservation or life is, moreover, the only object of natural right not transferred to the sovereign in the initial social contract, since "no man can transfer or lay down his right to save himself

---

29. Hobbes. *Leviathan*. I.xiv.1.

from death."[30] Locke similarly grants the *"right of self-preservation"* a foundational place in his account of the state of nature,[31] and consistently gives the right to "life" pride of place in his listing of the primary objects of right which governments are instituted to protect and preserve.[32] This fact is not particularly surprising, since life is a necessary precondition for exercising liberty, acquiring property or pursuing happiness. Conceiving the right to life or self-preservation in this way, however, might seem to indicate that life constitutes a primary object of natural right *because* it is presupposed by the further rights of liberty, property or the pursuit of happiness. While for Hobbes the right to self-preservation stems from the most powerful human passion, the fear of violent death, for Locke the right to self-preservation may appear instrumental to the further rights of liberty or property. In either case the right to life does not immediately appear to follow from the fact of self-ownership.

By attending carefully to Locke's initial formulation of the right to life as the right to "self-preservation," as well as Locke's subsequent identification of life (along with liberty and property) with the concept of "property,"[33] however, the close connection between the right to life and self-ownership comes into view. Locke himself did not, within the *Two Treatises*, elaborate a precise understanding of self-preservation which would connect the "self" in this formulation with the "self" of the *Essay*. Nor does Locke clearly indicate how one's life may be his own property given the fact that human beings are "his property, whose workmanship they are."[34] It is possible, however, to give a Lockean justification for the right to life as a basic implication of self-ownership.

There are many ways in which one might argue that one's life is not one's own, and therefore that while there may be a duty on the part of others not to take the life of another, there is no basis for a moral claim to one's own life which derives from the individual himself. The life of every human being is simply given by some combination of one's parents, natural causes or God. These progenitors of the individual human being, not the individual himself, would seem to possess a right to the life of the individual. As the "workmen" who produced the life of the individual, one's parents and/or God have a property in the life of the individual which is exclusive both of others and of the individual herself. However accurate this account may be,

---

30. *Ibid.*, I.xiv.29.
31. Locke, *Two Treatises*, II.ii.11.
32. *Ibid.*, II.vii.87; II.ix.123; II.xix.221.
33. *Ibid.*, II.ix.123.
34. *Ibid.*, II.ii.6.

Locke echoes an eminently commonsensical notion in characterizing one's life as her own property. This tension may be resolved by considering the life of the individual in terms of the same notion of concurrent univocal property utilized in reconciling self-ownership with Divine ownership with respect to the individual considered in general.[35]

Although the individual human being cannot claim to be the sole proprietor of his own life, there is indeed an aspect of the individual which is proximately and immediately of his own making: the self. The activity of self-consciousness, which constitutes the production of the self, depends upon human life and is a primary manifestation of this life. Human life in general is, on the other hand, separable from the activity of self-consciousness, as the most common example of sleep indicates. Human life, or the humanity of human beings, thus underlies the activity of self-consciousness and is ordered to the production of the self as one of its primary operations. Individuals do not have a right to life as the underlying condition for the production of the self, since the existence of the individual is coextensive with this life and is therefore in no way prior to it, but they do have a right to the actual self which depends upon this life. The actual self is the primary object of natural right since it is the object owned in the relation of self-ownership; the "substance" and "man" aspects of the individual point beyond the individual considered as the locus of bases for moral claims. Human life, moreover, is more closely associated with the humanity of the individual, or the individual considered as a locus of powers and potentialities rather than of operations and activities.

Thus the right to life ought to be understood as the right to the actual self which depends upon the continuance of life. Considered in this way, the right to life is more properly termed the right of "self-preservation," since it is the "self" rather than the life of the individual which is, strictly speaking, the object of the natural right. In this way Locke's characterization of one's life as "property" may also be understood in a more precise manner than Locke's language indicates; life is one's property in an extended or derivative sense since the self, which is undoubtedly one's property, depends upon life in general for its continued existence. The destruction of another's life is thus a violation of the other's natural right, or an injury *to* the other, primarily insofar as the actual self is implicated in this destruction.

There is, in addition, a secondary and related sense in which one may be said to have a right to one's life. Although life is not originated or produced by the individual, it is in a certain sense appropriated and transformed in

---

35. See Chapter 1.

the production of the actual self. The actual self, or the individual insofar as she is self-conscious, recognizes its dependence upon the continuance of life, and is concerned to preserve its life as a result of this dependence. In Locke's terms the activity of self-consciousness "reaches" or extends to the life upon which it depends and "joins" this life to itself.[36] In this way the life upon which the activity of self-consciousness or the actual self depends becomes, in fact, significantly different from life considered in general. Life, insofar as it is reached by self-consciousness and joined to it, enters into a relationship with the potential self which possesses the characteristics of ownership. The life of which one is self-conscious is transformed from life simply to life as a virtual part of self-consciousness, and life in this second sense is originated or produced by the activity of self-consciousness. Considered in this way, life is not simply a precondition for the existence of the actual self but rather a part of the actual self. Since one possesses a natural right to the actual self, one also possesses a natural right to the parts of the actual self; therefore, on this account as well, life is a primary object of natural right.

Liberty

Liberty, as a primary object of natural right, must be understood in the "negative" sense,[37] since the justifications for varieties of "positive" liberty are derived from considerations extending beyond the individual. In this negative sense, liberty denotes a control of one's own actions to the exclusion of the control of others. One's own actions, moreover, are precisely that: one's *own*. As Locke states in the *Essay*, the extension of self-consciousness to one's actions renders the self the exclusive owner of these actions.[38] In much the same way as life may be considered to be a part of the actual self, one's interaction with the external world through actions becomes a part of the actual self during the course of the activity of self-consciousness. Just as one is concerned for one's life as an object to which self-consciousness immediately extends, so one is concerned for one's actions insofar as they are joined to self-consciousness.

Consciously performed actions are significantly different from those performed unconsciously; the potential self, or the individual considered in light of the reflective capacity, is a cause of the existence of the former but

---

36. Locke, *Essay*, II.xxvii.17.
37. Berlin, "Two Concepts of Liberty."
38. Locke, *Essay*, II.xxvii.17.

not of the latter. Since the potential self produces conscious actions through its own activity of self-consciousness, the potential self enters into a relation of ownership with these actions. This relation of ownership, and the ordering fact upon which it is based, is contravened when another interposes between the potential self and its conscious actions; it is this interposition which is commonly termed "coercion" or "restraint." In this case, the potential self cedes a measure of causality with respect to conscious action to factors external to the self. By purporting to cause one's conscious action, such external factors usurp or interrupt the fundamental cause-effect relationship between the potential self and conscious action. This introduces moral implications since the ordering fact of this relationship is contravened by another's action. There is, therefore, a basis for a moral claim to liberty deriving from the individual.

Property

The natural right to property is here understood as the right to property in external objects, or what Locke sometimes refers to as "estates." The status of the natural right to property, both in itself and in its specific treatment by Locke, remains highly controversial. Tully understands Locke's natural right to property as a right of "usufruct," or the right of a "trustee" with respect to God's property and God's purposes.[39] Even this weakened right to property is, moreover, merely the "completion" of the natural right to self-preservation and is "conditional on . . . the performance of positive duties to God."[40] Thus, although Tully admits the presence of a natural right to property in Locke's account, the object of the natural right lies in a significantly weakened notion of property, and the right itself is merely instrumental and conditional.

Tully's understanding of Locke's natural right to property is challenged by Zuckert, who emphasizes the "transformative" and "immensely creative power of human labor."[41] Human beings do not simply use God's property, but rather produce "[t]hings that were never in the world . . . from what was there."[42] The natural right to property is thus the right not of the trustee to use the product of another but rather the right of the workman in his workmanship. This natural right is, moreover, intimately connected with

---

39. Tully, *A Discourse on Property*, 122.
40. Ibid.
41. Zuckert, *Natural Rights and the New Republicanism*, 264–65.
42. Ibid., 264.

the human activity of self-consciousness; it is because human beings labor "self-consciously" that their labor is better described as transformative creation than mere use. On this account, property as the object of the natural right is taken in its strongest form, and the right itself has an intrinsic status rather than a merely instrumental one.

By following Zuckert's interpretation of the connection between self-consciousness and the natural right to property in Locke's account, it is possible both to explain and justify the natural right to property as a consequence of the fact of self-ownership. The connection between self-consciousness, labor and the natural right to property constitutes the crux of Locke's argument; a point missed, for example, by Nozick in his description of Locke's theory of acquisition.[43] Nozick takes Locke's terminology of "mixing" one's labor with external objects in a literal sense which obscures Locke's meaning. Nozick asserts that, for Locke, ownership of one's labor "seeps over into" other objects, and challenges this Locke by asking: "Why isn't mixing what I own with what I don't own a way of losing what I own rather than a way of gaining what I don't?"[44] Comparing one's labor to a "can of tomato juice," Nozick questions whether spilling this juice on an object grants a title to ownership of the object or simply results in an empty can of juice. While it is clear that much is lost in this analogy, and that self-conscious labor is a very different sort of thing from tomato juice, how Locke's "mixing" is to be understood is far less clear.

Locke, as Nozick recognizes, rests the right to property on the prior ownership of one's actions or labor. Ownership of one's actions or labor stems, moreover, from one's self-ownership. In a manner parallel to the extension of ownership from one's self to one's actions, ownership is further extended from one's actions to external objects which are consciously appropriated. The individual owns his actions, and hence possesses a natural right to liberty, because conscious actions are directly produced by the potential self. It would seem, however, that in the case of appropriating external objects, such as Locke's acorns or apples, these objects have already been produced by causes beyond any individual, and hence that the criteria for ownership in a strong sense cannot be met by the appropriating individual. Gathering acorns or picking apples appears only to change the place of these objects, not alter them sufficiently to introduce an owner-owned relationship. For this reason, it is plausible that objects given by nature may only be appropriated for one's use, and thus that the natural right to property in such

---

43. Robert Nozick, *Anarchy, State, and Utopia* (New York: Basic Books, 1974), 174–76.
44. Ibid., 175.

objects either doesn't exist at all, or must be understood as a kind of "tenant" property.

In the case of objects which have been significantly altered by human art, such as a chair or house, it is more plausible to speak of a producer-product relationship. In these cases, the product has been sufficiently transformed by the human workman to warrant a plausible claim of ownership on the part of the workman. Even in these cases, however, the workman can only claim to own, in a sense stronger than mere use-ownership, whatever additional characteristics he has produced beyond the materials simply given by nature. This creates the rather awkward situation in which the carpenter owns the shape, arrangement, texture, color, etc., of the chair without owning the materials out of which the chair was fashioned. The carpenter thus owns many of the characteristics or features of the chair without actually owning the chair itself as a whole; he appears, in Nozick's terms, to have lost his labor rather than gained a chair.

It is thus difficult to speak of a natural basis for or right to property, if property is to be understood in the meaningful sense extending beyond mere use. By connecting the right to property to the activity of self-consciousness and the fact of self-ownership, however, it is evident that the case of property in external objects follows the model of property in one's own actions or labor. In the case of ownership of one's actions, the crucial distinction lay between actions considered simply and conscious actions. While the former owe much to external factors and material dispositions, the latter are produced directly and completely by the potential self. In the same way, acorns, apples, chairs or houses considered solely in themselves are not directly and completely produced by any individual. Considered in connection with self-consciousness, however, these objects owe their existence to the potential self and the activity of self-consciousness. When an apple becomes "my apple," much more has changed than the apple's location. This apple becomes attached to my self-consciousness in such a manner that it becomes, like conscious actions, a virtual part of the self. As a self-conscious individual, I have plans for this apple and am concerned for it in the same way, though perhaps to a lesser degree, that I am concerned for my life or liberty. Self-consciousness directly produces "my apple" in this sense, and "my apple" began to exist from the moment of conscious appropriation. It is not the mere mixing of physical labor which grants a title to property, but rather the mixing of the self-consciousness attached to conscious labor with the external object which grants such a title. The self-consciousness which previously extended only to one's conscious actions extends further to the objects of these actions in the external world.

External objects thus become transformed into components or virtual parts of the self, and are implicated in one's self-ownership. In this way, property may be understood as a primary object of natural right.

CONCLUSION

On this understanding, self-ownership as a natural right is of very great, but not absolute, moral weight. The presence of a basis for a moral claim deriving from the individual does not preclude the simultaneous presence of a basis for rejecting this claim in any given instance. For example, a convicted criminal retains the natural right to liberty even after being sentenced to incarceration; the fact of his self-ownership has not been altered by the judgment against him. Retaining the basis for a moral claim to liberty does not, however, imply the decisiveness of such a moral claim in this particular case. When confronted with the bases for constraining the criminal's liberty, the basis for the claim to liberty deriving from the criminal, though it remains, loses its moral implications.[45]

The claiming of a natural right is thus a beginning, rather than an end, of moral discussion and adjudication. First, it must be determined that the claim follows from the possession of a natural right; the right-claim must be shown to derive from the proper basis of such claims in the fact of self-ownership through self-consciousness. Secondly, this basis must be shown to be decisive in the given instance, and thus to have the full array of moral implications emanating from the possession of the natural right. Although natural rights are important components of human morality, their objects are much fewer than is usually supposed; and even when an appropriate object may be identified, such rights are not the absolute "trumps"[46] which they are commonly taken to be.

There is, moreover, an inherent order of importance or priority among particular natural rights arising from their respective proximity to the concept of self-ownership. The natural right to life holds the first place in this order, since one's life is either understood to be identical with one's self or is the most immediate object to which self-consciousness extends. The natural right to liberty holds the second place, since actions or operations, with which liberty is concerned, presuppose only life, and therefore

---

45. This example of the basis for a moral claim deriving from the individual losing its moral implications, or becoming a basis upon which nothing may be constructed, has a certain kinship to the type of nonmoral natural rights described by Zuckert as "proto-rights" in *The Natural Rights Republic* (73–75).

46. Ronald Dworkin, *Taking Rights Seriously* (Cambridge: Harvard University Press, 1978).

self-consciousness extends in the next place to these objects. The natural right to property, finally, is the farthest removed from the concept of self-ownership since self-consciousness may only appropriate external objects after it has joined itself to life and liberty. Other, secondary objects of natural right may be similarly ordered on the basis of the closeness of their derivation from self-ownership.

This order of priority matches up closely, moreover, with common understandings of natural rights; the natural right to property is constantly trumped by competing considerations relating to the common benefit (through taxes, for example) and the natural right to liberty is frequently, though with much more care, overridden by considerations relating to public safety, while the natural right to life is very seldom treated as less than decisive. Locke's succinct yet eloquent statement of the order of priority among the objects of natural right thus remains largely uncontroversial in the contemporary context.[47]

---

47. I am referring here to Locke's repeated listing of natural rights in the order of "life, liberty, and property" throughout the *Second Treatise*.

CHAPTER THREE

From Natural Rights to the Natural Law

By arguing for the existence of natural rights (or, more precisely, of a natural right to a few important objects) on the basis of self-ownership, I would seem to have lent substantial support to modern idealizations of human autonomy.[1] Self-ownership, and the natural right to liberty it grounds in particular, clearly implies a privileged moral status for self-direction. Self-direction represents, in fact, the primary manifestation of the underlying fact of self-ownership; it is a kind of dynamic self-ownership, or self-ownership in action. But to what extent does this notion of self-direction open the door to a "broader moral freedom . . . a realm of personal sovereignty or free choice" that is commonly taken to emanate from the possession of natural rights?[2]

Most conceptions of human autonomy or of realms of moral freedom, personal sovereignty, and free choice are not, of course, as open-ended as they might initially seem. As an example, for Nozick one's realm of autonomy created by the possession of rights is limited by its intersection with the realms of autonomy enjoyed by others. The rights of others enter as "side constraints" that circumscribe the otherwise potentially boundless area of individual autonomous self-direction.[3] Rawls, in *A Theory of Justice*, famously operationalized this conception through his construction of the "original position" and his formulation of the first principle of justice. J. S. Mill, even earlier, posited his influential "no harm" principle as

---

1. For examples of this, see Joseph Raz, *The Morality of Freedom* (Oxford: Oxford University Press, 1986); Stephen Macedo, *Diversity and Distrust: Civic Education in a Multicultural Democracy* (Cambridge: Harvard University Press, 2003); John Rawls, *A Theory of Justice* and *Political Liberalism*.
2. Zuckert, *Launching Liberalism*, 185.
3. Nozick, *Anarchy, State, and Utopia*.

84   CHAPTER THREE

an important boundary circumscribing autonomous, self-directed action.[4] Gewirth has provided perhaps the most systematic formulation of the built-in limits to individual autonomy with his Kantian "Principle of Generic Consistency," which affirms that since "all prospective purposive agents have rights to freedom and well-being," one must "act in accord with the generic rights of your recipients as well as of yourself."[5]

Most, if not all, proponents of individual autonomy thus acknowledge the principle of "side constraint autonomy:" I am morally entitled to make my own rules for action or form my own "life-plan" so long as these rules or this plan do not prevent any other individual from doing the same. The realm of individual autonomy may not possess any inherent shape in the form of direct constraints, but whatever shape it does take is limited by rubbing up against adjacent realms of individual autonomy. Side-constraint autonomy is widely palatable since it escapes the obvious difficulties of the Hobbesian "right to everything," enables living in society, and mimics basic features of more robust moral-religious systems. Side-constraint autonomists (which includes most inhabitants of Western liberal democracies today), however, generally do not have persuasive or rationally defensible justifications for the purported moral status of self-direction upon which their superstructures rest. The "value" of self-direction, whether expressed in terms of human dignity or the possession of rights, is normally placed beyond discussion in the nonrational realms of religious faith, common moral intuition, immediate apprehension or unavoidable deontic judgment.[6] Side-constraint autonomists have, in other words, found themselves unable to follow the path of justification through the gateway from "ought" to "is," and thus have focused more on where the moral decisiveness of self-direction might end than on where it begins.

A very different picture regarding the implications of the moral status of self-direction stemming from self-ownership emerges, however, when one considers this status in light of its justification as this has been explicated in the last two chapters. Attributing a moral status or "value" to self-direction commits one to accepting the validity of the proper reasons for this attribution, assuming such reasons exist (as I have argued they do). Accepting these reasons, in the form of (1) the distinction between the humanity of the individual and her unique selfhood, and (2) the ordering fact underlying

---

4. J. S. Mill, *On Liberty*, chap. 1.
5. Gewirth, *Reason and Morality*, 48, 135.
6. This is not to say the meaning or significance of self-direction is not debated and discussed, but that its value is commonly either assumed or inferred from its being valued by individuals.

self-ownership in the (individual as) potential self-(individual as) actual self relation, moreover, turns out to come at the cost of affirming individual autonomy. It is, in other words, inconsistent to simultaneously affirm a moral status for self-direction stemming from self-ownership or the possession of rights and the truth of individual autonomy. If human beings possess natural rights, if we are self-owners, and if we are properly self-directing agents, we are *ipso facto* not autonomous. We do not ultimately make our own rules and we are not morally free to proceed according to a "life-plan" of our choosing, at least at the most general level; our self-direction is subject to direct constraints, rather than mere side constraints, and therefore falls short of autonomy. The possession of natural rights does result in a "realm of personal sovereignty," but this realm is itself circumscribed by and contained within a wider heteronomy.[7] In order to affirm the former, one must simultaneously affirm the latter.

IMPLICATIONS OF SELF-OWNERSHIP FOR SELF-DIRECTION

Recalling the Lockean distinction between the humanity and the unique selfhood of the human individual, the genesis and structure of the unique self as traced in the preceding chapter is clearly rooted in the overarching context of one's humanity. In order to become a unique self, one must first be distinct from nonbeing, i.e., a substance in Locke's terms. One must, further, be a certain kind of being, since not every kind of being is capable of becoming a unique self. In fact, among all of the animals, human beings are the only kind of being that appears capable of performing this feat. The operation of becoming, or being, a unique self is also one that naturally, or "always or for the most part," is engaged in by human beings.[8] Moreover, every human being who engages in this operation characteristic of a unique self does so in precisely the same way. It is not as if John has his preferred way of being a unique self, Mary has hers, Tom has his, and so on. Every human individual is constrained not only to become a unique self, but to do so in precisely the same way. In this way, the humanity of the individual stands above and encompasses one's unique selfhood.

The simply given, or natural, way in which human individuals become unique selves consists in the dynamic structure of self-consciousness as an

---

7. I am using this term in its simple etymological (not strictly Kantian) sense as law stemming from a source other than oneself.
8. Aristotle, *Physics*, II.2.

operation of the capacity for reflection.[9] This dynamic structure results, as I have argued, in the fact of self-ownership and the possession of a natural right with respect to certain general objects. The crucial step in this argument consisted, further, in the discovery of the ordering fact of the potential self-actual self relation, which simultaneously provides the descriptive basis and normative implications for self-ownership (and thus its status as a natural right). Thus the path to human dignity and the possession of natural rights for human beings necessarily passes through the ordering fact of the potential self-actual self relation, which is in turn generated by the natural operation of self-consciousness. This ordering fact, consisting in the relation between the potential self and the actual self, is, moreover, itself firmly rooted in the humanity of the individual. While the actual self is, of course, characteristic of unique selfhood, both the potential self and the relationship between the two is located within one's humanity. This may be illustrated by considering the givenness and universality of the manner in which the actual self is produced by the reflective operation of the potential self. The transition from the potential self to the actual self does not vary across individuals, but is identical between them—a defining characteristic of the humanity, rather than the unique selfhood, of the human individual. While individuals as actual selves are unique, they necessarily begin at the same place and use precisely the same mode of transportation to arrive at this destination. A fundamental similarity at the level of the potential self, or the individual considered in light of the capacity for reflection, terminates in a diversity of actual selves.[10] At the level of the ordering fact of the potential self-actual self relation, therefore, one notices most conspicuously the manner in which the humanity of the individual stands above and encompasses one's unique selfhood.

The unique "location" of this ordering fact on the boundary, as it were, between the unique selfhood and the humanity of the individual enables it to perform the double function of justifying an area of personal sovereignty or free choice and of indicating direct limitations on the exercise of this agency. The idea of self-ownership that expresses this ordering fact is thus a double-edged sword, guaranteeing the moral inviolability of individual self-direction vis-à-vis other individuals on the one hand, and placing moral limits upon the exercise of individual self-direction vis-à-vis one's given humanity on the other. This double function of self-ownership has a certain

---

9. See preceding chapter.

10. Charles Taylor's conception of the self begins from this subsequent diversity of actual selves and their particular self-interpretations.

intuitive appeal, possessing clear analogues within ordinary experience. If someone owns a pit bull, for example, the fact of ownership legitimately excludes others from the use or destruction of the animal. The same fact of ownership, however, is also commonly recognized to include within it the responsibility of the owner for his pit bull; there are clear limitations on and requirements attaching to the owner's use of his pit bull following from the same owner-owned relationship that excludes others from such use. It would, for example, seem somehow inconsistent if the owner were to claim exclusive ownership of the animal while at the same time disavowing responsibility for the animal's training. Along similar lines, someone who commits a crime while intoxicated is properly assigned responsibility for his actions in direct proportion to the degree of self-ownership he is assigned. Insofar as he was not an actual self-owner at the time of the action, he is relieved of responsibility; insofar as he is normally a self-owner, he is blamed.[11] While it is not difficult to perceive the commonsensical connection between freedom and responsibility in general, the manner in which this connection is specifically forged through the ordering fact of the potential self-actual self relationship remains to be shown.

THE BEGINNING OF HETERONOMY

The relationship between the potential self (the individual considered in light of the capacity for reflection) and the actual self (the individual considered in light of the activity of self-consciousness) has been depicted as fixed and ordered, and hence as an ordering fact. It has been argued that this fixed and ordered relationship is a particularly strong instance of the general relationship between causes and effects, warranting its description in terms of ownership. What has not been explicitly indicated, however, is that this relationship is also inherently hierarchical. Of course, hierarchy is implied in every relationship of priority and posteriority or cause and effect. This hierarchical element becomes more pertinent, however, in the particularly close relationship between owner and owned. While the general superiority of a cause to its effect may only possess an abstract ontological relevance, the superiority of an owner to a thing owned possesses, in addition, a concrete, practical and normative relevance. Just as self-ownership has a concrete normative relevance with respect to the relationship between the self-owner and other individuals, it also has a concrete normative relevance with respect to the relationship between the self as owner and the self as

---

11. Aristotle, *Nicomachean Ethics*, III.1.

owned. In the former instance, it is primarily the uniqueness and intimacy of the relationship between owner and owned that is morally relevant; in the latter, however, it is primarily the hierarchy implicit in this relationship that is morally relevant.

While certain kinds of legal or conventional ownership might not clearly reflect an inherent superiority of owner to owned, the case of natural or pre-political ownership is very different. Since natural ownership results from the activity of workmanship or "transformative labor," a rigid and clear hierarchy is implied in the relation of natural ownership. The thing owned would not exist if not for the activity of the owner, and is thus radically dependent upon the owner. The superiority of the owner to the thing owned is, in this instance, an essential condition of ownership rather than a concomitant characteristic. There is no question, therefore, of the inherent superiority of the owner to the thing owned in the case of natural ownership. What does it mean, however, for the potential self to be superior to the actual self, and what possible implications could this hierarchy have for concrete human action?

The potential self, as explained above, refers simply to the individual human being considered as potentially reflective, or considered in light of the capacity for reflection. The actual self, on the other hand, refers to the individual human being considered as actually reflective or self-conscious. Thus the individual considered in light of the capacity for reflection is superior to, and owns, the individual considered as actually reflective or self-conscious. The capacity for reflection pertains, moreover, to the humanity of the individual while actual reflective activity pertains to one's unique selfhood. The ordering fact justifying the possession of natural rights, therefore, clearly implies the superiority of the humanity of the individual with respect to this unique selfhood. In order to better understand the practical normative implications of this conclusion, it is necessary to revisit and clarify the distinction between the humanity and unique selfhood of the individual.

At the broadest level this distinction reflects the difference between the "given" and "made" aspects of the individual; no one creates himself *ex nihilo*, and yet everyone participates in something like Taylor's identity formation through the accumulation and integration of self-conscious thought and action. Commonly recognized distinctions between "nature" and "nurture," between genetics and environment, or between talent and work ethic, are broadly parallel to the human-being/unique-self distinction. Individual human beings are a compound of (1) characteristics and capacities that are shared with all, or nearly all, other human individuals and which are simply "given," and (2) a self-consciousness of thought and action by means of which the individual separates himself from all other individuals through a form of self-"making." This broad point is rather difficult to deny, since it is immediately obvious that both elements of this compound do in fact somehow exist in all, or nearly all, individual human beings.

It may be objected, nevertheless, that this distinction is so abstract and removed from the concrete unity of the individual human being as to be rendered merely metaphorical. No less an authority than Aristotle, in fact, repeatedly denies that it is possible for someone to be unjust to himself precisely on the grounds of this concrete unity, conceding only the "metaphorical" possibility of speaking in such terms.[12] If this distinction is taken sufficiently literally, on the other hand, it may also invite comparison to the rigid dualism of Plato or Descartes. Combining these two possible lines of criticism, the distinction between the humanity and the unique selfhood of the individual seems to be either too far removed from concrete reality to have any real relevance, or to be simply a false depiction of a concrete reality characterized by unity. The account of this distinction provided attempts to steer a middle path between these two critiques, in fact following a distinctively Aristotelian approach in so doing. This approach is Aristotelian in two ways: (1) it denies that these two aspects of the individual comprise distinct substances, affirming rather that they represent two intellectually distinguishable ways of considering a single substance; and (2) it acknowledges that an intellectual analysis of unified substances in terms of their diverse aspects, such as the universal and the particular or form and matter, may nevertheless be true and meaningful.

How, then, is it meaningful or practically relevant to divide the human individual into her humanity and her unique selfhood, and to say that the individual as a human being is superior to the individual as a unique self? The superiority of the potential self to the actual self does not seem to possess any normative implications for the relationship between these two aspects of the individual, since it is difficult to conceive how contravening action would be possible in this instance. The general superiority of the humanity of the individual to his unique selfhood may, however, possess such normative implications if this humanity contains other elements whose relationship to unique selfhood admits of contravening action. If, in other words, the individual were able to act *in spite of* the superiority of his

---

12. Aristotle, *Ethics*, V.11.

humanity to his unique selfhood or *as if* this relationship of superiority did not subsist, an ordering fact with its normative implications would be present.

A SECOND ORDERING FACT

We have already uncovered one ordering fact that resulted in the possession of natural rights: the relationship between an element of the individual's humanity, i.e., the potential self, and an element of her unique selfhood, i.e., the actual self, is fixed, ordered, and admits of contravening action by others. Others may act *in spite of* this relationship or *as if* it didn't exist through coercion. If it is possible similarly for the individual herself to act in contravention of the superiority of her humanity to her unique selfhood, a second ordering fact will have been shown to exist. In other words, if it is possible for the individual to "make" herself through self-conscious thought and action in a manner contrary to some blueprint "given" by her humanity, this would constitute contravention of the superiority of her humanity to her unique selfhood. That some such blueprint exists, and that such contravention is possible, is widely attested in one way or another by numerous moral and political philosophers spanning the entire history of ideas.

Plato's Socrates, at the dawn of moral and political philosophy in the West, offered perhaps the most famous illustration of a given blueprint for self-conscious thought and action in his extended analogy between the Ideal city and the individual in Plato's *Republic*. Aristotle, in the *Nicomachean Ethics*, derived his account of happiness and virtue from the "function" or "work" given to human beings.[13] Locke, despite his many differences with both Plato and Aristotle, defined the "law of nature" in terms of reason as a human being's "only Star and compass," similarly acknowledging some blueprint for action in a given supply and arrangement of human capacities.[14] Such a blueprint need not be determinative or inflexible; each of these thinkers, in fact, are content to speak of this blueprint in extraordinarily general and even vague terms throughout their works.

It is clear from common experience, moreover, that if such a blueprint for human action or self-making exists, it is possible for individuals to deviate from this blueprint in their actions. This is indicated by the diversity of principles of action and "life-plans" followed by human beings, and is

---

13. Aristotle, *Ethics*, I.7.
14. Locke, *Two Treatises*, I.58.

universally attested by every thinker who acknowledges the existence of any sort of given blueprint for human action. While other animals appear to follow their respective patterns for living uniformly and unreflectively, human beings appear either to not possess such a given pattern or to be able to act as if they did not.

That there are other elements of the individual's humanity beyond the reflective capacity (or potential self), elements plausibly capable of constituting such a pattern or guideline for human action, is not difficult to surmise. It is clear that human beings have more in common with one another than the ability to engage in the activity of self-consciousness, even if this ability is one of the more important elements of humanity. Human beings are each given (i.e., not produced by the individual who possesses them) a similar supply and arrangement of capacities or powers that are determinate and limited, no matter how widely their similarity, determination and limitation are construed. Despite the great distance separating a Sir Isaac Newton or a Michael Jordan from the majority of human beings, these unusual individuals obviously do not possess idiosyncratic capacities or abilities but rather the usual capacities or abilities to an unusually high degree. All, or nearly all, human beings can understand principles of physics in a basic manner and jump at least a couple of inches off the ground. Given human capacities are also determinate, insofar as one can distinguish an ability to feel emotion from an ability to do a math problem or an ability to run a mile. Contrary to the Rousseauian idea of infinite perfectibility, moreover, given human capacities are inherently limited and circumscribed within some finite area of perfectibility, however large this area may be. Without these limitations, it is difficult to know what one would mean by the terms "human," "capacity," or "perfectibility;" the significations of these terms are necessarily attended by some form of limitation.

The humanity of the individual thus includes a number of identifiable elements in addition to the capacity for reflection, and these elements taken together constitute what I, following the traditional terminology, will call "human nature." This human nature contains a pattern or blueprint for action along the lines generally indicated by Plato, Aristotle, Locke and many others, a blueprint from which human beings may—and often do—deviate in their actions. Since the fixed and ordered relationship between one's humanity and one's unique selfhood thus appears capable of contravention by human action, this relationship does indeed constitute a second ordering fact. As the moral implications of the ordering fact of self-ownership constituted natural rights, so the moral implications of this second, and inextricably related, ordering fact constitute the natural law.

NATURAL LAW

It may seem strange to characterize the moral "shadow" of the second ordering fact in terms of the natural law, since the path traveled thus far looks quite different from those normally frequented by natural law thinkers. An argument for natural law would be expected to grow out of a discussion of the good rather than one of the right, or of a teleological discussion rather than a deontological one. It will be argued, nevertheless, that the term "natural law" is an eminently fitting one for describing the moral implications of the second ordering fact. The crux of this argument lies in the relationship of superiority between one's human nature and one's self, such that the human nature instantiated in individuals constitutes a legitimate superior to the individual considered in terms of particular self-consciousness. This legitimate superior issues rationally discernible commands in the form of the aforementioned blueprint it contains for self-conscious activity, and provides intrinsic rewards and penalties for compliance or deviation from this blueprint. Lastly, its commands are directed towards the good of its addressees.[15]

Although the road that has led our account to this point has indeed been unmarked by the footsteps of previous natural lawyers, it is precisely in recovering the "old" natural law of Aquinas and his predecessors that our own account of the natural law will be completed. This old natural law substantiates the existence of a blueprint for action in human nature and the possibility of contravening the second ordering fact, as well as each of the other features of the natural law mentioned above. The old natural law persuasively establishes the rational discernibility (and thus its promulgation as well as its pertinence to reason) of the guidelines for action contained within human nature, the commanding character of these guidelines, the existence of intrinsic rewards and punishments attached to these commands, and the direction of these commands to the human good or virtue. The insights of Aristotle, Cicero and Aquinas that comprise the old natural law are distinctively premodern insights whose contribution to a notion of natural morality will infuse a new and important moral direction to complement the moral baseline provided by modern liberalism and its idea of natural rights.

---

15. These components of the definition of "law" are drawn from the conceptions of both Locke and Aquinas, as well as commonsensical notions of law. The criterion of the "legitimate superior" is taken from Locke's *Questions Concerning the Law of Nature*, while the direction of law towards the good is taken from Aquinas's *Summa Theologica*. These criteria for the existence of law are chosen with a view to securing the widest possible assent.

THE CICERONIAN–ARISTOTELIAN NATURAL LAW

Although Cicero has recently begun to receive the attention he deserves as a philosopher in his own right, he is still commonly discounted as a natural law thinker in his own right.[16] By placing his thought in conversation with Aristotle on the one hand and Aquinas on the other, however, Cicero's crucial importance to the natural law tradition begins to clearly emerge. The specific points upon which Cicero's thought converges with both Aristotle and Aquinas correspond, moreover, with the distinguishing features of the account of the natural law contained herein. Cicero elaborates upon Aristotle's account of human nature as including a hierarchical order within it, an order that individual human beings are obliged to instantiate in their actions, in a manner that lays the groundwork for Aquinas's later doctrine of natural law. Taken together, Aristotle, Cicero and Aquinas confirm the existence of the second ordering fact outlined above and justify its description in terms of natural law.

Cicero's concept of human nature is founded upon a consideration of the specific place of human beings within a hierarchy of natures. In the beginning of the *De Officiis*, Cicero describes the natural characteristics and "instincts" of "every species of living creature."[17] These instincts primarily include self-preservation and reproduction, along with other instincts which are instrumental to these two. Although man possesses these animal impulses, he also exhibits the "marked difference" of "reason."

This description echoes Cicero's statement in the *De Legibus* that "reason, which alone raises us above the level of the beasts ... is certainly common to us all;"[18] in our terminology, Cicero might have said that reason constitutes an element of the humanity of human beings as opposed to their unique selfhood. In both accounts, Cicero begins by descriptively listing the proper capacities and inclinations inherent in reason. Reason's proper capacities include the ability "to draw inferences,"[19] "to discuss and solve problems,"[20] "perceive the causes of things,"[21] and "connect and associate the present and the future."[22] The proper inclinations of reason include the impulse to

---

16. S. Adam Seagrave, "Cicero, Aquinas and Contemporary Issues in Natural Law Theory," *Review of Metaphysics* 62, no. 3 (March 2009): 491–523.
17. *De Officiis* 1.11.13.
18. *De Legibus*, 1.30.329.
19. Ibid.
20. Ibid.
21. *De Officiis*, 1.11.13.
22. Ibid.

form communities with other human beings, to "provide a store of things"[23] both for himself and others in his care, and to "search after truth."[24]

Cicero also follows this discussion of reason in both accounts with a similarly descriptive one of the "evil tendencies"[25] inherent in human nature. These tendencies which run counter to the good of reason are generally subsumed under the heading of "sensual pleasure."[26] Sensual pleasure, moreover, is associated with "cattle and other beasts" which are "impelled" toward its pursuit in an irrational and unreflective manner.[27]

The crucial point here is that both inclinations, those pertaining to reason and those pertaining to the sensual appetite, are natural to human beings, or comprise distinct elements of humanity.[28] The problem of deciding between these inclinations in correctly determining one's actions does not exist for Cicero for the simple reason that man's rational aspect is clearly superior to his animal one. Thus Cicero explicates the virtue of "propriety" and its corresponding "duty," which involves the general one to live in agreement with nature, by stating that

> the essential activity of the spirit and also nature is twofold: one force is appetite . . . which impels a man this way and that; the other is reason, which teaches and explains what should be done and what should be left undone. The result is that reason commands, appetite obeys.[29]

Although this passage appears in the context of Cicero's discussion of the virtues, it is strikingly reminiscent of many formulations of the natural law throughout Cicero's writings. One is immediately reminded of Laelius's definition: "True law is right reason in agreement with nature . . . it summons to duty by its commands, and averts from wrongdoing by its prohibitions."[30] For human beings, living in agreement with the blueprint contained within human nature simultaneously implies the presence of virtue and obedience to the natural law.

---

23. Ibid., 1.12.15.
24. Ibid.
25. *De Legibus*, 1.31.331.
26. Ibid.
27. *De Officiis* 1.105.107.
28. On this point of Cicero's account of human inclinations, see Nicgorski, "Cicero's Paradoxes," 564–66.
29. *De Officiis*, 1.101103. I have altered the translation of the first clause in order to include "nature," which is present in the Latin.
30. Cicero, *De Re Publica*, trans. C. W. Keyes. Loeb Classical Library (Cambridge: Harvard University Press, 1970), 3.33.211.

Cicero thus derives both the natural law and the virtues from the single "fountain-head" of human nature.[31] This derivation appears to be a prime example of the "naturalistic fallacy" that, according to some, decisively refutes "the most popular image of natural law" and necessitates the project of the new natural law theorists.[32] Cicero does, in effect, build a normative theory of the virtues and the natural law using only a descriptive account of human nature. Since, however, Cicero's descriptive account of human nature involves both a definite blueprint for action in the superiority of reason to the sensual appetites along with the possibility of acting contrary to this blueprint, Cicero's account includes the elements necessary for qualifying as an ordering fact. Cicero's blueprint consists in the simple formula: "reason commands, appetite obeys," a formula that can be and often is reversed in particular human actions.

For Cicero the notion of law arises out of this descriptive account in two related ways. In the first and primary way, the blueprint for action contained within one's humanity becomes a lawful command when it confronts the contingent power of choice at the level of individual self-consciousness.[33] In other words, for Cicero, the possibility of contravening action against our second ordering fact gives rise to the moral implications characteristic of the commands of law.

According to Cicero, the rule of acting in accordance with the guidelines included in one's humanity possesses the form of a command, rather than a counsel or recommendation, because it includes the threat of punishment and the promise of reward (the proper effects of the notion of a command).[34] The punishment threatened by the command of one's humanity consists primarily in the alienation of oneself from one's nature, or the failure to be in actuality what one is fundamentally and potentially, which for Cicero is the harshest of penalties. This penalty, although it appears light as a result of its remoteness from tangible experiences of physical or material harm, is necessarily more painful than these since the most fundamental desire of any natural being consists in the preservation of its nature. In this manner the command of one's humanity also includes the reward of virtue, that is,

31. *De Legibus*, 1.18.317.

32. Finnis, *Natural Law*, 33; Robert P. George, "Natural Law and Human Nature," in *Natural Law Theory: Contemporary Essays*, 32.

33. See Cicero's derivation of "law" from the idea of "choosing" as one of the elements of its proper notion in *De Legibus* 1.19.317.

34. In this way one may, as Cicero does, establish the existence of a law or command from the existence of its proper effects (effects that could follow only from law or command). This is a kind of effect-to-cause (*quia*) argument which Fortin, for example, does not allow for in his discussion of the lawfulness of the natural law in "The New Rights Theory."

the eminently desirable fulfillment and completion of nature. This command is, moreover, delivered from within the individual human being himself, who knows upon reflection that the fulfillment of his nature requires acting at the behest of reason, or in accordance with the pattern for action contained within his humanity. Thus the natural law consists in a general command issuing from one's humanity which may be either followed or rejected, includes intrinsic rewards and penalties attaching to compliance or deviation,[35] and is universally promulgated to knowing subjects.

In the second way, the natural law exists by way of its instantiation in the particular commands for action which are issued by the reason of the individual in response to particular circumstances. It is in this second way that "Law . . . is the mind and reason of the prudent man, the standard by which Justice and Injustice are measured."[36] Whereas the subject of the natural law in the first way is the human being considered in light of his particular self-consciousness, in the second way its subject is the human being's sensual appetite. Since the nature of reason, including its proper inclinations, entails directing the actions of the whole human being, it must issue particular commands to the lower appetite and enlist its support. This appetite, however, is wont to oppose reason's commands and is capable of determining human actions in spite of them. This power of opposition and resistance, as in its first and more general manifestation, eliminates the possibility of a kind of despotic determination and necessitates a rule by law.[37] Therefore in this second way the individual, by following the injunctions of the primary and most general manifestation of natural law, issues commands to his appetite which possess the character of the natural law in the manner of particular participation or instantiation.

Absent this explicit derivation of the natural law, Cicero's account of the primary elements of humanity is, moreover, remarkably consonant with that provided by Aristotle. In the *Physics*, Aristotle defines "nature"

---

35. The distinction between "intrinsic" and "externally imposed" penalties and rewards is centrally important to an understanding of the natural law. Although punishments and rewards are indeed the proper effects of command and law, these need not be imposed by some external "observer," as Crosson, Fortin and many others would have it. If a law commands some good, disobedience of this law necessarily entails the deprivation of good. This penalty is an internal consequence of the act of disobedience itself, and not something appended to disobedience after the fact.

36. Cicero, *De Legibus*, 1.19.317–19. I have replaced "intelligent" in the translation with "prudent" to render the Latin more accurately.

37. For comparison see Aristotle's statement in the *Politics* that "the intellect rules the appetites with a constitutional and royal rule," in *The Basic Works of Aristotle*, ed. Richard McKeon (New York: Random House, 1941), 1254b4.

in general both in contradistinction to luck and chance as what is "always or for the most part,"[38] and as inhering in beings as the source or cause of their movement and rest.[39] The latter aspect, which constitutes the essential definition of "nature," is identified with a thing's matter in the sense of potency or necessary substratum for motion or change, and is identified with the form (that is, the soul) in the sense of actuality or fulfillment of this motion.[40] Applying this discussion of nature in general to human beings in the *Ethics*, Aristotle begins, as does Cicero, by placing human nature within a hierarchy of other natures.[41] Giving human nature the same proper (formal) element identified by Cicero, that of reason, Aristotle goes on to derive the notions of human happiness and virtue. In the course of this derivation, Aristotle portrays the same blueprint for action consisting in the superiority of the rational element of one's humanity, and attempts to explain the frequency of contravening action against this blueprint by individual human beings. Aristotle does so by dividing the human soul (which is human nature in the sense of form) into rational and irrational elements, with the irrational element being "naturally opposed"[42] to the rational principle" and apt to "fight against and resist that (the rational) principle."[43] Thus Aristotle already possesses an account of a blueprint for human action arising from the hierarchical relation of various elements of one's humanity, as well as an account of the frequency of contravening action against this blueprint, that is strikingly similar to Cicero's later account in terms of natural law.

A doctrine of natural law is, in fact, adumbrated by Aristotle's brief mention of "unrestrained people" in this context as well as in his further discussion of restraint and unrestraint in Book VII. In this latter discussion, Aristotle describes "unrestraint" with reference to "the facts of human nature."[44] These facts indicate the simultaneous presence within the individual of a "universal opinion" that either commands or forbids according to reason, and an "appetite" that resists this command.[45] In this way "a man behaves unrestrainedly under the influence (in a sense) of a rule and

---

38. Aristotle, *Physics*, in *The Basic Works of Aristotle*, 195b30–200b10.
39. Ibid., 192b22.
40. Ibid., 193a1–193b22.
41. Aristotle, *Nicomachean Ethics*, in *The Basic Works of Aristotle*, 1097b25–1098a5.
42. While Aristotle and Cicero would say "naturally opposed," St. Thomas would describe this frequent opposition as an effect of the Fall, and therefore the opposition would be "natural" in the sense of fallen nature, but not natural in the sense of original nature.
43. Aristotle, *Ethics*, 1102b13–30.
44. Ibid., 1147a25.
45. Ibid., 1147a30–35.

an opinion, and of one not contrary in itself . . . to the right rule."⁴⁶ For this reason Aristotle also states that the "lower animals are not unrestrained" precisely because "they have no universal judgment," which pertains only to reason.⁴⁷ The presence of reason and its universal judgment, in addition to the particular desires of the sensual appetite, introduces the contingent power of choice and the unique possibility of acting contrary to the pattern contained within one's humanity.

Aristotle's recognition and complex discussion of the phenomena of restraint and unrestraint adds an important dimension to his moral philosophy that is often overlooked by scholars who attempt to dissociate Aristotelian "natural right" from the idea of natural law. It is within this discussion that Aristotle presents an analysis of human action in general as the product of or conclusion from universal premises and a particular premise. The universal premises consist in propositions expressing some practical truth, such as "dry food is good for every man" or "such and such food is dry."⁴⁸ These universal premises join to form general commands or prohibitions formulated by reason and addressed to the human being as an agent concerned with particular actions. In Aristotle's example, there may be a "universal opinion . . . present in us" not only indicating that we should refrain from performing some action, but actually "forbidding" us to perform the action.⁴⁹ Since Aristotle does not indicate that his analysis of human agency in this place applies only to restrained or unrestrained persons, one may assume that the person of "practical wisdom" discussed in the book immediately preceding similarly possesses universal premises for action that have this commanding/forbidding character. The prudent man, then, is distinguished from the restrained man only in this: since his appetites or passions have been properly habituated, they do not give rise to competing premises that may impede the efficacy of the "right rule."

Aristotle's depiction of human agency in his discussion of restraint and unrestraint corresponds with the second or more particular manifestation of Cicero's natural law, that in which "Law . . . is the mind and reason of the prudent man." This particular manifestation consists in the concretization of the general and primary command of the natural law to act in accordance with the superiority of reason, in accordance with what Aris-

46. Ibid., 1147b.
47. Ibid., 1147b4–6.
48. Ibid., 1147a5–7.
49. Ibid., 1147a32. Although Aristotle's term here (*koluousa*) may be translated less strongly as "checking" or "preventing," it is most often, and not by an unwarranted license, translated as "forbidding."

totle terms the "function" of human beings,[50] or in accordance with the blueprint for human action produced by the hierarchical relation of various elements of one's humanity. In his analysis of human action, then, and that of the human soul on which it is based, Aristotle does indeed seem to approach a concept of natural law. Although Aristotle did not explicitly arrive at this concept himself, Cicero shows in his writings that the notion of law is indeed implicit in an Aristotelian account of human nature.[51] In this way, then, Cicero lays the foundation for the old natural law on the soil of Aristotle's nature.

FROM THE CICERONIAN–ARISTOTELIAN TO THE THOMISTIC NATURAL LAW

Armed with an understanding of the Ciceronian-Aristotelian conception of natural law, it is now (and only now) possible to provide an adequate interpretation of the culminating statement of the old natural law in the writings of St. Thomas. In his *Summa Theologica*, St. Thomas, like Cicero, attempts to derive the natural law inductively from a rational encounter with objective reality and an Aristotelian account of human nature.

St. Thomas's so-called "Treatise on Law,"[52] is, of course, not a proper "treatise" at all but rather a relatively small group of questions which occur in the middle of a much larger enterprise. The subject of the *Summa* is the science of "sacred doctrine," whose "chief aim . . . is to teach the knowledge of God."[53] St. Thomas gives a broad outline of this carefully structured work in Question 2 of the First Part, indicating that he will treat of "God," of "the rational creature's movement towards God," and of "Christ, Who as man, is our way to God."[54] Under the second topic of inquiry St. Thomas considers both "the last end of human life" and "those things by means of which man may advance towards the end, or stray from it."[55] The latter subject concerns "human acts," the treatment of which is first divided into "universal" and "particular" considerations.[56] Under the "universal" heading,

---

50. Aristotle, *Nicomachean Ethics*, I.7.
51. The question of whether Cicero read Aristotle's works himself, or was merely familiar with the thought of his followers in the Peripatetic school, is not of crucial importance to this particular argument (assuming a sufficient amount of continuity between the two sources). However, it seems that Cicero did read Aristotle's works himself from *De Finibus* 3.10.227.
52. St. Thomas, *ST*, I-II.90–108.
53. Ibid., I.2.prooemium.
54. Ibid.
55. Ibid., I-II.1.prooemium.
56. Ibid., I-II.6.prooemium.

St. Thomas plans to treat of "human acts themselves" and "their principles."[57] The discussion of the principles of human acts begins in Question 49 of the Prima Secundae, where this subject is once again divided into "intrinsic" and "extrinsic" principles.[58] We finally arrive at the questions regarding law in the treatment of the "extrinsic" principles of human acts, which are identified as the "devil" and "God."[59] The devil inclines human actions to evil through "temptations," while God inclines human actions to good through "Law" and "Grace."[60]

In surveying the overall structure and orientation of the *Summa*, as well as the context of the natural law discussion within the category of "extrinsic" principles of human acts, it is easy to deny the purely natural character of St. Thomas's natural law, or the location of the immediate source of his natural law in humanity rather than God. Such a denial is parallel to the claim that by making philosophy the "handmaiden"[61] of sacred doctrine or theology St. Thomas does violence to the proper sphere of the former in the interests of propounding the latter.[62] The notion that St. Thomas's method is not truly philosophical and that his natural law smacks more of a divine or eternal law has long enjoyed widespread currency.[63] It is not surprising, then, that St. Thomas's natural law doctrine is a particular focus of those who attempt to refute the idea of natural law in general by arguing that it requires faith in a legislating God (and is *ipso facto* not merely natural). This would be the case if a legislating God, rather than human nature, were the immediate source for St. Thomas's natural law, a point that will be contested in what follows.

It is first important to note that the questions on law are preceded not only by a treatment of God but also a thorough inquiry into the nature of human beings. This inquiry is of crucial importance for understanding the manner in which St. Thomas's natural law is "natural." Although many contemporary interpretations of St. Thomas's natural law rightly emphasize the importance of the article concerning "Whether the Natural Law

---

57. Ibid.
58. Ibid., I-II.49.prooemium.
59. Ibid., I-II.90.prooemium.
60. Ibid.
61. Ibid., I.1.5,ad.2.
62. See Fortin's translation of *ancilla* as "slave" in "St. Thomas Aquinas," in *History of Political Philosophy*, 271. While "slave" is a possible translation of *ancilla*, the connotations of this translation run counter to the spirit of St. Thomas's use of philosophy throughout the *ST*.
63. See, for example, Fortin, "St. Thomas Aquinas," as well as "Thomas Aquinas as a Political Thinker," *Perspectives on Political Science* 26 (Spring 1997): 92–7; see also Crosson, "Religion and Natural Law," 8–13.

Contains Several Precepts, or One Only,"[64] a disproportionate focus on this article often leads to an understanding of "nature" or the "natural" that distorts St. Thomas's conception of these terms in the case of human beings.

It is in this article that St. Thomas advances his well-known theory of the "natural inclinations" which are "naturally apprehended by reason as being good." If this article is read as St. Thomas's single, definitive statement of the natural law, it seems that "natural" means something like "pre-reflective," "instinctual," or "built-in." It seems, too, that by distinguishing the "practical reason" from "speculative reason"[65] prior to the discussion of inclinations within the article, St. Thomas means to dissociate the former from the latter and exclude the role of speculative reason or contemplative reflection in the workings of the natural law. If this reading is correct, three conclusions relevant to our purposes follow: (1) St. Thomas's natural law is not derived from the inductive philosophical understanding of human nature that precedes it in the *Summa*; (2) St. Thomas's natural law stands in contrast, rather than continuity, with the Ciceronian-Aristotelian version which does derive the principles of morality or natural law from such an understanding of human nature; and (3) St. Thomas's natural law doctrine is in fact quite different from that offered herein. In order to combat these conclusions and the reading on which they are based, it is necessary to discuss St. Thomas's inductive philosophical treatment of human nature in some detail and determine the role that this treatment plays in his understanding of the natural law.

Although the subject of the First Part of the *Summa* is "God," St. Thomas includes in his consideration of God an account of "the procession of creatures from Him."[66] This procession occurs, moreover, in the threefold manner of "production," "distinction" and "government."[67] Within the second heading, St. Thomas considers the distinction of corporeal and spiritual creatures; after treating each of these, he arrives at "the composite creature, corporeal and spiritual, which is man."[68] St. Thomas divides his consideration of human beings into a discussion of their "nature" and one of their "origin." While the second discussion explicitly relates the human creature to the transcendent God of theology, the discussion of man's "nature"

---

64. *ST*, I-II.94.2.
65. Although the extent to which St. Thomas means to distinguish the two applications of reason even in this article is open to question, since the distinction occurs within a discussion of the similar or analogous character of the two types of reasoning.
66. St. Thomas, *ST*, I.2.prooemium.
67. I.44.prooemium.
68. Ibid.; also I.75.prooemium.

is wholly philosophical and devoid of any theological premises. St. Thomas relies heavily in this section on "the Philosopher," Aristotle, and his account of human nature as derived from the *Physics, De Anima, Posterior Analytics,* and *Ethics.*

St. Thomas's discussion of human nature centers on a consideration of its "powers," which provides the basis for his later inquiry into the manner in which the rational creature approaches God. The "powers" of which St. Thomas speaks are such not in the sense of *potestas* (ability or might), but rather *potentia* (potentiality) and *virtus* (virtue or excellence).[69] In these senses the powers of the human soul are intrinsically ordered to operation as potentiality is ordered to actuality.[70]

Approving the classification of "the Philosopher," St. Thomas distinguishes five genera of powers in the human soul: the vegetative, sensitive, appetitive, locomotive and intellectual.[71] In addition to their mere distinction, these kinds of powers exist in a hierarchical order which corresponds with the order among the various types of natural beings in a manner essentially identical to the accounts of Cicero and Aristotle.[72] The vegetative, sensitive and intellectual powers in fact determine distinct types of "soul" and "modes of living" which are proper to plants, animals and human beings respectively.[73] The order among these types of soul and the corresponding modes of living arise out of the degree to which each "surpasses the operation of the corporeal nature."[74]

In determining the level of superiority of a certain type of soul to corporeal nature, St. Thomas employs Aristotle's definition of "nature" as the principle of motion. The proper principle of the motion of matter lies in its receptivity to an "extrinsic" impetus by which it is moved. The proper principle of motion attaching to animate beings (that is, beings with immaterial souls), on the other hand, lies in an "intrinsic" principle by which it moves itself.[75] Therefore, each type of soul exceeds materiality to the degree to which it enables self-motion. Further, since the operation of self-motion admits of degree according as it is accomplished independently of determinate material instruments, a lesser dependence on materiality corresponds to a greater degree of self-motion. The intellectual soul, which

---

69. See I.75.prooemium and I.77.prooemium.
70. I.77.3.
71. I.78.1.
72. Ibid.; see also I.77.4.
73. I.78.1; see also I.18.3.
74. I.78.1.
75. Ibid.

distinguishes human beings from other animals and plants, surpasses materiality to the greatest degree since it does not require any material organ as its instrument.[76] Thus human beings, insofar as they are human (that is, possess an intellectual soul), move themselves by the intrinsic principle of intellectuality.

Despite the role of intellectuality[77] in distinguishing and elevating human nature with respect to other natures, it is important to keep in mind the fact that it remains but one kind of power among five existing in a soul which is the substantial form of a body.[78] The most important consequence of the latter aspect is that all intellectual knowledge acquired by human beings occurs *per viam sensus*, "by way of the senses."[79] Since it is invariably necessary that human knowledge arise in this way,[80] human beings are intellectually inferior to the angels who do not require phantasms produced by the senses.[81] The former aspect further underscores the composite character of the human being by placing his intellectuality within the context of his fundamentally "animal" nature. Although the intellect raises human beings above all other animals, it does not do so to the extent of abandoning the proper characteristics attaching to lower animal natures.[82] The properly human element of man coexists with the properly animal and vegetative elements. Again following Cicero and Aristotle very closely, St. Thomas includes each of these elements as well as the hierarchical relation between them within his account of human nature, or of the humanity of the individual human being. In light of these considerations, St. Thomas states that "the human soul . . . is on the confines of spiritual and corporeal creatures, and therefore the powers of both meet together in the soul."[83]

St. Thomas further distinguishes two "ends" proper to the intellect which follow on its apprehension: the "consideration of truth" and the direction to operation. This difference in the application of the intellectual power results in the distinction between the "speculative" and the "practical"

---

76. Ibid. While the intellectual soul does not require any material organ as its instrument, this does not deny the necessity of the material sense organs to the operation of the intellect since all knowledge comes *per viam sensus*.

77. St. Thomas's *intellectus* is a close equivalent to Cicero's *ratio* and Aristotle's *logos* in relation to a conception of human nature.

78. I.75.5 and I.76.1.

79. I.76.5.

80. At least while in the natural state. See I.89.1–2.

81. I.85.1; also I.79.2.

82. For an interesting comparison, see Cicero's criticism of the Stoic position in Book IV of *De Finibus*.

83. I.77.2.

intellects.[84] Since these two intellects are really only accidental differences within the intellectual power itself, there is a close correspondence between the respective habits by which they are disposed to act. Both the speculative and the practical intellects must begin with indemonstrable first principles which are knowable immediately upon an intellectual encounter with being; these first principles are held by the habits of "understanding"[85] and "synderesis,"[86] respectively. From these starting points, both manifestations of intellect proceed by combination to produce conclusions, which are held by the habits of "science"[87] and "prudence."[88]

Despite the close analogy between the two manifestations of intellect, an important difference arises in connection with their relation to virtue. Virtues, defined in Aristotelian fashion as habits that dispose to the good, are divided by St. Thomas into two types: those which confer "aptness in doing good" and those which, in addition, confer "the good use" of this aptness.[89] The virtues of the speculative intellect belong to the former category, while those of the practical intellect belong to the latter. The disjunction between habit and act, to which this distinction in virtue answers, has its source in the indeterminacy of the appetite. The virtues of the practical intellect lead directly to good actions precisely because they "presuppose the rectitude of the appetite."[90] The indeterminacy of the appetite thus necessitates the cultivation of virtues by which its "rectitude" is secured.

In his Prologue to the Second Part of the *Summa*, St. Thomas explains that after treating primarily of God in the First Part, " . . . it remains for us to treat of His image, that is, man, according as he too is the principle of his actions, as having free choice and control of his actions." The power of "free choice," falling under the general appetitive power, arises from the fact that "reason in contingent matters may follow opposite courses."[91] That man

---

84. I.79.11–12.
85. I-II.57.2.
86. I.79.12. St. Thomas's term "synderesis" is normally left untranslated due to the lack of a sufficiently precise English equivalent. Although it is commonly understood in a loose manner as "conscience," it cannot be translated as conscience since St. Thomas speaks of *conscientia* in the next article. Joseph Cardinal Ratzinger (now Pope Benedict XVI) interestingly proposed "translating" *synderesis* with the Greek word "anamnesis" in his paper "Conscience and Truth" (presented at the 10th Workshop for Bishops, February 1991, in Dallas, TX. See http://ewtn.com/library/CURIA/RATZCONS/HTM).
87. I-II.57.2.
88. I-II.57.4–5.
89. I-II.57.1.
90. I-II.57.4.
91. I.83.1.

"has control of his actions," that is, that they are "voluntary," similarly results from the "rational appetite" by which human beings are capable of acting for an intellectually apprehended end.[92] In both discussions of the way in which human beings contain the principles of their actions within themselves, it is the indeterminacy of the practical reason (or intellect) that plays the decisive role.

A further indeterminacy in human action arises when the intellect, which is proper to human beings, confronts the other powers of the human soul that are shared in common with the animals. Since the sensitive power is also an apprehensive one (like the intellect), it gives rise to its own appetite whose object may contradict that proposed by the intellectual appetite.[93] Thus, in defending the distinction between moral and intellectual virtue from the Socratic position,[94] St. Thomas states that "the appetitive part obeys the reason, not blindly, but with a certain power of opposition."[95] It is for this reason that the "rectitude of the appetite" includes both the intellectual appetite and the sensual appetite; the former is perfected by justice and prudence,[96] while the latter is perfected by temperance and fortitude.[97]

In transitioning from his discussion of the virtues and vices to his consideration of law, St. Thomas appears to transition from internal principles of human action to external ones. This is, however, only partly true. The distinction between intrinsic and extrinsic principles in the realm of human action is not as clear as it appears at first glance, as St. Thomas himself indicates at the outset of his discussion of the subject. In treating the question of "whether there is anything voluntary in human acts," St. Thomas states that

> it is not contrary to the nature of the voluntary act that this intrinsic principle be caused or moved by an extrinsic principle, because it is not essential to the voluntary act that its intrinsic principle be a first principle.[98]

---

92. I-II.6.1.
93. I.80.1.
94. At least as interpreted by Aristotle in the *Ethics*, 1144b19.
95. I-II.58.2. Note that this is essentially a paraphrase of Aristotle's description of this situation in the *Ethics*.
96. See I-II.61.1.
97. I-II.61.2.
98. I-II.6.1, ad. 1.

In other words, there is a sense in which even human beings and their actions are wholly dependent on an extrinsic principle insofar as they are dependent on the first cause of all being, that is, God. In the beginning of his discussion of law, moreover, St. Thomas does not list "law" as one of the extrinsic principles with which he is concerned. The only extrinsic principles indicated are "the devil" and "God." Each of these extrinsic principles operates through certain instrumental causes; the devil through "temptations," and God through "law" and "grace." Grace, however, is earlier described as a "habit," that is, an internal principle of human action, which resides in the soul's essence.[99] It simply does not follow that because God is an extrinsic principle of human actions he may only act by means of purely extrinsic instrumental causes. There is nothing, therefore, in the structure of the *Summa* itself which indicates a priori whether St. Thomas's notion of law will prove to be wholly extrinsic, primarily intrinsic, or some combination of both.

This is not, however, meant to imply that the location of the natural law discussion within the framework of extrinsic principles is merely by accident or coincidence. St. Thomas enters his consideration of the natural law armed with philosophical proofs for the existence of a transcendent God who governs the entirety of His creation. This renders possible a derivation of the natural law within the context of its relation to the eternal law of God. That which is present in Cicero's derivation of the natural law in a relatively superficial and conjectural manner is thus present in a fundamental and certain manner for St. Thomas. Since St. Thomas is certain of the "coherence of the whole"[100] both by the light of faith and the testimony of reason, he views the natural law in the same manner in which he views creation as a whole, namely, "in the light of eternity."[101]

It is therefore consistent with St. Thomas's general perspective to define the natural law as the "participation of the eternal law in the rational creature."[102] This inclusion of the eternal law in the very definition of the natural law leads many commentators to dismiss the true "naturalness" of the latter. Upon closer examination, however, the rational participation described by St. Thomas is in fact quite different from the Divine coercion with which it is often equated.

---

99. I-II.50.2.
100. James V. Schall, "The Uniqueness of the Political Philosophy of Thomas Aquinas," *Perspectives on Political Science* 26 (Spring 1997), 89.
101. Fortin, "Thomas Aquinas as a Political Thinker," 92.
102. St. Thomas, *ST*, I-II.91.2.

Although St. Thomas defines law in general as something "pertaining to reason,"[103] he distinguishes two ways in which this relation to reason may occur: first, "as in one that rules," and secondly, "by participation, as in one that is ruled."[104] The eternal law clearly pertains to reason in the first sense since it is "the very Idea of the government of things in God."[105] As the eternal law applies to creatures which do not possess intellect or reason, it has the character of law simply by virtue of the Divine Reason as an external principle. If the lawfulness of the natural law were similarly derived only from the Divine Reason associated with the eternal law, St. Thomas's treatment of it as a kind of law distinct from the eternal law would be largely inexplicable. From the definition of the natural law, however, it is clear that it attains recognition as a law by pertaining to reason in the second sense, that is, "by participation."[106] For the rational creature, that part of the eternal law which applies to him externally is internalized by the power of the intellect apprehending the order established within human nature by the Eternal Reason. This order is manifested in the "order of natural inclinations" within human beings, the discussion of which closely parallels Cicero's regarding the "instincts" pertaining to the various levels of natural being.[107] This order constitutes a given blueprint for action that is both (1) contained within the humanity of every individual and (2) inductively accessible to all or nearly all human beings. Thus the natural law is that by which "we *discern* what is good and what is evil"[108] rather than simply that by which our true good and perfection is externally prescribed.

This argument may also be illustrated by an analogy in the realm of speculative reason. Suppose someone were to draw a right triangle on a sheet of paper and post this sheet on a bulletin board for all to see (or perhaps on the Google homepage). After seeing this triangle a number of times and forming an image of it in their minds, everyone would know its basic characteristics, namely, that the hypotenuse is greater than either of the other the two sides, that the right angle is wider than either of the other two, and so on. The keenest minds would go much farther than this, deducing that the right angle is equal to the sum of the other two angles, the square on the

103. I-II.90.1.
104. I-II.90.3, ad. 1.
105. I-II.91.1.
106. See I-II.91.2, ad. 3.
107. St. Thomas's discussion occurs in I-II.91.2 and in I-II.94.2. Cicero's similar discussion occurs in the *De Officiis*, beginning in 1.11.13.
108. I-II.91.2 (my emphasis).

hypotenuse is equal to the sum of the squares on the other two sides, and so on. This entire body of knowledge, however, is derived from and implicit in the manner in which the triangle was originally drawn. In fact, the one who drew the triangle happened to be Euclid, who did so with a knowledge not only of its most complex attributes, but also those of many other types of figures which may be drawn. Since the knowledge which now exists in the observers of the triangle preexisted in Euclid and was, in part, extrinsically caused by his action of drawing it, ought we to deny these observers the internal possession of this knowledge? Did Euclid infuse the theorems relating to the triangle in its observers by the mere fact of drawing it in this manner? Is it not more reasonable to concede that, while Euclid's action was an extrinsic principle of the observers' knowledge, this knowledge is now the shared possession of both Euclid and those who rationally encountered his triangle?

This discussion illuminates the manner in which St. Thomas's natural law is truly natural, i.e., not dependent *in the order of knowledge*[109] on the eternal law or the Divine Reason from which the eternal law emanates. Since the eternal law is reflected in the objective order within and among created beings, including the human being, all that is required for understanding the first principles of the natural law is the intellectual procedure of induction from objective reality.[110] While God is indeed the ultimate source of St. Thomas's natural law, human nature or humanity as it is apprehended through induction is its immediate source. Since, moreover, this apprehension proceeds through induction rather than demonstration, the principles of the natural law are indeed *per se nota* and *indemonstrabilia*, although not in the manner in which these terms are understood by many new natural law theorists.[111]

For St. Thomas "every knowledge of truth is a kind of reflection and participation of the eternal law,"[112] and so falls within the definition of the natural law insofar as this truth directs the human being to the good of its nature. The most basic truths that are relevant for human action, such as the superiority of the intellect to the sensitive powers (corresponding to the

---

109. At this point the distinction Finnis draws between the "epistemological" and "ontological" orders, which is present both throughout the *ST* and in Aristotle's *Physics*, becomes relevant.

110. See I-II.93.2.

111. The understanding of indemonstrable principles by the new natural law theorists does not include any positive explanation, such as that provided by the process of induction, but only the negative assertion of indemonstrability.

112. I-II.93.2.

superiority of human beings to the other animals), or the hierarchy among the elements of humanity that constitute a blueprint for action, are apprehended through induction by the intellect and held habitually by *synderesis*. Thus the fundamental precept of the natural law consists for Aquinas in the general command that "good is to be pursued and done, and evil is to be avoided."[113] St. Thomas explicates the meaning of this first precept by stating that "whatever the practical reason naturally apprehends as man's good belongs to the precepts of the natural law."[114] The "good," then, consists first and foremost in the general state of living according to the blueprint contained in one's humanity (that is, acting at the promptings of intellectual apprehension). In this way St. Thomas's natural law also possesses the twofold and flexible character of Cicero's derivation; from the first and most basic injunction to follow reason, the more particular applications of reason also acquire the character of law by commanding the appetites of individuals involved in concrete actions.

The natural law tradition, extending from Cicero's Aristotelian account of human nature to St. Thomas's doctrine, provides a persuasive account of a blueprint for action in one's humanity that may be—and often is—contravened by human beings. This blueprint emerges from an account of certain elements of human nature, besides the capacity for reflection, that are hierarchically ordered and capable of instantiation or contravention in particular human actions. Among the general capacities or elements of one's humanity, reason or intellect stands above and is superior to the emotions or passions, an order of superiority that can be either followed or deviated from. Aristotle, Cicero and Aquinas join to show persuasively that one's humanity does, indeed, include certain guidelines for action that stand as a measure of one's unique selfhood. In this way the natural law tradition substantiates the existence of the second ordering fact, cohering with and providing specificity to the account of the natural law provided herein.

IS THIS NATURAL LAW REALLY A "LAW"?

The old natural law tradition, with which the account provided herein purports to be in fundamental agreement, is often critiqued on the basis of a supposed tension between its "naturalness" and its "lawfulness." As Fortin asserts, "the term 'natural law' could well be a misnomer of sorts" since it is difficult to conceive how it could be a genuine law if it is genuinely natural,

---

113. I-II.94.2.
114. Ibid.

and vice versa.[115] Even granting all of the foregoing arguments regarding the existence and implications of the second ordering fact, why are these implications described in terms of "natural law" rather than in terms of natural standards for behavior or classical "natural right"?[116]

Sources of law are generally conceived to be personal agents distinct from those who are simply subject to the law. In the case of the natural law, this personal agent is usually assumed to be God. If God is the legislating source of the natural law, however, it seems this law would cease to be strictly natural—but what other options for a natural legislator are there? Although one's own humanity cannot constitute a personal agent distinct from the individual human being herself in the manner normally required to qualify as a legislator, it is not a merely metaphorical extension of language to speak of one's own humanity as a legitimate superior to one's unique selfhood, and thus as a potential legislator with respect to this unique self. While one's humanity does not constitute a substance distinct from the individual considered in terms of actual self-consciousness, or as a unique self, it does possess the central characteristics of a distinct personal agent to an extent sufficient to warrant its more-than-metaphorical description as the legislating source of the natural law.

Human nature is, to follow Aristotle rather than Plato, always instantiated in particular human beings. One need not, in other words, speak of some separate "Humanness" in which individuals participate to speak of human nature. At the same time, however, individual examples of instantiated human nature, or the humanity of individual human beings, are identical with one another. Although there is no separately existing Humanness in which both John and Mary participate, the human nature instantiated in each of them is identical. This is simply to say that human beings are individual members of a certain kind of being, and thus that whatever else may render them unique, their humanity does not. Although one may speak of the human nature instantiated in this particular human being as different from the human nature in that particular human being, this is only a trivial difference in number.

This humanity that is identical across individual human beings exists independently of each of these individuals; their particular existence or nonexistence does not affect human nature in any way. Individual hu-

---

115. Fortin, "The New Rights Theory and the Natural Law," 610.
116. See E. A. Goerner, "On Thomistic Natural Law: The Bad Man's View of Thomistic Natural Right," *Political Theory* 7, no. 1 (February 1979): 101–122; "Thomistic Natural Right: The Good Man's View of Thomistic Natural Law," *Political Theory* 11, no. 3 (August 1983): 393–418.

man beings, on the other hand, obviously cannot exist independently of humanity. In this way the human nature instantiated in the individual, or the individual's own humanity, is different from and superior to everything that individuates him or is unique to him as an individual. Although this particular instance of human nature comes into being and passes away simultaneously with this individual human being, humanity both preexists and outlives every individual human being. Therefore, while this particular instance of human nature cannot even be conceived independently of this particular individual, humanity itself can be distinguished to some meaningful extent from the individual human being. In other words, the hypothetical nonexistence (or death) of one human being does not entail the nonexistence of human beings as such; the same (different only in number) human nature that was instantiated in the one human being will continue to exist in each of the others. It is evident, therefore, that the human nature instantiated in an individual human being—his humanity—is to a meaningful extent distinct from the individual considered as a unique self or in light of his particular self-consciousness.

This instantiated human nature may, in addition, be conceived to a meaningful, more-than-metaphorical extent as itself a personal agent. On Aristotle's definition, nature in general is a "principle of motion and change,"[117] belonging along with intelligent action to the class of causes that act "for the sake of an end."[118] That this characterization of nature in general may be applied to our definition of human nature is evident from our account of the phenomenon of self-consciousness. Like Aristotle's example of the frequency of rain in winter, the universality of human beings' production of the actual self through the operation of self-consciousness is the sort of thing that one would attribute to purpose-driven action rather than mere coincidence.[119] Aristotle is far from alone, moreover, in characterizing nature as an intelligent agent in a more-than-metaphorical sense. Among his more notable companions in this effort are Cicero, Locke and Jefferson, to name only a few. None of these thinkers understand the personification of nature as mere poetic license or rhetorical flourish; while nature does not seem to actually be a personal agent, it does in fact behave in ways strikingly similar to such an agent.

In the case of human nature in particular, its instantiation in the individual human being draws it closer to personal agency than in the case of

---

117. Aristotle, *Physics* II.1; III.1.
118. Ibid., II.8.
119. Ibid.

other instantiated natures. An individual's humanity is, after all, the cause of her unique selfhood, and is itself appropriated and joined to this unique selfhood. It is, in fact, through the activity of self-consciousness characteristic of the unique self that humanity actually becomes fully instantiated in this particular individual and distinguished in number from other instances of humanity. Insofar as individual human beings are conscious of their humanity, or identify themselves as members of humankind, their humanity is included within or subsumed under their unique selfhood. Thus instantiated human nature, while not itself a person with agency, becomes personal, or closely associated with and made a part of a person, through the formation of the unique self in the activity of self-consciousness. In this way as well, then, one's humanity approaches the status of a personal agent to an extent beyond the merely metaphorical.

We may thus speak of one's humanity as a Lockean "legitimate superior" or Thomistic "community caretaker" with respect to individual self-conscious human beings in a sense sufficient to qualify this humanity as the source of a law. It is not here implied that one's humanity is somehow on par with a personal God in terms of the distinct personal agency and superiority requisite to be the source of law. It is asserted, however, that the depiction of one's humanity as a personal agent distinct from each individual human being is much more substantial than a mere metaphor. Since, as has been shown, this humanity in fact issues commands to human beings as individuals that are directed toward their good, include rewards and penalties, and are sufficiently promulgated, we may speak of human nature as a legislator and of the moral implications of the second ordering fact as a natural law.

Identifying human nature as the legislating source of the natural law also serves to effectively distinguish the natural law from another type of law with which it has sometimes been confused; namely, the law of nations or *ius gentium*. The idea of the *ius gentium* originated with the Roman jurists (following Cicero) as a way of navigating the potential tension between nature and convention, or the *ius naturale* and the *ius civile*.[120] The primary distinguishing criterion for different types of law, according to the Roman jurists' account, would be extent of application rather than natural/conventional status. The *ius naturale* applied to animals and human beings in common, the *ius gentium* applied to all human beings in common, and the *ius civile* applied to human beings within particular societies.[121] As Grotius

---

120. For an excellent discussion of this point see Zuckert 1994, 129–34.
121. Tierney 1997, 136.

argued, however, human nature is sufficiently distinct from all other animal natures to warrant its own particular *ius naturale*.[122] If this is the case, as our account similarly holds, extent of application as a criterion for distinguishing types of law fades away, and the nature-convention distinction reasserts its significance.

Attending to this distinction reveals the crucial difference between the natural law and the law of nations: the natural law is natural, and the law of nations is conventional. The legislating source of the natural law is one's humanity, while the legislating source of the law of nations is the agreement between particular human beings in particular societies. The law of nations tends to "look" like the natural law because of its universality; the greater the number of particular human beings and particular societies included within an agreement, the more their agreement seems to be independent of any of them. This is, however, a mere optical illusion, and the nature-convention distinction continues to separate the natural law equally from both particular positive laws and the law of nations.

NATURAL LAW AND NEW NATURAL LAW

Having fully set forth our exposition of the natural law, it is possible to indicate the ways in which this natural law differs from that offered by the "New Natural Law" (NNL) theorists such as Robert George and John Finnis, as well as to explain the significance of this exposition of the natural law for the direction of contemporary natural law thinking. Since NNL theorists begin from the assumption of the near-sacred inviolability of the logical separation between "is" and "ought," they will of course tend to disagree with the approach to deriving the natural law taken above root and branch. Beside our initial disagreement regarding the permeability of the logical barrier between is and ought, moreover, a number of illuminating contrasts may be drawn subsequent to this initial disagreement between our respective conceptions of the natural law. During the course of indicating these contrasts, the questionability of a few key assumptions of the NNL theory as well as the resulting shortcomings in its expositions of the natural law will become evident. As a result of these shortcomings, and the manner in which the account of the natural law offered herein succeeds in avoiding them, it will be argued that the NNL theory, despite having much to commend it, ultimately represents a wrong turn in natural law thinking.

---

122. *De Jure*, Prolog.6; Cf. Zuckert 1994, 136.

The signpost for this wrong turn consists in the seriousness and intransigence with which the NNL theorists treat the is-ought divide. Although Finnis has much to say on this issue in his *Natural Law and Natural Rights*, perhaps the most illuminating statement by an NNL theorist on the is-ought issue is provided by George in his essay "Natural Law and Human Nature." In response to Henry Veatch's claim that "the very 'is' of human nature has an 'ought' built into it," and his indication that the NNL theorists are too straight-laced in their commitment to logical technicalities, George responds that the NNL theorists aspire to more than the "muddle" represented by Veatch's insufficiently precise analysis.[123] Treating Veatch in a manner strikingly similar to that in which the NNL theorists are wont to treat Aristotle and Aquinas, George condescendingly judges that Veatch's statement is "not flatly wrong," but "just muddled." In the place of such "muddle," George endorses the following, and purportedly less muddled, statement by Grisez: "The truth of practical knowledge with respect to its first principles is their adequacy to possible human fulfillment considered precisely insofar as that fulfillment can be realized through human action."[124]

Although the concept of ordering facts set forth here does aspire to accommodate and satisfy, at least to some extent and as far as possible, the analytic precision demanded by the NNL theorists and other philosophers of an analytic turn of mind, there is much to be said for Veatch's complaint regarding the technical strictness of the NNL theorists in their emphasis on the logical importance of the is-ought gap. The sort of technical zeal exhibited by the NNL theorists was, in fact, explicitly anticipated by Aristotle in his famous warning regarding the level of precision to be expected from a treatment of morality and politics at the outset of his *Nicomachean Ethics*.[125] Aristotle was right to warn his readers that on certain matters, in George's terms, "muddle is the best we can hope for." Not all muddle is created equal, however; Aristotelian or Thomistic muddle is likely to be better and truer than your or my (or, for that matter, Finnis's or George's) muddle. George's claim that something other than his conception of muddle is attainable in moral and political philosophy, and that he and the other NNL theorists have in fact risen out of the muddle through their adherence to the logical is-ought gap, is unwarranted.

123. George, "Natural Law and Human Nature," 38.
124. Ibid.
125. I.2.

A deeply problematic aspect of the NNL theorists' arguments arising directly from this assumption consists in the sharpness of their distinction between speculative and practical reason, "metaphysics" and "intelligent grasping," or "understanding from the outside" and "experiencing from the inside."[126] The NNL theorists are very careful to exclude any speculative, metaphysical, or factual propositions regarding human nature or any other aspect of descriptive reality from their account of the manner in which the basic goods are initially grasped or ought to be subsequently pursued. Beside the general is-ought divide this exclusion maintains, the NNL theorists conceive of human nature as open or indeterminate and thus as basically silent on practical matters relating to the individual actions of human beings. As George puts it, "Human nature . . . is not a closed nature," and thus "many . . . possible intelligent purposes remain as yet unenvisaged."[127] It is not only that one need not and ought not consult some speculative concept of human nature in order to determine the morality of some action; it is also that this speculative concept would have nothing to add to felt inclinations and practically grasped goods. Abstract moral philosophy is thus an alien "appendage" added to practical experience after the fact by idiosyncratic groups of individuals who set up knowledge as their preferred basic good.[128] The foregoing exercises in reflective speculation, while they may be true enough from a metaphysical perspective and prove interesting to those with a knowledge-dominant "life-plan," have little to do in any case with practical moral judgment or "practical reasonableness."

This distinction, central in many ways to the NNL project, in fact represents a false dichotomy, and sets up metaphysics as a mere "straw man" whose predictable demise automatically issues in the victory of the only remaining alternative. According to the depiction of the NNL theorists, there are only two rigidly distinct modes of understanding human nature: there is the highly developed, abstract, complex sort of speculative or metaphysical understanding uniquely cultivated by the philosopher, and then there is the irreducibly simple, immediate, and concrete sort of practical understanding possessed by all human beings.[129] Moral reasoning or judgment is, obviously, the kind of thing that we want to attribute to human beings as such, and not only to some small and elite subsection of human beings. Therefore, the basic rules for action involved in moral reasoning or

126. Finnis, *Natural Law and Natural Rights*, 33–34.
127. George, "Natural Law and Human Nature," 39.
128. Finnis, *Natural Law and Natural Rights*, 36.
129. This distinction is clearly present throughout Finnis's *Natural Law and Natural Rights*.

judgment (expressed in terms of the natural law) must be the object of the irreducibly simple, unified and concrete sort of practical understanding as opposed to the kind cultivated by philosophers.

Although this reasoning appears persuasive enough once the initial dichotomy between the respective understandings of idiosyncratic metaphysicians and the bulk of humanity is accepted, this dichotomy entirely misses a crucial form of understanding situated somewhere in between these two extremes. This form of understanding consists in that described by Aristotle in his *Posterior Analytics* as induction, or the basic process of abstraction by which the first universal concepts, however vague or simple, are formed in the mind of the individual from the variety of particulars presented to his immediate experience of beings.[130] Through the inductive activity of the human understanding, intellect, or reason, the notions of commonality and individuality, as well as those of human nature in general and of an individual human being in particular, are insensibly but actively formed by all or nearly all human beings. This inductive activity works in a seemingly automatic manner both on external encounters with other human beings and on one's internal experience of oneself. One need not, in other words, be a card-carrying metaphysician to possess a definite speculative or reflective understanding of what it means to be a human being, of the difference between what one has in common with other human beings and what is particular to himself, and of the relevance of these basic understandings for one's own actions. Ordinary human beings could not, in fact, avoid possessing a basic understanding of these notions even if they wanted to.

It is at this level of understanding, between abstruse metaphysics and unreflective instinct (or grasp of practical "reason"), that moral reasoning and judgment ought to, and does in fact, occur. All or nearly all human beings understand, however vaguely, that humanity, or human nature, is something both larger than and contained within each individual human being. Ordinary human beings also, I submit, routinely mediate their evaluations of goods, even basic ones, as well as their pursuit of them, through such an inductive-speculative understanding of human nature. The foundational account of the natural law provided above is, therefore, a more developed and detailed explanation of a basic inductive-speculative understanding possessed by all or nearly all human beings, and not a superfluous "speculative appendage"[131] with respect to the actual moral reasoning of ordinary human beings.

---

130. Aristotle, *Posterior Analytics*, II.19.
131. Finnis, *Natural Law and Natural Rights*, 36.

The addition of inductive operations to an account of human understanding provides something similar to what the NNL theorists are grasping for in their depiction of the immediate intelligent apprehension of practical reason without extending the notion of "reason" or "intelligence" beyond the limits of a discernable meaning or appealing to a problematic version of self-evidence. Including a merely inductive understanding of human nature and of oneself as an individual human being as a component of moral reasoning and judgment makes such reasoning and judgment available to all human beings, and not just metaphysicians or philosophers. Inductive understanding is also far less obtrusive with respect to the ordinary process of moral reasoning than the "metaphysical propositions about human nature" that the NNL theorists strive to exclude.[132] Indeed, the inconspicuousness of such an exercise of speculative and reflective understanding goes very far toward explaining its neglect by the NNL theorists and many other moral philosophers. Most importantly, however, the process of induction is capable of issuing in ordering facts that bridge the gap between "is" and "ought."

By interposing an inductive understanding of human nature between the pre-rational or instinctive inclinations toward various objects and the activity of moral reasoning and judgment, we are able to include a number of crucial features in our account of natural law that are problematically absent from that offered by the NNL theorists. First, our account of the natural law is more fully "law" in the sense that it possesses much more clearly than the NNL version the obligatory character that moral rules are thought to possess. The moral rules comprising the NNL theorists' version of the natural law consist in merely procedural considerations, or a kind of due process requirement following from their (rather vague) notion of "reasonableness."[133] The explanation for why one should be praised for following the natural law, blamed for acting contrary to it, or in any way beholden to its requirements remains unclear. Our account of the natural law, on the other hand, includes a conception of a lawgiver, a Lockean "legitimate superior" or a Thomistic "community caretaker," that issues actual commands in the form of a blueprint against which individual actions are measured. Conformity with this blueprint is rewarded, and contravention is punished. The source of obligation to the natural law is clear: one's humanity is necessarily superior to one's unique self, and its commands contain the specifically human good.

132. Ibid., 33.
133. Ibid.

Secondly, our account of the natural law allows for a clear distinction between real and merely apparent goods, or justifiable and mistaken desires or inclinations, and thus enables a clarity of moral judgment that is problematically absent from the NNL version.[134] On the NNL account, the commonsensical distinction between real and apparent goods or justifiable and mistaken desires dissolves in the absence of any single standard according to which these goods might all be measured. The basic goods are utterly incommensurable and irreducibly plural, and as a result their realization through the actions of individual human beings contains a very wide range of morally indistinguishable variation. While this may more comfortably reflect the Rawlsian "fact of reasonable pluralism" and avoid a thorny confrontation with the empirical variation among the life-plans of different individuals, it leaves us with a far weaker apparatus for moral reasoning and judgment than a theory of the natural law would be expected to provide. Our account of the natural law, on the other hand, includes a definite means of distinguishing between real and apparent goods or justifiable and mistaken inclinations in the blueprint for action contained within human nature. While the task of discerning such distinctions in practice requires a certain amount of thought and reflection, the concept of human nature and the pattern it contains secures the existence of these distinctions in principle. In this way our account of the natural law, assisted by the possibility of inductive understanding, is capable of providing a much more clear and definite guide to moral judgment and promises to issue in more meaningful evaluations of individual actions.

The NNL theory has indeed performed the very valuable task of persuasively confronting more extreme or "progressive" manifestations of contemporary liberalism and illuminating a more palatable, sensible and moderate liberal alternative while incorporating important elements of communitarian-type critiques of liberalism. It has done so, however, on the basis of the needlessly constraining assumptions of pluralism and the is-ought divide, assumptions which problematically isolate contemporary moral and political philosophers from their predecessors. The foregoing account of the natural law, on the other hand, is unfettered by these assumptions, and is thus able to reconnect with the historical natural law tradition and genuinely resurrect its central insights. We are thus able, as the NNL theorists have not been, to recover the force and distinctiveness of the "old"

---

134. On the importance of making this distinction for a natural law doctrine, see Michael Zuckert, "The Fullness of Being: Thomas Aquinas and the Modern Critique of Natural Law," *Review of Politics* 69 (February 2007): 28–47.

natural law that reached its culmination, rather than finding its beginning, in the thought of St. Thomas Aquinas.

CONCLUSION

It has been shown in this chapter that the distinctively modern idea of natural rights explained in the preceding chapter in fact necessarily entails—rather than invalidates, renders obsolete or simply contradicts—the distinctively premodern idea of natural law epitomized in the thought of St. Thomas. The natural law tradition, extending from Cicero's Aristotelian account of human nature to St. Thomas's doctrine, provides a persuasive argument for the existence of a blueprint for action located within one's humanity that one may contravene. This blueprint emerges from an account of certain elements of human nature, besides the capacity for reflection, that are hierarchically ordered and capable of instantiation or contravention in particular human actions. Among the general capacities or elements of one's humanity, reason or intellect stands above and is superior to the emotions or passions, an order of superiority that can be either followed or deviated from. In this way the natural law tradition substantiates the existence of the second ordering fact, cohering with and providing specificity to our account of the natural law.

By carefully attending to the twofold structure of the individual as both a human being and a unique self, a structure intimated most clearly by Locke, it has become possible to conceive the relationship between a modern idea of natural rights and a pre-modern idea of the natural law as one of fundamental complementarity. Since this complementarity is organic rather than artificial—arising immediately out of the inductively observable structure of the human individual—these two concepts in fact join to form the composite concept of natural morality.

CHAPTER FOUR

Natural Morality

It is often noted that natural rights and the natural law, even if they were once content fellow travelers, have developed in widely divergent or even contrary directions.[1] While there have been many important recent attempts to show that these two concepts possess important areas of overlap, grew up together historically, or may be coherently defined in terms of one another, these attempts have generally come at the cost of recognizing the real disparities between natural rights and the natural law conceived as foundations for morality meaningfully distinct from and essentially independent of one another.[2] The clearest manner of showing compatibility would, of course, be to argue that one of these concepts is simply derivative from the other, as continuity-compatibility theorists most often do. There is indeed a pervasive sense that the realm of natural morality isn't big enough for the two of these concepts conceived as independently valid sources for moral justification. It is often thought that the two must inevitably encroach on each other's province, with natural rights demanding a degree of personal freedom that the natural law cannot grant, and the natural law demanding a level of submissive obedience that runs directly counter to the assertion of natural rights.[3]

Before proceeding to an explication of the manner in which the foregoing account of natural rights and the natural law simultaneously addresses these issues of compatibility and mutual independence, it will prove helpful to briefly revisit the recent continuity-compatibility projects undertaken

---

1. One important signpost indicating this divergence consists in the transition from "natural" rights to "human" rights.
2. Here I have in mind, respectively, Christopher Wolfe, *Natural Law Liberalism*, Brian Tierney, *The Idea of Natural Rights*, and John Finnis, *Natural Law and Natural Rights*.
3. Zuckert, *Launching Liberalism*, 185.

by John Finnis, Christopher Wolfe and Brian Tierney. While each of these scholars have made significant contributions to the general task of thinking through the relationship between the concepts of natural law and natural rights, a task that is indeed pursued herein, they have each fallen short of accomplishing their purported aims of reconciling the modern idea of natural rights with the premodern one of the natural law. Each, moreover, has fallen short in a broadly similar manner; namely, by failing to properly recognize and accurately describe the modern idea of natural rights. In other words, the continuity arguments upon which their compatibility accounts rely define natural rights in a manner that ignores the developments of this concept since the medieval period. Although they may claim to effect a reconciliation of the two disparate traditions, they each end up simply defending one at the direct expense of the other.

Throughout his discussion of rights in *Natural Law and Natural Rights*, Finnis too easily dismisses the Hobbesian legacy of modern natural rights doctrines consisting in the separation of rights from law, asserting that "the ordinary modern idiom of 'rights' does not follow Hobbes all the way" to this stark separation.[4] While subsequent natural rights thinking indeed has not followed Hobbes's radical path "all the way," it is difficult to disavow the influence of the Hobbesian separation on subsequent liberal thinkers such as Locke, J. S. Mill and even John Rawls. It is also difficult to assert with Finnis that Hobbes's separation of rights and law may be wholly rejected while retaining his definition of "a right" as a liberty that is subjectively possessed by individuals prior to civil society and the institution of government. The notion of *jus* or "a right" as "essentially something someone *has*" rather than something that is assigned to someone according to a legal judgment certainly appears to be intimately connected with a rejection of the notion that all rights are strictly derivative from legal duties.[5] This connection, moreover, is clearly evidenced by the contemporary use of human or natural rights language in legal and political contexts, as well as in ordinary usage. While the language of pre-political human rights possessed by individuals abounds in liberal democracies throughout the world, the language of natural law remains unfashionable, taboo, or even politically incorrect within these societies. By attending too closely to the use of rights language by lawyers in ordinary legal contexts, within which positive rights deriving from positive laws predominate, Finnis is led to summarily dismiss

---

4. Finnis, *Natural Law and Natural Rights*, 208.
5. Ibid., 207–8.

the pressing claim of modern *natural* rights doctrines since Hobbes that such rights are separate from and prior to any corresponding natural law.

In *Natural Law Liberalism*, Wolfe provides his clearest statement of the manner in which liberalism's conception of rights is compatible with the natural law tradition by stating that "If it is *wrong* for A to hit B, then B can be said to have a *right* not to be hit by A. If it is a principle of justice that A *ought to* give x to B, then B can be said to have a *right* to x from A."[6] In response to Fortin's objection that such an analysis fails to address the priority question in dispute between ancients and moderns, or natural lawyers and liberals, Wolfe states that this dispute may be circumvented simply by specifying an understanding of rights as derivative from natural law duties. While this understanding of natural rights in general as derivative from natural law duties may be the ultimately true one (although I have argued that it is certainly not the whole truth), by subscribing to this version of natural rights Wolfe significantly alters course from showing the compatibility between the liberal and classical natural law traditions to arguing for the natural law position *as opposed to* the liberal one. In so doing Wolfe, like Finnis, attempts to sweeten his natural law philosophy with the Splenda of rights language while subtly jettisoning the pure cane of modern natural rights doctrines.

Tierney's notable attempt to reconcile modern natural rights with traditional natural law, like those of Finnis and Wolfe, conspicuously overlooks and problematically understates the profound disparities between contemporary understandings of natural rights and medieval ones. This problem is even more clear in Tierney's attempt than in Finnis's or Wolfe's as a result of the historical method he utilizes; the evident difficulty Tierney has in finally tracing early medieval ideas of natural rights to contemporary ones unfolds as if in slow motion. The shortcomings of Tierney's analysis also aid in pinpointing the most appropriate historical location for the parting of natural rights from the natural law and the resulting formation of a distinctively modern natural rights doctrine in the thought of John Locke. By missing the transformative contribution of John Locke's natural rights doctrine to the history of natural rights thinking, and hence failing to fully recognize the import of modern ideas of natural rights, Tierney is precluded from effecting a genuine reconciliation of modern natural rights with the natural law.

The account of the compatibility of natural rights and the natural law offered herein purports to significantly improve upon the accounts offered

6. Wolfe, *Natural Law Liberalism*, 189.

by Finnis, Wolfe and Tierney by responding to a single decisive criticism of their work in this area, a criticism that notices and exploits the shortcoming indicated above. This criticism is that each of their attempted reconciliations either ignore or too readily dismiss a central feature of modern natural rights doctrines; namely, the implicit claim of such doctrines that natural rights are prior to and independent of the duties or obligations stemming from the natural law conception of the common good. This criticism, stated most clearly and forcefully by Michael Zuckert in *Launching Liberalism*, represents a cogent liberal, or natural rights-based, response to the continuity arguments of Finnis, Wolfe and Tierney.

In a chapter of *Launching Liberalism* that addresses the same question raised briefly and perfunctorily by Finnis, namely, "Do Natural Rights Derive from Natural Law?"[7] Zuckert argues that modern natural rights doctrines, and particularly the seminal one of John Locke, are in fact premised upon a decisive break from the understanding of rights within the classical natural law framework. The very "launching" of liberalism, on this account, is associated with the newfound independence of natural rights from the natural law. For this reason the task of reconciling the two traditions, if it is possible at all, must involve far more than a substantial restatement of the early efforts of the Spanish Thomists to graft a notion of subjective rights onto St. Thomas's natural law.

Zuckert identifies the natural law and natural rights as "ultimate normative standards for judgment and action," and admits that "it would have been relatively easy" for Aquinas to have spoken in terms of rights.[8] The rights of which Aquinas could have spoken, however, are clearly not "the kind of rights the liberal tradition affirms."[9] These latter rights, by focusing on the "self-assertion of agents" or the "realm of personal sovereignty" over which such agents exercise legitimate control, stand outside of and in tension with the classical Thomistic natural law doctrine.[10] While allowing for potential areas of overlap and agreement between classical natural law and modern natural rights doctrines, Zuckert cogently argues with the aid of examples such as the "right to suicide" that modern natural rights cannot be explained in terms of a straightforward derivation from natural law duties. Regardless of the manner in which one may choose to define or interpret natural rights, the classical Thomistic natural law is nevertheless

---

7. Zuckert, *Launching Liberalism*, 169.
8. Ibid., 169, 183
9. Ibid., 185.
10. Ibid.

"unpromising raw material" from which to derive the understanding of natural rights affirmed by liberal thinkers since Locke.[11]

It is thus somewhat misleading for Finnis, Wolfe, Tierney and others with similar continuity-compatibility aims to claim to effect a reconciliation between natural rights and the natural law. While these scholars may argue that modern natural rights such as those described by Zuckert are not valid normative foundations at all and that their interpretation of natural rights is the only one compatible with the truth of the matter, the fact remains that such scholars take their stand *against* modern natural rights doctrines since Hobbes and Locke. The reconciliation attempted herein between natural rights and the natural law improves significantly upon those of Finnis, Wolfe, Tierney and others by responding to Zuckert's criticism and moving beyond the nearly intractable debate between them and the perspectives they represent. This has been accomplished by granting each moral foundation independence from the other while placing both upon a common basis in an inductive encounter with observable reality. This common basis, consisting in the single fact of self-ownership through self-consciousness, underlies and engenders the ordering facts that respectively give rise to natural rights and the natural law. By discovering this form of compatibility between natural rights and the natural law, both the "priority problem" and the "foundational problem,"[12] two issues that have profoundly divided the natural law orientation and the modern natural rights perspective since the early modern period, may finally be brought to a satisfactory resolution.

The existence of a common descriptive source for natural rights and the natural law secures their formal compatibility in two ways: (1) it ensures that apparent contradictions between their respective particular applications may be resolved in principle by appealing back to this common source; and (2) it limits and constrains the range of particular applications for each concept as well as their inherent implications through the descriptive character of this common source, effectively ensuring that each leaves sufficient "room" for the other. In addition to these formal means of guaranteeing some measure of compatibility, it may also be shown that natural rights and the natural law are compatible in a more substantial and concrete manner. The possession of natural rights by individual human beings represents a very important practically relevant truth grasped by reason; as such, respect for natural rights itself constitutes a precept of the natural law. Fol-

---

11. Ibid., 187.
12. Ibid., 174–75.

lowing the precepts of the natural law, moreover, requires the exercise of the natural right to liberty.

COMPATIBILITY FROM COMMON DESCRIPTIVE SOURCE

Since the respective ordering facts immediately underlying natural rights and the natural law both follow directly from a single fact or descriptive phenomenon, apparent tensions in their applications to particular circumstances may in principle be defused by carefully tracing each application back to this common source. This may be expressed analytically as follows: If (1) B and C are propositions each validly derived from some more general proposition A; and (2) D is a proposition validly derived from proposition B, while E is a proposition validly derived from proposition C; then (3) propositions D and E cannot contradict one another. This argument hinges upon the ultimate unity of proposition A and the validity of each of the subsequent connections among the derivative propositions. If there were two initial propositions, A and A', each giving rise to separate lines of derivative propositions, there would of course be no guarantee that subsequent propositions D and E would not be in contradiction with one another. If the unity of the initial proposition and valid subsequent derivation conditions hold, however, it is indeed the case that the two lines of derivative propositions cannot be supposed to be in contradiction with one another at any level removed from the single ultimate proposition from which they stem.

In the present case, assuming that each of the two ordering facts has been validly derived from the fact of self-ownership through self-consciousness (step 1), it follows that any apparent conflicts between subsequently derivative propositions regarding natural rights and the natural law (contradictory of step 3) may in principle be resolved by discovering an invalid derivation of these subsequent propositions from their respective ordering facts (contradictory of step 2). An apparent moral dilemma pitting natural rights against the natural law, such as a "right to do wrong,"[13] is not evidence for the existence of a tragically self-contradictory moral universe demanding groundless decisions by hapless individuals, but rather a simple indication that something has gone wrong in step 2. This is not to imply that it is always, or even usually, easy to correctly perform this step or to determine that one has correctly done so. It is only to say that failures of step 3, or apparent contradictions between natural rights and the natural law in their

---

13. See, for example, Jeremy Waldron, "A Right to Do Wrong," *Ethics* 92 (October 1981): 21–39.

more particular applications or wider implications, should not invite the shrugging of the shoulders or throwing up of the hands, since they are *in principle* traceable to corresponding and remediable failures in step 2.

Since, moreover, the common ultimate source for natural rights and the natural law is a descriptive or factual one, the potential concrete applications and broader implications of each are limited and constrained in a way that they would not be if this source were normative. The factual character of self-ownership through self-consciousness provides an anchor, as it were, for the respective spheres of influence of natural rights and the natural law. The reason for this is that descriptive or factual propositions tend to be more determinate, more widely accessible, and more sensibly verifiable than normative ones, and thus better able to check and restrain the production of derivative propositions and conclusions. For example, the proposition "one ought to act reasonably," however true it may be, admits a wide range of interpretations with nearly boundless applications and potential implications when taken by itself or as a grounding principle for morality. Its interpretation, application and potential implications are, as Rawls might say, issues on which reasonable people may differ. The proposition "human beings are self-conscious," on the other hand, cannot accommodate wide differences in interpretation; its determinate meaning is readily understood once the relevant definitional knowledge and experience are obtained.

Although the transition from the descriptive source for natural rights or the natural law to normative conclusions does introduce the potential for varying interpretations of the possible extent or reach of each concept, these interpretations are necessarily limited by the grounding of each concept in a descriptive proposition. It is much easier, for example, to determine whether individualism is a necessary implication of the idea of natural rights or merely a superfluous extension of it if natural rights stem from the fact of self-ownership through self-consciousness than if they stemmed from individual right-claims or subjective value judgments. Without a connection to a descriptive basis, it is difficult to determine where one ought to begin and end in the tasks of either drawing out the necessary implications of natural rights and the natural law or properly applying each to concrete reality. It is for this reason that some scholars are confused as to whether all animals have the rights normally ascribed to human beings, or whether there is in principle any limit to the proliferation and extension of objects of human rights.[14] It is also for this reason that scholars are divided into

---

14. See, for example, Peter Singer, *Animal Liberation: A New Ethics For Our Treatment of Animals* (Avon Publishers, 1976).

contending campus according to the primacy they bestow on either natural rights or the natural law; since each of these concepts are taken to represent much broader orientations or clusters of values, they are bound to incessantly clash with one another.

To take one example, it is often thought that proponents of natural rights and the natural law provide clearly different answers to the questions of the natural sociality of human beings and the natural foundation of government in virtue of their primary commitment to one or the other foundational concept. This becomes far less clear, however, when natural rights and the natural law cease to be conceived in terms of nebulous value orientations and become tethered to a particular descriptive phenomenon. If natural rights and the natural law represent the moral shadows of ordering facts, which are themselves directly derived from an ordinary observable fact, it is a far simpler task to confirm or deny the legitimacy of any asserted implication of either. In the case of the example cited, it would seem that natural sociality and the naturalness of government may indeed be necessary implications of the natural law, but that the contraries of these positions possess a contestable connection to natural rights. Whether or not this particular point may be substantiated by detailed argument, it is at least evident that many of the purported implications of natural rights or the natural law could be readily exposed as extraneous to these concepts themselves by determining the relation between the supposed implication and the clear fact to which it must be linked.

A similar point may be made with respect to the extension of natural rights and the natural law into concrete reality, or their respective applications to practical matters. Just as legitimate implications must be defended on the basis of their relation to the clear fact of self-ownership through self-consciousness, so legitimate applications must be so defended. Particular claims of natural rights are no longer associated with and validated by the tenets of liberal secularism or any other broad value orientation, and particular applications of natural law are no longer bound up with religious or faith-based values. Particular applications of these general moral concepts must, rather, be evaluated solely on their relation to the much more clear, readily accessible, and sensibly verifiable touchstone of descriptive reality. Replacing a normative foundation with a descriptive one in this manner significantly restrains the practical applications of natural rights and the natural law and diminishes the number of particular objects or circumstances to which they might be connected. What is apparently lost in practical utility, however, is more than gained in clarity and truth (and much is, in fact, gained in practical utility as well, as will be shown in the final chapter).

By reining in the broader implications and more particular applications of both concepts, the descriptive character of the common source for natural rights and the natural law contributes greatly to establishing their compatibility. Confining each to a more modest, if clearer and more definite, sphere has the effect of making philosophical "room" for both to be included in a coherent account of natural morality. There is much less danger that natural rights and the natural law will irreconcilably conflict with one another if each is kept on the shorter leash of descriptive reality than the more easily extendable one of a supposed purely normative reality. Natural rights and the natural law need not be caught up in a clash between progressive and traditional, or secular and faith-based, orientations seen as clusters of irreducible "values." Rather, the broader meanings and concrete applications of each may be determined with reference solely to the (at least more) common realm of descriptive reality.

A similar move to make room for both natural rights and the natural law by tethering each more closely to descriptive propositions is in fact, as previously intimated, made by John Locke. Locke is primarily concerned in his treatment of this subject with making room for a robust doctrine of natural rights by diminishing the sphere of the natural law, for the general reason that his natural rights are the newcomer to the scene of natural morality while the sphere of natural law morality had been nourished for centuries. Locke's attempt at this task is made most fully and directly in his *Questions Concerning the Law of Nature*, in which Locke replaces (with respect to his treatment of the natural law) the God of Faith as contained in the Bible with the God of natural theology, or the "potter-God."[15] This explicit replacement provides a clear instance of restraining the metaphorical reach of the natural law by means of placing it on a purely descriptive foundation.

SUBSTANTIAL COMPATIBILITY

In addition to the ways in which the common descriptive source for natural rights and the natural law contributes to the possibility for their compatibility, this compatibility is further ensured by the inextricable connections forged between these general moral concepts themselves during the course of their derivation. In a manner parallel to that in which the humanity of the individual is superior to and stands above her unique selfhood, so

---

15. See Chapter 1.

the natural law in a sense stands above and encompasses natural rights.[16] This is not to say that natural rights are derived from the natural law; but rather, as noted briefly above, that the possession of natural rights by individual human beings neatly fits the description of a practically relevant truth. There is, moreover, a way in which natural rights encompass the natural law, since the liberty or self-direction that is an object of natural right constitutes a significant precondition for acting in accordance with the natural law.

The natural law, it will be remembered, consists in the primary command to act in accordance with reason or intellectual apprehension, and in secondary commands resulting from the application of true practically relevant propositions to particular actions. True propositions of practical relevance thus serve as the conduit through which the natural law becomes applicable to concrete and particular actions. For example, the true proposition that human beings are animals issues in the practical consequence that procreation is in accordance with reason. Similarly, the true proposition that human beings are rational issues in the practical consequence that seeking knowledge is in accordance with reason. And, moreover, the true proposition that there is an objective hierarchy between human beings and other animals issues in the practical consequence that truths relating specifically to the former ought to be given more weight in directing one's actions than truths relating solely to the latter.

If it is a true proposition that individual human beings possess natural rights, this would of course include a considerable amount of practical relevance. The fact that human beings possess natural rights, unlike the fact that the interior angles of a triangle add up to a straight angle, is a very useful one for directing one's actions. While there isn't normally a very great difference between acting in accordance with or contrary to geometrical propositions regarding triangles, there is often a very great difference between acting in accordance with the proposition that human beings possess rights and acting contrary to it. The natural law thus contains a general command to act in accordance with the proposition that human beings possess natural rights, and such action may be commonly termed respect for the natural rights of others or respect for the dignity of individual human beings. This does not mean, of course, that the general command to act in accordance with the natural rights proposition is invariably operative in determining right action in any particular instance. To take a common example, a judge may be acting in accordance with the natural rights proposition

---

16. See Chapters 1 and 3.

in condemning a criminal to the loss of her liberty; in this instance, however, the natural rights proposition is superseded or overruled by other true propositions of practical relevance.

In this way natural rights give significant content to the natural law, and provide an important example of the manner in which the natural law's primary command to act in accordance with reason becomes instantiated in particular actions. The natural rights proposition constitutes, in fact, one of the fundamental channels through which the primary command of the natural law acquires concrete relevance. The reason for this is that human beings always or nearly always live in proximity to and community with other human beings, and thus the majority of one's actions involves or affects other human beings. True propositions regarding individual human beings, such as the natural rights proposition, are thus likely to be of very great practical relevance for action. The importance of the natural rights proposition within our account of the natural law also resonates with otherwise very different accounts of natural and supernatural morality that possess a similar emphasis on supra-individual grounds of morality. The "moral sense" philosophy of Hutcheson, for example, privileges natural rights as crucially important components of the general good despite his predominant focus on the good of the "system" as a whole.[17] The "integral humanism" of Jacques Maritain goes even further than Hutcheson in emphasizing the importance of respect for the dignity of the human person within a predominantly communitarian perspective.[18] The NNL theorists similarly include a robust notion of respect for individual self-direction and natural rights within their account of the natural law.[19] It is not, therefore, surprising that our account of the natural law should include within it such an emphasis on the importance of natural rights.

In addition to this significant intersection between natural rights and the natural law, their substantial compatibility is further secured by the manner in which the natural law fits within our account of natural rights. The clearest way in which this occurs involves the natural right to liberty. This application of subjective natural right stems from the extension of self-ownership to one's self-conscious actions, resulting in ownership of these actions themselves. Such ownership of one's actions constitutes, moreover, an essential precondition for acting in accordance with the natural law. The

---

17. Francis Hutcheson, *Inquiry into the Original of Our Ideas of Beauty and Virtue*, ed. Wolfgang Leidhold (Indianapolis: Liberty Fund, 2008).

18. Jacques Maritain, *Man and the State* (Washington, DC: Catholic University of America Press, 1998).

19. Finnis, *Natural Law and Natural Rights*.

reason for this is that acting in accordance with the natural law involves acting on the basis of one's apprehension of the true propositions relevant to a given set of circumstances. Acting on the basis of one's own apprehension of these propositions requires, of course, that one not be coerced into acting on the basis of anything other than one's own apprehension of practical truth. As aforementioned, a slave, insofar as he is a slave, is restrained from acting in accordance with the natural law as a result of his inability to act on the basis of such apprehension.[20] It is for this reason that the idea of voluntary action as a prerequisite for moral agency and responsibility is of such crucial importance for moral philosophers from Aristotle and Aquinas up to the present time. In more common terminology, one may say that as the first mode of substantial compatibility consists in the duty to respect rights, so this mode of compatibility consists in the right to do one's duty.

The strong compatibility between natural rights and the natural law, arising as it does from the ultimate unity of the individual human being, justifies the inclusion of both within a broader concept of natural morality. The intellectual historical relevance of the foregoing arguments may be encapsulated in the "discontinuity-compatibility" position described at the outset; neither of the primary competing positions are entirely correct (nor, for that matter, are they entirely incorrect) regarding the relationship between premodern ideas of the natural law and modern ideas of natural rights, since these ideas are simultaneously independent of one another (discontinuous) and compatible with one another. This intellectual historical point issues, however, in an additional and more directly philosophical one: since natural rights and the natural law are conceived neither as two versions of the same concept, nor as two incompatible concepts, but rather as two fundamentally complementary concepts, the resulting composite concept of natural morality constitutes a newcomer on the scene that may itself now be placed in conversation with preceding, related concepts.

One such concept is that of an ideal standard for human action lying beyond each individual human being—or the conventions of the society in which they happen to live—in some notion of human nature, a concept normally associated with the ancients and often termed "natural right." This human nature was conceived by the ancients to include general guidelines for action within it; following these guidelines defined virtue, and straying from them defined vice.[21] The medieval period witnessed the addition of

---

20. Chapter 2.
21. The most well-known proponents of this general idea include Plato, Aristotle, and Cicero.

a dimension of command and prohibition following from the pattern contained within human nature, and hence the dimension of law. The ancient and medieval periods provide, in general, explorations of supra-individual foundations for morality; classical natural right and medieval natural law express the moral implications of that which individual human beings have in common or that which lies beyond each individual. That which is unique to the individual as an individual is of moral interest primarily insofar as it is capable of deviating from or adhering to these supra-individual normative foundations.

The modern period, on the other hand, saw the emergence of the idea that the individual human being, considered as an individual, actually contains certain normative foundations within himself. Given its first widely known expression by Hobbes and placed on a more secure foundation by Locke, this characteristically modern insight attends to that which is unique to the individual in a manner largely overlooked by medieval and ancient moral and political philosophers. This is not, of course, to say that the concept of the individual was somehow unknown or wholly unappreciated before the modern period; after all, the Spanish Thomists such as Suarez had already attempted to extract a notion of subjective rights from Aquinas's texts, and subjective understandings of rights were in existence even before St. Thomas.[22] Before Hobbes, however, the individual in his uniqueness or as an individual was not conceived to be a source of normative foundations himself, but rather to have particular subjective relations to such a source lying somewhere beyond him. The modern period thus claims an original insight in asserting and exploring the implications for morality stemming from the individual considered in terms of that which is unique to him rather than as a part of a larger whole.

In comparison with the concept of natural morality argued herein, both characteristically ancient/medieval and modern conceptions of normative foundations might be said to emphasize one "side" of natural morality at the expense of the other: the ancient/medieval conceptions focus on supra-individual sources to the neglect of purely individual ones, while modern conceptions are often guilty of precisely the reverse offense. Such one-sided emphases have led to and enabled the development of extreme versions of each type of conception, with the supra-individual perspective occasionally supporting various forms of oppression and the purely individual one giving rise to excessive individualism and the erosion of salutary restraints

---

22. See Tierney, *The Idea of Natural Rights* and "Historical Roots."

on individual self-direction.[23] While valuable attempts have been made to combine typically ancient/medieval and modern conceptions of normative foundations, thereby enabling each to moderate and balance the other to some extent, such attempts tend to maintain a clear emphasis on one or the other conception as an ultimate or primary foundation. The foregoing account of natural morality, founded as it is on the independent pillars of natural rights and the natural law, purports to improve both upon these more recent attempts as well as upon many characteristically ancient/medieval and modern conceptions of normative foundations considered in themselves.

CONFRONTING OBJECTIONS

During the course of establishing the compatibility of natural rights and the natural law from which the composite concept of natural morality arises, it is necessary to answer a few important potential objections to the foregoing account in general and to emphasize the points on which this account significantly differs from other attempts to render natural rights and the natural law compatible with one another. The most important objections that may arise from the foregoing account include (1) the objection that one or the other of these concepts remains essentially derivative from the other, and (2) the objection that the natural law, in the final analysis, overshadows natural rights to the extent that the latter become relatively insignificant as a foundation for morality. Each of these objections will be presented and addressed in turn before clarifying the manner in which this account of natural rights and the natural law improves upon those advanced by Finnis, Wolfe and Tierney.

The first objection regarding derivation may be restated in terms of dependence and independence, where derivation necessarily implies some

---

23. The extreme to which the modern, purely individual perspective has given rise is of the sort famously described by Solzhenitsyn in his 1978 Harvard commencement address. Solzhenitsyn correctly associates the historical transition from supra-individual sources for morality to purely individual ones with a parallel transition from spiritualism to materialism—from an emphasis on the importance of the soul to an emphasis on the needs and desires of the body. This association of an undue focus on the individual with an undue focus on the body is given a clear explanation on our account, particularly in Chapter 2. The activity of self-consciousness there described prominently includes the experience of embodiment or "embeddedness" as a necessary component, and the body is the first and most permanent of self-consciousness's appropriations. The body is thus placed in a more favorable light when one attends to individual self-consciousness than it is when one attends to supra-individual sources for morality. Attending exclusively to the latter, as the ancients and medieval did, encourages a negative view of embodiment as a result of the body's association with the passions.

sort of dependence and its absence some sort of independence. An objection of this type may take one of two obvious general forms: either (1) natural rights are derived from and dependent upon the natural law, or (2) the natural law is derived from and dependent upon natural rights. The first might be argued on the basis of the hierarchical relation of dependence between the individual as an individual, or a unique self, and the individual as a human being, or in terms of her humanity. It has been argued that the latter stands above and encompasses the former, giving rise to it in the manner of an immediate efficient cause. Natural rights, moreover, pertain to the individual primarily considered as a unique self while the natural law pertains to the individual primarily considered as a human being. The natural law is thus more closely associated with that aspect of the individual that stands above and encompasses the aspect more closely associated with natural rights. Therefore, the natural law itself stands above and encompasses natural rights; that is, natural rights are derivative from and dependent upon the natural law.

This form of objection may be answered in a manner similar to that in which Locke, as I have argued, navigated the superiority of Divine ownership to self-ownership without relegating the latter to merely derivative status.[24] This was accomplished by means of the concept of "nesting" property, which allowed for the higher or more noble status of Divine ownership while maintaining the proper importance of self-ownership considered by itself. Although the two relationships of ownership were connected in an ontological sense, neither entered into the definition of the other or possessed an epistemological priority with respect to the other. The concept of "nesting" effectively captured this situation by reflecting the ontological compatibility or "fit" between the two relationships of ownership as well as the hierarchical character of this fit, while simultaneously reflecting the manner in which each remained independent of the other. Similarly with respect to our account of natural rights and the natural law, the ontological priority of the natural law does not imply that natural rights are derived from or dependent upon the natural law in an epistemological sense. The natural law does not enter into the definition of natural rights, so that one need not know the existence of the natural law in order to know the existence of natural rights. Natural rights, though eclipsed ontologically in a sense by the natural law, maintain an epistemological independence from the natural law and in this way are not derived from or dependent upon it.

24. Chapter 1.

The second form of the general objection, namely, that the natural law is derived from or dependent upon natural rights in the foregoing account, appears to draw clear support from the very order in which the two concepts have been treated. On this account, natural rights have been first derived from the fact of self-ownership through self-consciousness in a manner independent of the teleology associated with the natural law, or in what one might now call a "deontological" mode of argument. These natural rights have then been connected with the natural law through a kind of middle term provided by the notion of self-direction or the natural right to liberty.[25] A defensible justification for natural rights, it has been argued, implies the existence of the natural law and indicates the manner of establishing its existence. It seems, then, that the natural law has grown out of and is dependent upon natural rights in a manner that problematically undermines my claim to have genuinely recovered crucial insights of the old natural law.

This form of the objection may be answered by clarifying the relationship between the derivations of natural rights and the natural law offered herein, and particularly by briefly revisiting the transition between the two in order to determine whether the natural law has in fact been derived from natural rights. This transition was effected not by noticing that the natural law was implied by or followed from the existence of natural rights, but rather by noticing that the natural law was implied by and followed from the same underlying fact of self-ownership through self-consciousness that generated natural rights. The natural law was then derived by considering this single fact from a different angle and attending to another ordering fact arising therefrom. In the terms of the analytic illustration above, the cogency of the foregoing accounts of natural rights and the natural law in no way depends upon whether B = natural rights and C = natural law or the other way around. The order in which each has been treated makes no substantial difference; I might have begun with a derivation of the natural law and proceeded to a derivation of natural rights without departing from the account provided of either.

Even if, however, neither concept has been derived from the other, it may nevertheless be objected that the natural law overshadows and encompasses the concept of natural rights on this account to the extent that the latter is relegated to an insignificant status as a component of natural morality. First, the ordering fact giving rise to the natural law is related to that giving rise to natural rights as the general to the particular—the human-being/ unique-self relationship includes the potential-self/actual-self relationship

25. Chapter 3.

within it. As a result of this general-particular relation, it would seem that the concept of natural rights represents a superfluous addition to the concept of natural morality once the natural law is taken into account. Secondly, the substantial compatibility between natural rights and the natural law may be argued to have been established on the basis of relegating the former to merely secondary status. As providing content to the natural law in the form of the natural rights proposition, the concept of natural rights appears as one of the more important subsidiary elements of the natural law; as supplying an essential prerequisite for performing one's natural law duties, natural rights appear as merely ancillary or preparatory to the natural law and essentially ordered to it.

While it is true, as has been noted, that the natural law does possess a measure of ontological superiority to natural rights despite their epistemological independence from one another, this measure of superiority does not render the concept of natural rights superfluous or insignificant as a component of natural morality. First, the underlying fact of self-ownership through self-consciousness issues in two, and only two, ordering facts, and these ordering facts are clearly distinct from one another. Although the potential-self/actual-self relationship is included within the more general human-being/unique-self relationship, the moral implications of the former relationship pertain primarily to the further relation between one individual (considered as a whole) and others, while the moral implications of the latter relationship pertain primarily to the relation between an individual (as a unique self) and himself (as a human being). Thus the two ordering facts, though related descriptively as general and particular, are not so related in their normative or moral implications.

This distinction between the natural law and natural rights that ensures the importance of the latter in itself and beyond its connections to the natural law reflects what one might call the intersubjective two-sidedness of natural morality. The two-sidedness of natural morality follows from the two-sidedness of the individual as a human being and as a unique self. This dimension of natural morality is expressed by the natural law. The two-sidedness of natural morality becomes intersubjective when the individual is conceived in relation to other similar individuals within a community. This further dimension of natural morality is expressed by natural rights. A complete account of natural morality must include both the relationship between the two sides of the individual considered primarily in isolation and the further relationship between this individual and other similar individuals.

The idea that natural morality has this bipolar, multidimensional character is not a novel one, and was given a particularly clear expression by Aristotle in his *Nicomachean Ethics*. Aristotle draws an intriguing distinction in this work between two general senses of justice: (1) justice as comprising "virtue entire," or "the actual exercise of complete virtue," and (2) justice as "a part of virtue" and as divided into its distributive and rectificatory applications.[26] Although Aristotle's distinction does not, of course, perfectly mirror that represented in the foregoing account of natural morality, it does possess an important basic similarity to the intersubjective two-sidedness of morality described above. While justice in the first sense, as complete virtue, does include for Aristotle a relation to other individuals, its identification with complete virtue indicates that it primarily concerns the relationship between the reason and passions of the individual himself, and not that between the individual considered as a unit and other individuals. Since, for Aristotle, human beings are by nature social and by nature form political communities, and since one's relationship with oneself will nearly always affect other individuals within a political community in some way, justice in the expansive sense becomes essentially concrete or applied virtue. Virtue in general is, moreover, conceived by Aristotle in terms of acting according to the determinations of the rational principle rather than according to the extremes preferred by particular passions. This conception of virtue, and of justice as complete virtue, thus corresponds closely with our account of the natural law insofar as it is concerned primarily with the relationship between an individual (as an individual with particular passions) and herself (as a human being endowed with reason), and not with the relationship between individuals considered as wholes or units.

Aristotle's second sense of justice as "a part of virtue," on the other hand, is concerned primarily with the relationship between individuals considered as wholes or units and objects considered in the same way. The terms according to which Aristotle analyzes circumstances of distributive and rectificatory justice are individuals considered as irreducible wholes and objects to be distributed or adjusted. Distributive justice does, admittedly, overlap with justice as complete virtue insofar as the "merit" of the individual according to which the distribution occurs may depend upon his possession of justice in the expansive sense. Rectificatory justice, however, treats individuals as equal units regardless of their merit in any sense of the term. It is for this reason that rectificatory justice is defined according

---

26. Aristotle, *Ethics*, Book V. Cf. Zuckert, *Launching Liberalism*, 183.

to simply arithmetical rather than geometrical proportion; the relation between an individual and herself is almost entirely set aside in order to attend to the relation between one individual and others. Both types of justice considered as a part of virtue, and especially rectificatory justice, thus attend primarily to the intersubjective character of justice as described above by focusing on the relationship between one individual and others.

In this way the idea of the intersubjective two-sidedness of morality traces back to Aristotle's account of justice and may also be discerned in the thought of many others throughout the history of moral and political philosophy. A crucial characteristically modern insight lies in exploring the intersubjective character of morality more deeply than ancient and medieval philosophers (including Aristotle), and uncovering the source of this feature of natural morality in the individuating aspects of the human being rather than generic or supra-individual ones. Once this source is discovered, the idea of natural rights arising from it achieves an importance by underpinning the essentially intersubjective character of natural morality independently of the natural law that underpins its two-sided character. Recovering this modern insight thus guarantees that supra-individual sources of natural morality, such as the natural law, cannot engross or eclipse the importance of natural rights, or the moral relevance of the individual as an individual, as they often were permitted to do in ancient/medieval conceptions.

POLITICAL APPLICATIONS: SHIFTING EMPHASIS WITHIN COMPATIBILITY

Despite the ontological superiority of the natural law to natural rights as an ultimate moral foundation, when it comes to enforcing compliance with the two ordering facts, or action in accordance with either natural rights or the natural law, natural rights are rightfully accorded pride of place by the liberal tradition. The reason for this has been intimated with respect to the task of interpreting Locke's emphasis on self-ownership and natural rights in the *Second Treatise* despite his recognition of the ontological superiority of Divine ownership and the natural law.[27] This reason consists in three characteristics of natural rights with respect to the natural law: (1) the enforcement of natural rights is more urgent for the maintenance of political society than the enforcement of the natural law in general, (2) the security of natural rights is a condition for individual action in accordance with the

27. Chapter 1.

natural law and (3) a particular instance of contravening action is usually clearer and more readily discernible in the case of natural rights than in the case of the natural law.

The first characteristic of natural rights is perhaps the most obvious. Although there are many other true propositions of practical relevance whose enforcement is indeed urgent for the maintenance of political society, the enforcement of the natural rights proposition is the most urgent. Although government should be, and in practice always turns out to be, more than simply a guarantor of the security of the lives, liberty and property of its citizens, this basic role must be fulfilled prior to pursuing any other purposes. While governments and political societies may collapse over time as a result of neglecting to enforce many other injunctions of the natural law, neglecting to enforce the particular injunction to respect natural rights would result in the immediate dissolution of any society. If individuals in a society weren't forcibly restrained by law from violating the natural rights of others, that society would cease to exist long before questions such as the equal distribution of government benefits were even considered. If there were no enforcement of laws against murder, for example, the reform of the health care system would be the last thing on anyone's mind.

The second characteristic mirrors the first on the individual level. As noted earlier, a slave is prevented from acting according to the natural law since she does not possess the liberty that is a precondition for doing so. The possession of each of the other objects of natural right, i.e., those objects that are implied by self-ownership, is similarly a prerequisite for individual action in accordance with the natural law. The third characteristic is also fairly obvious; it is much easier for the external observer to discern whether one's natural rights have been violated than it is for such an observer to discern whether one has acted in accordance with the natural law. In fact, while it is in most cases relatively easy to perceive a violation of natural rights, it is in most cases quite difficult to be sure of a violation of the natural law.

In addition to these characteristics, it is often correctly noticed that the content of the natural law is in most cases contingent upon particular circumstances and that the natural law contains very few precepts that may be singly and directly applied to such circumstances. The natural law does not contain some definite "natural table of obligations" that may be codified and enforced in a straightforward manner.[28] While it is the task of legislators

---

28. Zuckert, *Launching Liberalism*, 187.

to ensure that human laws are derived from the natural law, i.e., from true propositions of relevance to the practical circumstances under consideration rather than from passionate or particularistic sources, the question of whether human laws have been correctly derived from the natural law is often open to debate and difficult to finally resolve. There are, however, a very few true propositions of practical relevance that do apply in a near-universal manner, among which the natural rights proposition must be counted. Aquinas himself seems to agree with this assessment in a general way, admitting that most of the actual content of the natural law is in fact changeable according to circumstances, but that the principle that "one should do harm to no man" is one of the "common" or most universally applicable principles of the natural law.[29]

As a result of these considerations, Thomas Jefferson (and Locke before him) was indeed correct to affirm that the first purpose of government is "to secure these rights" rather than "to enforce the natural law." While the two purposes are, as has been argued, entirely compatible with one another in theory, the former is both a more urgent and a more attainable goal for political power. It is thus fitting that political and legal discourse is dominated by rights talk rather than natural-law talk—so long as one knows what one is talking about. Since discovering this knowledge has been the task of the preceding arguments and discussions, it is now possible to return to the practical realm and to indicate the manner in which the foregoing account of natural morality might be applied to issues of contemporary social and political relevance.

---

29. *Summa Theologica* I-II.94.5; 95.2.

CHAPTER FIVE

Practical Applications

Assuming the correctness of the foregoing arguments, natural morality would enjoy the same ontological status even if it were entirely ignored by all human beings at all times, and ordering facts themselves would in no way be damaged by contravening action. This independence does not, however, work both ways: ordinary practical judgments remain entirely dependent upon natural morality for the extent of correctness or truth they possess. Without this extra-conventional measure, one may argue that the entire sphere of human action would be thrown into profound confusion. In Strauss's apt phrasing, the absence of such a measure would create the deeply problematic situation of "retail sanity and wholesale madness."[1]

Tacitly acknowledging the undesirability of "wholesale madness," actual political and legal argumentation and deliberation, situated at the highest level of practical judgment, is invariably (if often implicitly) framed with reference to conceptions of natural morality. While many, if not most, scholars have difficulty affirming a concept of natural or extra-conventional morality from the perspective of their armchairs, almost everyone acknowledges this concept in practice. The conceptions of natural morality that are commonly applied to practical social/political issues are, however, problematically vague, undeveloped and incoherent, resulting in seemingly insoluble conflicts among such conceptions as well as the practical judgments deriving therefrom.

The understanding of natural rights and the natural law elaborated herein significantly clarifies the concept of natural morality by including and integrating crucial elements of a variety of common conceptions that routinely do battle with one another on the fields of theoretical argumentation

---

1. Strauss, *Natural Right and History*, 4.

and practical judgment. By carefully gathering the "grains of truth" contained within these conceptions and observing their connections with one another, this new understanding of natural morality contains the potential to shed fresh light on many issues of contemporary practical relevance that previously appeared more or less intractable. The remainder of this concluding chapter will begin the task of exploring this potential with respect to the issues of universal health care, same-sex marriage and the death penalty. In addition to indicating new ways of understanding these issues from a public policy standpoint, the following discussions will also show how the abstract concept of natural morality argued herein may be translated into the realm of practice.

UNIVERSAL HEALTH CARE

The issue of universal access to health care is one that has periodically captured the national spotlight off and on for the past two decades, and never more so than in the recent debates surrounding "Obamacare." Proponents of universal health care have long bemoaned the United States' stubborn refusal to follow the example of European liberal democracies in this respect, a refusal that has deep roots in the unique intellectual and cultural history of the US.[2] While some polls indicate that a clear majority of Americans are in favor of universal access to health care in theory, others indicate that many of these same Americans are opposed to the necessary practical means of implementing this universal access.[3] The issue of universal health care turns largely on the question of whether there are "positive" or "benefit" natural rights in addition to "negative" or "liberty" ones,[4] a question that our concept of natural morality is particularly well-equipped to answer.

---

2. Puneet K. Sandhu, "A Legal Right to Health Care: What Can the United States Learn from Foreign Models of Health Rights Jurisprudence?" *California Law Review* 95, no. 4 (August 2007): 1151–92; David Lazarus, "Is Healthcare a Privilege or a Right?" *Los Angeles Times*, March 30, 2012. For discussions of the roots of this refusal see Mark J. Cherry, "Review of Allen Buchanan, *Justice and Health Care: Selected Essays*," *Ethics* 121, no. 1 (October 2010); Daniel H. Fernald, "Natural Law and the 'Right' to Health Care," *American Thinker*, March 31, 2010.

3. See Sandhu, "A Legal Right to Health Care," 1154, and Cherry, "Review of *Justice and Health Care: Selected Essays*."

4. See Sotirios A. Barber, "Liberalism and the Constitution" and Michael P. Zuckert, "On Constitutional Welfare Liberalism: An Old-Liberal Perspective," in *Liberalism: Old and New*, ed. Ellen Frankel Paul, Fred D. Miller, Jr. and Jeffrey Paul (Cambridge: Cambridge University Press, 2007), 234–88. See also Jeff Jacoby, "What 'Right' to Health Care?" *Boston Globe*, September 13, 2009; Fernald, "Natural Law and the 'Right' to Health Care"; Lazarus, "Is Healthcare a Privilege or a Right?"; Cherry, "Review of *Justice and Health Care: Selected Essays*."

Universal health care, like other government assistance programs, is often claimed as a natural right in virtue of its close relationship to the right to life. For those who could not otherwise afford appropriate health care, the provision of government assistance secures their natural rights to life and liberty in the same way that the police powers of government secure this right. Menzel and Light place this point in exceptionally clear terms: "Access to medical services, regardless of income, is as necessary to individual freedom, opportunity and self-responsibility as is access to the protective services of fire or police departments."[5] On this understanding, legitimate government's duty to secure the natural rights of its citizens includes a consideration not only of the negative rights of noninterference, but also of positive rights that enable the effective exercise of one's rights.[6]

Opponents of universal health care, on the other hand, decry many forms of government assistance to individuals on the grounds that the additional taxes required to fund them are violations of the natural rights of others to their property. They also tend to deny that there is any natural right to health care at all, since natural rights are only of the negative or "liberty" kind. As Jacoby puts it, "The rights delineated in the Declaration of Independence and the Constitution are negative rights only—they protect our autonomy, allowing us to peacefully live life and pursue happiness, neither coercing others nor being coerced by them."[7] Fernald similarly states that "in the natural law and related philosophical traditions, the vast majorities of rights are 'negative' and consequently impose no affirmative obligations on others"; positive rights, on the other hand, are simply "counterfeit" rights.[8] This issue is thus appropriately framed in terms of the conflict between rival conceptions of natural rights as either including or excluding the positive or "benefit" variety. If this type of right is included in one's conception of natural rights, universal health care is much more plausibly construed as itself an object of natural right;[9] if all rights are of the negative

---

5. Paul Menzel and Donald W. Light, "A Conservative Case for Universal Access to Health Care," *Hastings Center Report* 36, no. 4 (July-August 2006): 36–45, 37.
6. Martha Nussbaum's "capabilities approach" to human development offers an interesting instance of this sort of reasoning (*Creating Capabilities: The Human Development Approach* [Harvard University Press, 2011]).
7. Jacoby, "What 'Right' to Health Care?"
8. Fernald, "Natural Law and the 'Right' to Health Care."
9. See, for example, Norman Daniels, *Just Health Care* (New York: Cambridge University Press, 1985); Barber, "Liberalism and the Constitution"; and Allen Buchanan, *Justice and Health Care: Selected Essays* (Oxford: Oxford University Press, 2009).

type, universal health care more plausibly involves only a violation of the natural right to property.[10]

Although this issue is framed primarily in terms of competing conceptions of natural rights, the positive rights position is much more closely associated with natural law-based perspectives than the negative rights position.[11] This is because positive natural rights entail correlative natural duties beyond the mere forbearance or respect required by conceptions of negative natural rights. To possess a positive natural right is to possess a moral basis for demanding the performance of some action by another, while the possession of a negative natural right is the possession of a moral basis for demanding forbearance from action by another. The natural law, by containing more robust commands (at least on most accounts) than mere forbearance from harming others, coheres well with the positive natural duties that correspond with positive natural rights. From a natural law–based perspective, in fact, one indeed possesses a moral basis for demanding the performance of actions commanded by this law, and thus possesses positive natural rights derivative from the natural law duties of others. In the case under consideration, for example, the natural law duty of those in charge of a community to provide for the basic well-being of its members engenders a corresponding positive natural right in these members to provision for their needs. The more extensive requirements of the natural law–based perspective, as well as the character of natural rights on this perspective as essentially derivative from natural law duties, thus fits much more readily with the positive natural rights conception than with a solely negative one.

The debate regarding universal health care pits two rival conceptions of natural rights against one another and, by association, a natural law–based one (positive natural rights) against a natural rights–based one (negative natural rights). Taking a positive natural rights conception, the natural right to health care clearly outweighs the natural right to property of other members of the community due to its close association with the natural right to life. Taking a negative natural rights conception, on the other hand, there is no natural right to health care. While there may nevertheless be a moral duty to assist those in need, the natural right to property retains its moral implications and presents a moral barrier to redistributive government as-

---

10. See, for example, Zuckert, "On Constitutional Welfare Liberalism: An Old-Liberal Perspective;" Fernald, "Natural Law and the 'Right' to Health Care;" and Jacoby, "What 'Right' to Health Care?"

11. On this point, Fernald's argument linking the natural law to negative rights is misguided.

sistance programs. On the positive natural rights view, refraining from enacting redistributive health care policies constitutes a violation of the very natural rights that government was instituted to protect. On the negative natural rights view, it is enacting redistributive health care policies that constitutes a violation of these very natural rights.

On our account natural rights are indeed only of the negative kind. This is because the ordering fact giving rise to natural rights does so only through the possibility of contravening action. While many actions may be in accordance with or congenial to self-ownership, the failure to perform such actions does not amount to contravention of this ordering fact itself. Distinguishing between contravening action and contravening omission in the description of the moral implications of ordering facts is appropriate due to the vast differences between these two ways of relating to ordering facts. While contravening action occurs in a direct manner, contravening omission occurs only indirectly. In the case of contravening omission, one's actions are directed toward other objects rather than the relevant ordering fact; in the case of contravening action, one's actions are directed against the relevant ordering fact. In the former case, contravention occurs as a side-effect or unintended consequence of one's actions; in the latter case, contravention occurs as a direct and intended consequence of one's actions. Failing to save someone's life, for example, possesses a vastly different relationship to the natural right to life than actively taking someone's life. Describing both of these instances as violations of the natural right to life risks blurring or losing entirely the real and important distinction between them. To do so would be similar to describing the failure to give someone a Christmas present and the stealing of one of their presents in morally equivalent terms as violations of the Christmas spirit. It is therefore appropriate to limit the definition of a natural right to a basis for claims against action contravening one's self-ownership rather than including a basis for claims to the performance of an indefinite range of actions in accordance with one's self-ownership. Only the possibility of contravening action, not of contravening omission, generates the moral implications of self-ownership and hence the possession of a natural right.

For this reason there is no natural right to health care that would justify government assistance in this area or override the natural rights to property standing opposed to it. This particular judgment, however, does not yet entail a judgment regarding the issue itself since other considerations may justify universal health care besides the presence of a natural right to it. As the natural law commands in all such cases, a judgment must be produced from a consideration of all (or as many as possible) of the true propositions of practical relevance to this particular issue. Here are a few that may initially come to mind:

> *Proposition 1*: Each individual within the society possesses a natural right to their property.
>
> *Proposition 2*: The physical well-being of individuals within a political society constitutes an important part of the common good that government seeks to secure.[12]
>
> *Proposition 3*: The stability of political society is threatened by the existence of vast differences in health care availability that correlate with differences in wealth or socio-economic class.

Although there are undoubtedly many other true propositions relevant to this issue, these few important ones will allow at least a provisional judgment on the issue.

There is only one natural rights proposition to be considered in connection with this issue (Proposition 1), and it is the "weakest" of the three primary natural rights in terms of the universality of its decisiveness in particular cases. It does, nevertheless, weigh on the side of refraining from providing government-subsidized health care since this requires overriding the natural right of some to their property through additional taxation. Propositions 2 and 3, however, weigh heavily on the other side of the issue. Healthy (and, of course, living) citizens are a vital component of a political community's ability to defend itself from foreign attack, perpetuate itself through reproduction, and sustain itself economically (Proposition 2). Significant deficiencies in the health of individual members of society, such as might be caused by sufficiently widespread unavailability of quality health care, would result in significant threats to a political community's very existence. Insofar as vast differences in health care availability correspond to differences in wealth, socioeconomic status, or other criteria that hierarchically divide large segments of society, differences in health care availability may also act as a catalyst for social disorder (Proposition 3). While a differential ability to purchase superfluities, claim certain privileges, or engage

---

12. This common good–based or communitarian proposition relating to the issue of universal health care has been effectively explored in "Universal Access to Health Care," *Harvard Law Review* 108, no. 6 (April 1995): 1323–40, as well as Charlene A. Galarneau, "Health Care as a Community Good: Many Dimensions, Many Communities, Many Views of Justice," *Hastings Center Report* 32, no. 5 (September-October 2002): 33–40.

in certain activities contributes to resentment between various segments of political society, a differential ability to preserve one's very life through medical care constitutes a particularly serious potential source for disruptions of social stability.

Taking these propositions together, it appears that our understanding of natural morality would support a policy of government assistance for the provision of health care to those who could not otherwise obtain it. This is not to say, of course, that direct government assistance is the only, or even the best possible, manner of securing the common good of political society against the threats mentioned above. If, for example, it were true that sufficiently widespread physical well-being and a sufficiently similar availability of health care to disparate segments of society could be secured without direct governmental assistance, our judgment would reverse. The addition of this proposition would remove the conflict between the normal implications of the natural rights proposition (Proposition 1) and Propositions 2 and 3. With the removal of this conflict, the moral implications of the natural right to property would be retained and would render additional taxation unjust (as a violation of this natural right).

The analysis of this issue according to our account of natural rights and the natural law contributes significantly to contemporary debates by incorporating the central contentions of both opposed stances on the issue—the positive rights stance as well as the negative rights one—in a manner that moves beyond and resolves their grounds of disagreement, grounds that are nourished by the long-standing conflict between natural rights and the natural law. The current position advocating positive natural rights loses its characterization as a natural rights position, but is nevertheless substantially incorporated in the process of practical political judgment through the application of the natural law in the form of bringing true propositions of practical relevance to bear on the issue. The current position advocating negative natural rights is relieved of its opposition to and conflict with the natural law while being accorded a privileged place in the practical political decision-making process undertaken according to the natural law's commands. The debate is thus transformed from a seemingly intractable clash of opposing conceptions of natural rights to a more dialogic and constructive undertaking through the increased clarity offered by our account of natural morality.

SAME-SEX MARRIAGE

The issue of same-sex marriage (or marriage equality[13]) is in even greater need of constructive dialogue undertaken on the basis of natural reason than that of universal health care, since both sides of current debates almost always lean heavily on nonrational (though not necessarily irrational) grounds—whether emotional or faith based—that impede genuine and effective persuasion. These debates provide a particularly clear illustration of the pathologies that have arisen in recent political discourse as a result of the failure of natural foundationalist moral perspectives—such as those of Strauss, Maritain and their successors—to stake out a unified and compelling approach to moral issues. These pathologies include the proliferation of foundationless rights talk as well as the abandonment of any intellectual middle ground between anti-foundationalist liberalism and religiously based conservatism. Our account of natural morality aspires to ameliorate these pathologies in the manner argued in the preceding chapter: by highlighting the ability of a basic process of induction to engender meaningful knowledge of the world and pointing out the way in which this knowledge can have normative implications through "ordering facts," our account tethers rights talk to a determinate nonreligious foundation. Because of this, our account is uniquely able to indicate a few important shortcomings of existing arguments on either side of the same-sex marriage debate as well as to provide a more dialogic and promising direction for its future.

As a recent political scientific study confirms, the issue of same-sex marriage is generally framed in terms of a conflict between "traditional values" and "equal rights."[14] In many ways this framing mirrors the two pathologies of recent political discourse mentioned above, since these "traditional values" usually represent supra-rational foundations for morality and these "equal rights" usually represent an instance of the proliferation of foundationless rights talk. While some of the more nuanced and thoughtful arguments on both sides of the same-sex marriage issue avoid these poles, this dominant framing pits two positions against one another whose short-

---

13. This term is generally preferred by those in favor of extending marriage to same-sex couples. See John Corvino and Maggie Gallagher, *Debating Same-Sex Marriage* (New York: Oxford University Press, 2012), 6.

14. Barry L. Tadlock, C. Ann Gordon and Elizabeth Popp, "Framing the Issue of Same-Sex Marriage: Traditional Values Versus Equal Rights," in *The Politics of Same-Sex Marriage*, ed. Craig A. Rimmerman and Clyde Wilcox (Chicago: University of Chicago Press, 2007), 193–214, at 199.

comings are readily identifiable from the perspective of our account of natural morality.

The "traditional values" frame—involving an appeal either to religious faith, the authority of custom or both—is problematic to the extent that it encourages an unwarranted retreat from the ground of natural reason (or the related realm of "public reason," if one prefers[15]).[16] While arguments from one's religious faith or the time-honored traditions of history are entirely legitimate in themselves, they become inappropriate when they are applied unilaterally to an issue regarding which purely rational argumentation is possible. Although this point is now fairly commonplace due largely to the influence of Rawls's political philosophy, it may, upon considering the interpretations advanced in Chapter 3 of the natural law tradition, be justly described as a—if not *the*—Thomistic principle: religious faith should pick up where natural reason leaves off, and not serve as an excuse to abandon natural reason entirely. Even if philosophy is ultimately the "handmaiden" to theology, it retains a sphere proper to itself. Arguments from custom or historical tradition are even more inappropriate, since the authority of custom must stem ultimately from some conception of its accumulated or aggregate rationality; it isn't mere time, but rather the presumed working of rationality upon experience over time, that establishes the authority of custom or tradition in the first place. Isolated appeals to custom or tradition are thus tantamount to arguing simply *that* some reason for one's position exists while remaining silent regarding *what* that reason is.

These shortcomings of the "traditional values" approach to the issue of same-sex marriage are highlighted particularly clearly by our account of the natural law in Chapter 3. According to this account, arguments from the natural law—an idea usually conceived to be in close harmony with religious beliefs and the authority of custom—should proceed on the basis of an inductive understanding of observable reality, or true propositions of practical relevance. Such truths regarding the world in which we live may,

---

15. John Rawls, "The Idea of Public Reason Revisited," *University of Chicago Law Review* 64, no. 3 (Summer 1997): 765–807.
16. For a trenchant critique of "traditional values" positions upon a generally Rawlsian ground, see David A. J. Richards, *Women, Gays, and the Constitution: The Grounds for Feminism and Gay Rights in Culture and Law* (Chicago: University of Chicago Press, 1998), 438–57. See also Michael R. Stevenson and Markie Oliver, "Deconstructing Arguments Against Same-Sex Marriage," in *Defending Same-Sex Marriage, Vol. 3, The Freedom-to-Marry Movement: Education, Advocacy, Culture, and the Media*, ed. by Martin Dupuis and William A. Thompson, ed. Mark Strasser (Westport, CT: Praeger, 2007), 77–86.

in turn, easily be conceived as elements of the "eternal law" of God or as truths progressively discovered over time and assimilated into customs and traditions—as they usually are by natural lawyers[17]—without losing their original status as inductively true propositions regarding the world. To cast an inductively true proposition exclusively in terms of religious beliefs or social traditions, however, implicitly denies its accessibility to reason. Since it does indeed seem that there are inductively true propositions regarding the nature of interpersonal relationships, the basic features of human society, and the purposes of government, that are relevant to the issue of same-sex marriage, implicitly denying the rational accessibility of these propositions significantly weakens and vitiates the "traditional values" approach to same-sex marriage.

The frame usually opposed to that of "traditional values"—that of "equal rights"—is, however, equally suspect from the perspective of our account of natural morality. Although, as one recent commentator asserts, "That individuals of every group except homosexuals have a fundamental right to marry is now uncontroversial,"[18] the existence of such a "fundamental" right to marry—as possessed by any individual—is not in fact supported by the account of natural rights provided herein. Because the case for a constitutional right to marry has, moreover, been built heavily upon the existence of such a fundamental right since the seminal argument provided by Chief Justice Warren in *Loving v. Virginia*,[19] this implication of our account of natural morality may have considerable significance for arguments regarding a constitutional right to marry as well.[20]

Regardless of the general policy question of whether someone should be able to marry someone else, it is clear from our account of natural rights that marriage does not constitute a possible object of such a right, and this

---

17. Maritain (*Man and the State*) provides a particularly clear example of these ways of conceiving the precepts of natural law.

18. Mark Carl Rom, "Introduction: The Politics of Same-Sex Marriage," in *The Politics of Same-Sex Marriage*, 6.

19. 388 US 1 (1967).

20. For explanations of the connection between the idea of fundamental rights, including most importantly the right to marry, and the history of same-sex marriage jurisprudence, see William N. Eskridge, Jr., *The Case for Same-Sex Marriage: From Sexual Liberty to Civilized Commitment* (New York: The Free Press, 1996), 123–52; David A. J. Richards, *Women, Gays, and the Constitution*, 438–57; David A. J. Richards, *Identity and the Case for Gay Rights: Race, Gender, Religion as Analogies* (Chicago: University of Chicago Press, 1999), 153–70; and Daniel R. Pinello, *America's Struggle for Same-Sex Marriage* (New York: Cambridge University Press, 2006), 33–101.

for at least a couple of compelling reasons. First, marriage—in the "civil" sense under political debate as the sum total of 1,138 legal privileges and responsibilities[21]—is, like universal health care, something provided by a government rather than something reserved from governmental infringement by individuals.[22] It is thus the object of a "positive" right rather than a "negative" right, and on account of this fact falls short of achieving the status of a natural or "fundamental" right in the same manner as the supposed fundamental right to health care. While individuals do indeed possess a natural right to liberty entailing forbearance on the part of others, including the government, from interference in their interpersonal relationships, this is distinct from a right to legal privileges or responsibilities such as those attending civil marriage. Secondly, natural rights, on our account, pertain only to individuals considered as individuals, since such rights are derived from the idea of individual self-ownership which is, in turn, derived from a consideration of the phenomenon of self-consciousness. Marriage, on the other hand, pertains properly to couples or the relationships between individuals. Couples and relationships, since they are not individual human beings, cannot possess any natural or fundamental rights on our account of natural morality; and thus no couple—heterosexual or homosexual—can be said to possess a fundamental right to marry. Since only individual human beings can possess natural rights, marriage is not a possible object for a natural or fundamental right.

If both of the dominant opposing approaches to the issue of same-sex marriage have been shown to be deeply problematic according to our account of natural morality, what approach is left to us? As in the case of universal health care, our account of natural morality dictates that recourse must be had to the most important true propositions of practical relevance to this issue. While, as in the case of universal health care, it is extremely difficult to ensure that one has actually collected all of the most important such propositions, the primary command of the natural law—to act in accordance with our rational apprehension of the world—demands that an attempt be made and acted upon. Some of the more nuanced and thoughtful arguments on both sides of the same-sex marriage debate indicate a few directly relevant propositions that provide an adequate starting point:

---

21. GAO-04-353R, Defense of Marriage Act (January 23, 2004), letter from GAO Associate General Counsel Dayna K. Shah to Senator Bill Frist, dated Jan. 23, 2004.

22. See S. Adam Seagrave, "Civil Marriage: The View from a State of Nature," *Public Discourse*, September 19, 2012.

> *Proposition 1*: The stability of relationships contributes significantly both to the private good of individuals and to the common good of society.[23]
>
> *Proposition 2*: Opposite-sex couples contain the potential for procreation while same-sex couples do not.[24]
>
> *Proposition 3*: It is the duty of government to provide for the common good of society.

While both proponents and opponents of same-sex marriage would be expected to admit the truth of each of these propositions, proponents tend to emphasize a combination of Propositions 1 and 3 and opponents tend to emphasize the importance of Proposition 2.

Proposition 1 applies to all sorts of close personal relationships—in addition to intimate couples, it would clearly apply to other familial relationships, friendships, and even professional partnerships. The crucial question is whether all relationships to which Proposition 1 applies trigger action on the basis of Proposition 3—i.e., whether governmental support should be extended to all such relationships—or whether there is some threshold relationships must cross in order to warrant governmental involvement. Some scholars propose a minimalist threshold according to which all "caring" relationships, intimate or not, are entitled to governmental support on the basis of Proposition 3.[25] Most proponents of same-sex marriage propose romantic relationships as the threshold, including both same- and opposite-sex couples but excluding non-romantic relationships. Opponents of same-sex marriage, on the other hand, hold that Proposition 2 provides the appropriate threshold, and that only relationships that contain the potential for procreation warrant governmental support on the basis of Proposition 3.

Of course, the application of any threshold at all involves "discriminating" between relationships (though not necessarily between the individuals within them) that meet the threshold and those that do not. In addition

---

23. John Corvino, "The Case for Same-Sex Marriage," in *Debating Same-Sex Marriage*, by John Corvino and Maggie Gallagher (New York: Oxford University Press, 2012), 180; Stephen Macedo, "Homosexuality and the Conservative Mind," *Georgetown Law Journal* 84 (1995): 261–300, 279.

24. Maggie Gallagher, "The Case Against Same-Sex Marriage," in *Debating Same-Sex Marriage*, 95, 177; Sherif Girgis, Robert P. George and Ryan T. Anderson, "What is Marriage?" *Harvard Journal of Law and Public Policy* 34, no. 1: 245–87, 246. S. Adam Seagrave, "Civil Marriage: The View from a State of Nature."

25. Elizabeth Brake, "Minimal Marriage: What Political Liberalism Implies for Marriage Law," *Ethics* 120, no. 2 (January 2010): 302–37.

to attending to the differences between the various types of relationships that contribute to the common good of society, determining an appropriate threshold for the application of Proposition 3 involves applying conceptions of the appropriate level of governmental involvement in civil society to this particular case. In other words, a justification for governmental regulation on the basis of Proposition 3 requires both Proposition 1 and some conception of the extent to which governments should involve themselves in actively supporting the common good they are duty bound to look after—after all, many things contribute to the common good of society without requiring active governmental assistance. A libertarian, therefore, may very well be expected to differ from a political liberal on this issue regardless of where the particular relationship threshold is located.

Positions on same-sex marriage should thus be expected to lie at the intersection between a particular relationship threshold and one's conception of the nature of the government's duty to provide for the common good. Regardless of where this intersection occurs, it is at least clear that Proposition 2 entails an intensification of Proposition 1 beyond the level achieved by other kinds of relationships, so that opposite-sex couples would logically be the first or most obvious form of relationship to warrant governmental recognition and support. While many argue for including other relationships besides opposite-sex couples within the category of civil marriage and widening the threshold for entrance into it, no one would argue for simultaneously including other sorts of relationships and excluding opposite-sex couples. Opposite-sex couples include (at least in theory or for the most part) each of the elements of other sorts of relationships that contribute to the private good of individuals and the common good of society—that fall under Proposition 1—while also including in addition the element represented by Proposition 2, that of giving rise to new life.

The foregoing analysis carried out in accordance with our account of natural morality has already accomplished two important objectives: that of clearly indicating the shortcomings of the existing debate and that of illuminating the contours of a much more dialogic and potentially constructive route to take in deciding this important issue. It remains "only" to determine the question of whether or not the intensification of Proposition 1 accomplished by Proposition 2 provides a sufficient and necessary difference in crossing a threshold for triggering governmental involvement on the basis of Proposition 3. This is, however, a question requiring a more extended discussion than is warranted here, and one that would involve bringing many more propositions of practical relevance to bear in order to reach a persuasive conclusion. Having sufficiently indicated a starting point and appropriate route for such a discussion, our account of natural morality has already accomplished its essential work.

Our consideration of this issue would be problematically incomplete, however, if we were to ignore the fact that the same-sex marriage debate is, for many of those involved, not ultimately about the 1,138 legal incidents of civil marriage at all. It is, rather, about what Richards has called the "moral slavery of homosexuals" or the "cultural construction of the dehumanization of the homosexual"; the idea that failing to extend civil marriage to same-sex couples indicates that homosexual individuals are second-class citizens who are not entitled to equal treatment with their heterosexual counterparts.[26] If this were in fact the case—if limiting marriage to opposite-sex couples reflected the "slavery" and "dehumanization" of homosexual individuals— our account of natural morality would likely provide clear support for Richards' conclusions. Richards' argument problematically neglects, however, the distinction between a negative natural right possessed by an individual and a positive right purportedly possessed by couples. The "right to intimate life" upon which Richards bases the "right to marriage" is a negative natural right possessed by an individual, one entailing forbearance from interference with individual liberty rather than the provision of particular recognition or legal status to a couple. The leap from the former to the latter is, therefore, much larger than that of a "reasonable corollary."[27] It may, in other words, be entirely consistent for the individual negative natural rights of homosexuals to be respected and affirmed—as they have been by the outcome of *Lawrence v. Texas* and the inclusion of sexual orientation in hate-crime legislation—without providing homosexual couples with positive rights extended to heterosexual ones.

The enormous leap that Richards' argument requires underscores the fact that the same-sex marriage issue may, at root, not actually be about civil marriage at all; civil marriage may merely serve as the ground upon which both sides of the debate have chosen to wage a contest over competing conceptions of morality. Richards, along with many other proponents of same-sex marriage, views the traditional conception of civil marriage as a vehicle for enforcing a sectarian moral framework that condemns homosexuality.[28] This is why most proponents of same-sex marriage would not

26. Richards, *Women, Gays and the Constitution*, 441, 447; see also Pinello, *America's Struggle for Same-Sex Marriage*, 164–66.
27. Ibid., 443.
28. This perception is particularly clearly indicated in Stevenson and Oliver, "Deconstructing Arguments Against Same-Sex Marriage," in *Defending Same-Sex Marriage*.

be satisfied by civil unions or domestic partnerships, even if these unions were able to mimic civil marriage perfectly (which they currently do not).[29] Disagreeing primarily with the moral framework standing behind civil marriage, proponents of same-sex marriage seek to combat it by eliminating what they take to be its legal manifestation. For their part, opponents of same-sex marriage have predictably rushed to support this supposed legal manifestation of a moral framework with which they agree. If, as this discussion would indicate, the same-sex marriage debate is ultimately not really about what it purports to be about—namely, the 1,138 legal incidents of civil marriage—then perhaps both sides of this debate should take a step back from the realm of political-legal argumentation into the moral realm. Within this moral realm, our account of natural morality may be expected to be of even more clear utility in articulating a persuasive view of the issue.

THE DEATH PENALTY

The death penalty has ceased to be an issue of contention in most Western liberal democracies with the general abandonment of the practice. It remains legal and supported by a large portion of the population in the United States, however, and is thus an issue of continuing relevance for contemporary American politics.[30] It is also, with respect to our purposes, an issue that promises to prove illuminating for the task of determining the practical applications of our understanding of natural morality. Justifications for the death penalty normally include one or both of the following propositions: (1) the commission of certain crimes entails the forfeiting of one's natural right to life, and (2) a concern for the natural rights of others, or the public safety, warrants the death penalty in the case of individuals who present a particularly serious threat to public safety.

The first justificatory proposition may mean either (1) that the criminal retains the natural right to life, but this natural right loses its moral implications when weighed against the severity of the crime committed; or (2) that the commission of the crime entails the loss of the criminal's natural right to life. On our definition of subjective natural right, (2) may be immediately rejected as a possible justification for the death penalty since

---

29. See *Perry v. Brown* (671 F.3d 1052).
30. See Tony G. Poveda, "American Exceptionalism and the Death Penalty," *Social Justice* 27, no. 2 (80), Criminal Justice and Globalization at the New Millennium (Summer 2000): 252–67.

the criminal's factual self-ownership, which forms the core of the definition of a natural right, is not altered by the commission of any crime. Natural rights are incapable of being forfeited and are indeed inalienable as a result of their primarily descriptive character. Meaning (1), however, represents a much more promising and interesting justification for this practice and is more difficult to pronounce upon. In order to do so, it will be necessary to apply our understanding of the natural law by collecting a few important propositions of relevance to this generic situation and determining whether these warrant overriding the criminal's natural right to life. Here are a few that may immediately come to mind:

Proposition 1: The criminal has committed some heinous crime, or at least has been convicted of this crime in accordance with the due process of law.
Proposition 2: Ensuring rectificatory justice constitutes a proper purpose of government.
Proposition 3: Protecting the natural rights of those subject to it constitutes a primary purpose of government.

Taking 1 and 2 together, it might be argued according to some notions of retributive punishment that the rectificatory justice required to restore equality[31] after certain crimes necessitates the criminal's loss of her life, and thus that governments are authorized to exact this punishment in pursuance of the purpose of ensuring rectificatory justice.[32] This argument possesses an undeniable resonance both with commonsensical notions of justice and with biblical ones. "An eye for an eye and a tooth for a tooth" is condoned by the Old Testament, and "let the punishment fit the crime" reflects our most basic grasp of justice as involving a precise correspondence (of some kind) between the offense committed and the punishment received. When faced with certain crimes, it indeed seems as if rectificatory justice could not be achieved by any punishment short of the loss of life, and sometimes even this might appear too lenient.

---

31. See Aristotle, *Ethics* V on the notion of justice as a restoration of equality. For contemporary elaborations and defenses of this basic Aristotelian notion see E. J. Weinrib, "Corrective Justice," *Iowa Law Review* 77 (1992): 403–25; and James Gordley, "Tort Law in the Aristotelian Tradition," in *Philosophical Foundations of Tort Law*, ed. by David Owen (Oxford: Oxford University Press, 1995).

32. See E. van den Haag, "Justice, Deterrence, and the Death Penalty," in *America's Experiment With Capital Punishment*, ed. by J. R. Acker, R. M. Bohm and C. S. Lanier (Durham, NC: Carolina Academic Press, 1998), 139–56.

There are, however, a number of potential problems with this kind of argument. First, there is the problem of accepting the criminal's life as the rectificatory equivalent for a wide variety of crimes.[33] In the simplest imaginable case, a criminal is given the death penalty in punishment for the premeditated murder of a single human being; one life is taken to rectify the taking of one life. If this criminal committed two or more such murders, however, what is to be done? If he is given the death penalty, he is only punished for the equivalent of one murder and effectively escapes unpunished for the others; on the one side is the single life of the criminal, and on the other are the multiple lives taken and affected by his actions. There are, in fact, many such cases in which it would appear simply impossible to restore rectificatory equality. Human beings possess a much greater capacity to inflict harm than to suffer it, and thus the governmental purpose described in Proposition 2 does not admit of perfect fulfillment even in theory.[34] An adequate justification for the death penalty must extend beyond the purpose of ensuring rectificatory justice (Propositions 1 and 2) since there are very few cases in which a persuasive case could be made that rectificatory justice is secured through this practice.

Secondly, Proposition 3 weighs strongly against government-sponsored taking of life, and may be interpreted as a restatement of the natural rights proposition relating to the criminal's natural right to life. As indicated in Chapter 2, life constitutes the most fundamental or important object of natural right, normally trumping rights to liberty and property. If a primary purpose of legitimate government is the protection of natural rights, and if the primary natural right is the natural right to life, a very strong presumption is created against the legitimacy of government-sponsored killing of any human being. Proposition 3 cuts both ways, however, since it may also be invoked on the side of justifying the death penalty and overriding the criminal's natural rights when one considers the natural rights of other members of the political society. It may be argued that the government is acting to protect the natural rights of the other members of society when it acts against the natural right of the single criminal to life. In Locke's terms the criminal has become like a wild animal with respect to the rest of

---

33. This problem of incommensurability is explored in Joseph Raz, *The Morality of Freedom* (Oxford: Oxford University Press, 1986), 348; and Cass Sunstein, "Incommensurability and Kinds of Valuation: Some Applications in Law," in *Incommensurability, Incomparability, and Practical Reason*, ed. by R. Chang (Cambridge: Harvard University Press, 1997).

34. See Seth R. M. Lazar, "Corrective Justice and the Possibility of Rectification," *Ethical Theory and Moral Practice* 11, no. 4 (August 2008): 355–68.

society, and may therefore be treated accordingly in order to ensure the safety of oneself and others.[35]

In his treatment of the death penalty in the *Second Treatise*, Locke downplays and neglects the first interpretation of Proposition 3, apparently assuming that the criminal's natural right to life is rendered morally irrelevant by other considerations such as the second interpretation of Proposition 3. In Locke's state of nature, *"every man hath a right to punish the offender, and be executioner of the law of nature,"* including "the right of war" which entails "a liberty to kill the aggressor" in certain circumstances.[36] When an individual threatens to violate the natural right of another to life, the moral value of his life becomes roughly equivalent to that of a *"lion,"* a *"tyger,"* a *"wolf,"* and other such "wild savage beasts."[37] This occurs as a result of the criminal abandoning "the common law of reason," i.e., the law of nature.[38] The formation of political society is, moreover, characterized chiefly by every individual resigning the executive power of the law of nature to the public.[39] Since the natural right to be executioner of the law of nature clearly includes the right to kill a criminal, and this right is transferred to the public with the formation of political society, it would indeed seem that political societies may justly take the life of criminals. This is further confirmed by Locke's initial definition of *"Political power"* as "a *right* of making laws with penalties of death. . . ."[40]

While Locke's judgment regarding the death penalty provides an illuminating example of the manner in which the natural rights of individuals interact with the natural law in his thought, this judgment is ultimately compromised by Locke's failure to take sufficient account of the criminal's natural right to life. Locke's repeated comparison of criminals to animals may, in fact, suggest the stronger claim that they have forfeited the natural right to life itself. At least on this single point, Hobbes's discussion appears more thoughtful and nuanced than Locke's, primarily by including this additional consideration.[41] Perhaps the best and most thorough treatment

---

35. Locke, *Two Treatises*, II.iii.1.
36. Ibid., II.ii.8; II.iii.19.
37. Ibid., II.ii.11; II.iii.16.
38. Ibid., II.iii.16.
39. Ibid., II.vii.89.
40. Ibid., II.i.3. For a more thorough exploration of the Lockean position on the death penalty, see Brian Calvert, "Locke on Punishment and Capital Punishment," *Philosophy* 68, no. 264 (1993): 211–29, and A. John Simmons, "Locke on the Death Penalty," *Philosophy* 69, no. 270 (1994): 471–77.
41. Hobbes, *Leviathan*.

of this issue in the early modern period, however, is provided by Cesare Beccaria. Beccaria argues against the death penalty at length, both on the basis of its justice and on the basis of its purported social utility.[42] With respect to the question of justice, Beccaria focuses on the natural right of the criminal to his life, arguing that, since no one possesses the right to take his own life, this right cannot be supposed to have been transferred to anyone else. With respect to the question of utility, which is closely connected with the purpose of protecting the rights of others within society, Beccaria argues at length that "perpetual slavery" or imprisonment would in fact better achieve the social effects hoped for from the death penalty.[43] Although Beccaria primarily focuses in his arguments regarding the death penalty on its use within political societies while Locke focuses on its primitive use within the state of nature, Beccaria's analysis provides in some respects a more faithfully Lockean treatment of the issue than Locke himself through his explicit consideration of the criminal's natural right to life.

Especially in the context of more developed nations such as the United States, Beccaria's argument for the alternative of perpetual imprisonment is rather persuasive. Assuming some reasonable threshold of prison security, incarcerating an individual for the remainder of his life is, with respect to the danger he presents to the natural rights of others, the practical equivalent of taking his life. While Proposition 3 may indeed be interpreted to support the death penalty, this support is thus often mitigated by other circumstances and directly conflicts with another possible interpretation of the practical relevance of this proposition. Taking the three propositions of practical relevance raised in connection with this issue together, along with the natural rights proposition consisting in the criminal's natural right to life, it appears on this analysis that the death penalty may be prohibited by natural morality in most contexts.

Applying our understanding of natural morality to the issue of the death penalty in this way, while it does not yield a universally definitive answer and is subject to revision based upon the introduction of additional propositions of practical relevance, does add substantial clarity to this issue. A predominantly natural rights–based perspective, focusing on the individual rather than society as a whole, would attend primarily to the natural right of the criminal to his life and generally assume the decisiveness of this natural rights proposition. A natural law–based perspective, on the other hand,

---

42. Cesare Beccaria, *On Crimes and Punishments*, chap. 28.
43. Ibid.

through the tendency of such a perspective to focus on the common good of society and to derive the rights of the individual from this good, would attend primarily to the social benefit derived from the practice and disregard the criminal's continued possession of the natural right to life. The analysis provided above, on the other hand, takes the inalienability of the criminal's natural right to life seriously without assuming the presence of the moral implications that normally attend this natural right. It admits the central contentions of both a natural rights–based and a natural law–based perspective, diffusing the potential disagreement between them, while offering the possibility of a clear judgment on the issue itself. Our understanding of natural morality is thus capable, on this important issue as well, of enabling a more broad-minded and dialogic treatment of such difficult issues than is normally available.

CONCLUSION: NATURAL MORALITY AND INTELLECTUAL HISTORY

It should not be surprising that this account of natural morality offers increased clarity on a number of contemporary social and political issues, since it draws together and unites two perspectives whose unreflective application in practice generally tends to widen the perceived gap between them. It has been argued herein that "modern" insights regarding natural rights as independent justificatory sources for morality are both defensible and in profound harmony with "premodern" insights regarding supraindividual sources for morality including the natural law tradition. These insights, if true, are presumably valid for all human beings at all times; natural rights liberalism is not a contingent preference of Western culture, and the natural law is not an obsolete historical curiosity.

If my account is persuasive, it would seem that moral and political philosophy has not actually "progressed" since the medieval period, or at least not in the manner this is commonly understood—nor, however, has it regressed. Although the emergence of modern political philosophy indeed occurred through an explicit rejection of many elements of premodern doctrines, the crucial insights regarding the natural rights of individuals and the connection of this conception to political legitimacy do not in fact imply a wholesale rejection of ancient and medieval moral and political philosophy. Natural rights are indeed a peculiarly modern insight, but their discovery complements rather than contradicts premodern insights regarding the natural law. The progression that has occurred in moral and political philosophy since the medieval period is much more like the discovery of a missing piece to a jigsaw puzzle behind a couch cushion than the purchasing of a shiny new puzzle to replace an old and faded one. In the excitement surrounding the initial discovery of this missing piece, early modern political philosophers such as Machiavelli and Hobbes began searching for a new puzzle to accommodate it. Although Locke cautiously yet cogently indicated the possibility that this newly discovered piece may in fact fit somewhere within the old puzzle, subsequent moral and political philosophers were already too taken with the prospect of a new puzzle to entertain this possibility.

The intellectual historical relevance of the foregoing account of natural morality, in terms of this admittedly crude analogy, has been to argue that this new piece (while it is indeed new) does, in fact, fit within the old puzzle. This account was rendered possible in large part by outlining the concept of ordering facts, a concept that enables the use of the justificatory tools required to place the doctrine of natural rights on a defensible foundation. Defending modern natural rights doctrines in this way entails, in turn, their reconciliation with premodern conceptions of the natural law. If natural rights are to make sense in themselves or be rationally defensible, in other words, they must be placed in a broader context that inextricably connects them with the traditional natural law.

This natural law tradition that extends from Aristotle to Aquinas through Cicero is not in need of updating to accommodate the idea of natural rights. Nor does the modern natural rights doctrine need to be relieved of its radical novelty in order to be rendered compatible with the natural law tradition. If my argument is persuasive, the traditional natural law remains as true and applicable today as it was in Cicero's time, and modern natural rights actually existed long before those such as Hobbes and Locke brought them to light. The coexistence of natural rights and the natural law as the complementary pillars of natural morality is, in fact, coextensive with the existence of human beings. Progress in moral and political philosophy, unlike progress in the empirical natural sciences, is not always marked by replacing the old with the new, the ancient and medieval with the modern and contemporary. The relationship between Rawls and Plato, J. S. Mill and Aristotle, or Locke and Aquinas is not like that between Copernicus and Ptolemy. The so-called "Copernican revolution" in the history of ideas did indeed introduce a radically new perspective on moral and political realities, but this perspective in no way invalidated the previously dominant perspective as Copernicus's heliocentrism invalidated Ptolemy's geocentrism. One might say that the ancients and medievals saw with one eye, and the moderns discovered the other by shutting the first. Recognizing the compatibility of natural rights and the natural law enables moving beyond these Cyclopic perspectives to view moral and political realities through a wider and more accurate lens—that of natural morality.

BIBLIOGRAPHY

Aquinas, Thomas. *Summa Theologica*. Translated by the Fathers of the English Dominican Province. New York: Benziger, 1948.
———. *Basic Writings of Saint Thomas Aquinas*. Edited by Anton C. Pegis. New York: Random House, 1945.
Aristotle. *The Basic Works of Aristotle*. Edited by Richard McKeon. New York: Random House, 1941.
———. *Nicomachean Ethics*. Translated by H. Rackham. Loeb Classical Library. Cambridge: Harvard University Press, 1994.
———. *Politics*. Translated by H. Rackham. Loeb Classical Library. Cambridge: Harvard University Press, 1998.
Arkes, Hadley. "That 'Nature Herself Has Placed in Our Ears a Power of Judging': Some Reflections on the 'Naturalism' of Cicero." In *Natural Law Theory: Contemporary Essays*. Oxford: Oxford University Press, 1992.
Ashcraft, Richard. *Revolutionary Politics and Locke's "Two Treatises of Government."* Princeton: Princeton University Press, 1986.
Barber, Sotirios A. "Liberalism and the Constitution." In *Liberalism: Old and New*. Edited by Ellen Frankel Paul, Fred D. Miller Jr., and Jeffrey Paul. Cambridge University Press, 2007.
Berlin, Isaiah. "Two Concepts of Liberty." In *Four Essays on Liberty*. Oxford University Press, 1969.
Bermudez, José Luis. *The Paradox of Self-Consciousness*. Cambridge: MIT Press, 1998.
Brake, Elizabeth. "Minimal Marriage: What Political Liberalism Implies for Marriage Law." *Ethics* 120, no. 2 (2010): 302–37.
Buchanan, Allen. *Justice and Health Care: Selected Essays*. Oxford University Press, 2009.
Calvert, Brian. "Locke on Punishment and Capital Punishment." *Philosophy* 68, no. 264 (1993): 211–29.
Cherry, Mark J. "Review of Allen Buchanan, *Justice and Health Care: Selected Essays*." *Ethics* 121, no. 1 (2010).
Cicero. *De Officiis*. Translated by Walter Miller. Loeb Classical Library. Cambridge: Harvard University Press, 2001.

———. *De Re Publica, De Legibus.* Translated by C. W. Keyes. Loeb Classical Library. Cambridge: Harvard University Press, 1970.

———. *De Finibus Bonorum et Malorum.* Translated by H. Rackham. Loeb Classical Library. Cambridge: Harvard University Press, 2006.

Coleman, Janet. "*Dominium* in Thirteenth- and Fourteenth-Century Heirs: John of Paris and Locke." *Political Studies* 33 (1985): 73–100.

Corvino, John, and Maggie Gallagher. *Debating Same-Sex Marriage.* New York: Oxford University Press, 2012.

Corvino, John. "The Case for Same-Sex Marriage." In *Debating Same-Sex Marriage.* Oxford, 2012.

Crosson, Frederick. "Religion and Natural Law." *American Journal of Jurisprudence* 33 (1988): 1–17.

Daniels, Norman. *Just Health Care.* New York: Cambridge University Press, 1985.

Dunn, John. *The Political Thought of John Locke: An Historical Account of the Argument of the "Two Treatises of Government."* Cambridge University Press, 1969.

Dworkin, Ronald. *Taking Rights Seriously.* Cambridge: Harvard University Press, 1977.

———. *Justice for Hedgehogs.* Cambridge: Harvard University Press, 2011.

Eskridge, Jr., William N. *The Case for Same-Sex Marriage: From Sexual Liberty to Civilized Commitment.* New York: Free Press, 1996.

Feinberg, Joel. "The Nature and Value of Rights." *Journal of Value Inquiry* 4, no. 4 (1970): 243–57.

Fernald, Daniel H. "Natural Law and the 'Right' to Health Care." *American Thinker,* March 31, 2010.

Finnis, John. *Natural Law and Natural Rights.* Oxford University Press, 1980.

———. "Natural Law and Legal Reasoning." In *Natural Law Theory: Contemporary Essays,* 134–57. Oxford University Press, 1992.

———. *Aquinas: Moral, Political, and Legal Theory.* Oxford University Press, 1998.

Finnis, John, and Germain Grisez. "The Basic Principles of Natural Law: A Reply to Ralph McInerny." *American Journal of Jurisprudence* 26 (1981): 21–31.

Fortin, Ernest L. "Augustine, Thomas Aquinas, and the Problem of Natural Law." *Mediaevalia* 4 (1978): 179–208.

———. "The New Rights Theory and the Natural Law." *Review of Politics* 44 (1982): 590–612.

———. "St. Thomas Aquinas." In *History of Political Philosophy,* 248–75.

———. "Thomas Aquinas as a Political Thinker." *Perspectives on Political Science* 26 (1997): 92–97.

Galarneau, Charlene A. "Health Care as a Community Good: Many Dimensions, Many Communities, Many Views of Justice." *Hastings Center Report* 32, no. 5 (2002): 33–40.

Gallagher, Maggie. "The Case against Same-Sex Marriage." In *Debating Same-Sex Marriage.* Oxford, 2012.

George, Robert P., ed. *Natural Law Theory: Contemporary Essays.* Oxford University Press, 1992.

———. "Natural Law and Human Nature." In *Natural Law Theory.* Oxford, 1992, 31–41.

———, ed. *Natural Law and Moral Inquiry: Ethics, Metaphysics, and Politics in the Work of Germain Grisez.* Washington, DC: Georgetown University Press, 1998.

———. *Making Men Moral*. Oxford: Clarendon Press, 1993.
Gewirth, Alan. *Reason and Morality*. Chicago: University of Chicago Press, 1978.
———. "Moral Rationality." Lindley Lecture. Lawrence: University of Kansas, 1972.
Girgis, Sherif, Robert P. George, and Ryan T. Anderson. "What Is Marriage?" *Harvard Journal of Law and Public Policy* 34, no. 1: 245–87.
Glendon, Mary Ann. *A World Made New: Eleanor Roosevelt and the Universal Declaration of Human Rights*. New York: Random House, 2001.
———. *Rights Talk: The Impoverishment of Political Discourse*. New York: Free Press, 1991.
Goerner, E. A. "On Thomistic Natural Law: The Bad Man's View of Thomistic Natural Right." *Political Theory* 7 (1979): 101–22.
———. "Thomistic Natural Right: The Good Man's View of Thomistic Natural Law." *Political Theory* 11 (1983): 393–418.
Gordley, James. "Tort Law in the Aristotelian Tradition." In *Philosophical Foundations of Tort Law*. Edited by David Owen. Oxford University Press, 1995.
Grotius, Hugo. *De Jure Belli ac Pacis Libri Tres* (1625). Classics of International Law 3. Edited by James Brown Scott. Vol. 1 (Washington, DC: 1913), Latin text, facsimile of 1646 edition. Vol. 2 (Oxford 1925), English text. Translated by Francis W. Kelsey et al.
Haakonssen, K. "From Natural Law to the Rights of Man: A European Perspective on American Debates." In *A Culture of Rights*. Edited by M. J. Lacey and K. Haakonssen. Cambridge University Press, 1991.
Hart, H. L. A. "Are There Any Natural Rights?" *Philosophical Review* 64 (1955): 175–91.
Hittinger, Russell. *The First Grace: Rediscovering the Natural Law in the Post-Christian World*. Wilmington, DE: ISI Books, 2003.
Hobbes, Thomas. *Leviathan*. Edited by Edwin Curley. Indianapolis: Hackett, 1994.
Holton, James E. "Marcus Tullius Cicero." In *History of Political Philosophy*, 155–75.
Horsley, Richard A. "The Law of Nature in Philo and Cicero." *Harvard Theological Review* 71 (1978): 35–59.
Horwitz, Robert. Introduction to John Locke's *Questions Concerning the Law of Nature*. Ithaca: Cornell University Press, 1990.
———. "John Locke's *Questions Concerning the Law of Nature*: A Commentary." Edited by Michael Zuckert. *Interpretation* 19 (1992): 251–306.
Hume, David. *A Treatise of Human Nature*. New York: Penguin Books, 1969.
Hutcheson, Francis. *Inquiry into the Original of Our Ideas of Beauty and Virtue*. Edited by Wolfgang Leidhold. Indianapolis: Liberty Fund, 2008.
Jacoby, Jeff. "What 'Right' to Health Care?" *Boston Globe*, September 13, 2009.
Keys, Mary. *Aquinas, Aristotle, and the Promise of the Common Good*. Cambridge University Press, 2006.
Laslett, Peter. Introduction to John Locke's *Two Treatises of Government*. Cambridge University Press, 1988.
Lazar, Seth R. M. "Corrective Justice and the Possibility of Rectification." *Ethical Theory and Moral Practice* 11, no. 4 (2008): 355–68.
Lazarus, David. "Is Healthcare a Privilege or a Right?" *Los Angeles Times*, March 30, 2012.

Locke, John. *An Essay Concerning Human Understanding.* Edited by Peter H. Nidditch. Oxford University Press, 1975.

———. *Two Treatises of Government.* Edited by Peter Laslett. Cambridge University Press, 1988.

———. *Questions Concerning the Law of Nature.* Edited and translated by Robert Horwitz, Jenny Strauss Clay, and Diskin Clay. Ithaca, NY: Cornell University Press, 1990.

———. *The Reasonableness of Christianity, as Delivered in the Scriptures.* In *John Locke: Writings on Religion.* Edited by Victor Nuovo. Oxford: Clarendon Press, 2002.

MacCormick, Neil. "Natural Law Reconsidered." *Oxford Journal of Legal Studies* 1 (1981): 99–109.

Macedo, Stephen. *Liberal Virtues.* Oxford: Clarendon Press, 1990.

———. *Diversity and Distrust: Civic Education in a Multicultural Democracy.* Cambridge: Harvard University Press, 2000.

———. "Homosexuality and the Conservative Mind." *Georgetown Law Journal* 84 (1995): 261–300.

MacIntyre, Alasdair. *After Virtue,* 2nd ed. Notre Dame, IN: University of Notre Dame Press, 1984.

Macpherson, C. B. *The Political Theory of Possessive Individualism: Hobbes to Locke.* Oxford: Clarendon Press, 1962.

Makinen, Virpi and Petter Korkman, eds. *Transformations in Medieval and Early-Modern Rights Discourse.* The Netherlands: Springer, 2006.

Mansfield, Harvey. "On the Political Character of Property in Locke." In *Powers, Possessions and Freedom: Essays in Honor of C. B. Macpherson.* Edited by A. Kontos. Toronto: Toronto University Press, 1979.

Martin, Rex. *A System of Rights.* Oxford: Clarendon Press, 1993.

McInerny, Ralph. "The Principles of Natural Law." *American Journal of Jurisprudence* 25 (1980): 1–15.

Menzel, Paul and Donald W. Light. "A Conservative Case for Universal Access to Health Care." *Hastings Center Report* 36, no. 4 (2006): 36–45, 37.

Mill, John Stuart. *On Liberty.* New York: Cambridge University Press, 1989.

Nederman, Cary. "Review of Brian Tierney, *The Idea of Natural Rights* and *Rights, Law and Infallibility in Medieval Thought.*" *American Journal of Legal History* 42 (1998): 217–19.

———. "Empire and the Historiography of European Political Thought: Marsiglio of Padua, Nicholas of Cusa, and the Medieval/Modern Divide." *Journal of the History of Ideas* 66 (2005).

Nicgorski, Walter. "Cicero and the Rebirth of Political Philosophy." *Political Science Reviewer* 8 (1978): 63–102.

———. "Cicero's Paradoxes and His Idea of Utility." *Political Theory* 12 (1984): 557–78.

Nozick, Robert. *Anarchy, State, and Utopia.* New York: Basic Books, 1974.

Nussbaum, Martha. *Creating Capabilities: The Human Development Approach.* Cambridge: Harvard University Press, 2011.

Oakley, Francis. *Natural Law, Laws of Nature, Natural Rights: Continuity and Discontinuity in the History of Ideas.* New York: Continuum, 2005.

Pangle, Thomas. *The Spirit of Modern Republicanism: The Moral Vision of the American Founders and the Philosophy of Locke*. Chicago: University of Chicago Press, 1988.

Pinello, Daniel R. *America's Struggle for Same-Sex Marriage*. New York: Cambridge University Press, 2006.

Poveda, Tony G. "American Exceptionalism and the Death Penalty." *Social Justice* 27, no. 2 (2000): 252–67.

Pufendorf, Samuel. *Elementorum Jurisprudentiae Universalis Libri Duo* (1660). Classics of International Law 15. Edited by James Brown Scott. Vol. 1, Latin text, facsimile of 1672 edition. Vol. 2, English text, translated by W. A. Oldfather. Oxford, 1931.

———. *De Jure Naturae et Gentium Libri Octo* (1672). Classics of International Law 17. Edited by James Brown Scott. Vol. 1, Latin text, facsimile of 1688 edition. Vol. 2, English text, translated. by C. H. and W. A. Oldfather. Oxford, 1934.

Putnam, Robert D. and David E. Campbell. *American Grace: How Religion Divides and Unites Us*. New York: Simon and Schuster, 2010.

Rawls, John. *A Theory of Justice*. Cambridge: Harvard University Press, 1971.

———. "The Idea of Public Reason Revisited." *University of Chicago Law Review* 64, no. 3 (1997): 765–807.

Raz, Joseph. *The Morality of Freedom*. Oxford: Clarendon Press, 1986.

Richards, David A. J. *Women, Gays, and the Constitution: The Grounds for Feminism and Gay Rights in Culture and Law*. Chicago: University of Chicago Press, 1998.

———. *Identity and the Case for Gay Rights: Race, Gender, Religion as Analogies*. Chicago: University of Chicago Press, 1999.

Rimmerman, Craig A., and Clyde Wilcox, eds. *The Politics of Same-Sex Marriage*. Chicago: University of Chicago Press, 2007.

Sandel, Michael. *Liberalism and the Limits of Justice*, 2nd ed. New York: Cambridge University Press, 1998.

Sandhu, Puneet K. "A Legal Right to Health Care: What Can the United States Learn from Foreign Models of Health Rights Jurisprudence?" *California Law Review* 95, no. 4 (2007): 1151–92.

Schall, James V. "The Uniqueness of the Political Philosophy of Thomas Aquinas." *Perspectives on Political Science* 26 (1997): 85–92.

Seagrave, S. Adam. "Identity and Diversity in the History of Ideas: A Reply to Brian Tierney." *Journal of the History of Ideas* 73, no. 1 (2012): 163–66.

———. "Cicero, Aquinas, and Contemporary Issues in Natural Law Theory." *Review of Metaphysics* 62 (2009): 491–523.

———. "Civil Marriage: The View from a State of Nature." *Public Discourse*, September 19, 2012.

Sigmund, Paul E. *Natural Law in Political Thought*. New York: University Press of America, 1971.

———. "Jeremy Waldron and the Religious Turn in Locke Scholarship." *Review of Politics* 67 (2005): 407–18.

Simmons, A. John. *The Lockean Theory of Rights*. Princeton: Princeton University Press, 1992.

———. "Locke on the Death Penalty." *Philosophy* 69, no. 270 (1994): 471–77.

Singer, Peter. *Animal Liberation: A New Ethics for Our Treatment of Animals.* New York: Avon Publishers, 1976.

Stevenson, Michael R., and Markie Oliver. "Deconstructing Arguments against Same-Sex Marriage." In *Defending Same-Sex Marriage*, vol. 3. *The Freedom-to-Marry Movement: Education, Advocacy, Culture, and the Media.* Edited by Martin Dupuis and William A. Thompson. Westport, CT: Praeger, 2007.

Strasser, Mark. ed. *Defending Same-Sex Marriage.* 3 vols. Westport, CT: Praeger, 2007.

Strauss, Leo. *Natural Right and History.* Chicago: University of Chicago Press, 1953.

Strauss, Leo and Joseph Cropsey, eds. *History of Political Philosophy*, 3rd ed. Chicago: University of Chicago Press, 1987.

Suarez, Francisco. *Selections from Three Works: De Legibus, ac Deo Legislatore* (1612); *Defensio Fidei Catholicae et Apostolicae Adversus Anglicanae Sectae Erores* (1613); *Opus de Triplici Virtute Theologico: Fide, Spe, et Charitate* (1621). Classics of International Law 20. Edited by James Brown Scott. Vol. 1, Latin text, facsimiles from original editions. Vol. 2, English texts, translated by Gladys L. Williams, Ammi Brown, and John Waldron. Oxford, 1944.

Sunstein, Cass. "Incommensurability and Kinds of Valuation: Some Applications in Law." In *Incommensurability, Incomparability, and Practical Reason.* Edited by R. Chang. Cambridge: Harvard University Press, 1997.

Swanson, Scott. "The Medieval Foundations of John Locke's Theory of Natural Rights: Rights of Subsistence and the Principle of Extreme Necessity." *History of Political Thought* 18 (1997): 399–458.

Tadlock, Barry L., C. Ann Gordon and Elizabeth Popp. "Framing the Issue of Same-Sex Marriage: Traditional Values Versus Equal Rights." In *The Politics of Same-Sex Marriage*, edited by Craig A. Rimmerman and Clyde Wilcox. Chicago: University of Chicago Press, 2007.

Tatum, Dale C. *Genocide at the Dawn of the 21st Century.* New York: Palgrave Macmillan, 2010.

Taylor, Charles. "Atomism." In *Powers, Possessions and Freedom.* Edited by Alkis Kontos. Toronto: University of Toronto Press, 1979.

———. *Sources of the Self: The Making of the Modern Identity.* Cambridge: Harvard University Press, 1989.

Thomson, Judith Jarvis. "A Defense of Abortion." *Philosophy and Public Affairs* 1 (1971): 47–66.

Tierney, Brian. *The Idea of Natural Rights: Studies on Natural Rights, Natural Law and Church Law 1150–1625.* Atlanta: Scholars Press, 1997.

———. "Natural Law and Natural Rights: Old Problems and Recent Approaches." *Review of Politics* 64 (2002): 389–406.

———. "Historical Roots of Modern Rights: Before Locke and After." *Ave Maria Law Review* 3 (2005): 23–43.

———. "Dominion of Self and Natural Rights Before Locke and After." In *Transformations in Medieval and Early-Modern Rights Discourse.* Edited by Virpi Mäkinen and Petter Korkman. New York: Springer, New Synthese Historical Library, 2005

Tuck, Richard. "Review: *Natural Law and Natural Rights*, by John Finnis." *Philosophical Quarterly* 31 (1981): 282–84.

———. *Natural Rights Theories: Their Origin and Development.* Cambridge University Press, 1979.

Tully, James. *A Discourse on Property: John Locke and His Adversaries.* Cambridge University Press, 1980.

———. *An Approach to Political Philosophy: Locke in Contexts.* New York: Cambridge University Press, 1993.

"Universal Access to Health Care." *Harvard Law Review* 108, no. 6 (1995): 1323–40.

van den Haag, E. "Justice, Deterrence, and the Death Penalty." In *America's Experiment with Capital Punishment.* Edited by J. R. Acker, R. M. Bohm, and C. S. Lanier. Durham, NC: Carolina Academic Press, 1998.

Veatch, Henry, and Joseph Rautenberg. "Does the Grisez-Finnis-Boyle Moral Philosophy Rest on a Mistake?" *Review of Metaphysics* 44 (1991): 807–30.

Villey, Michel. *La Formation de la Pensee Juridique Modern,* 4th ed. Paris, 1975.

Waldron, Jeremy. *God, Locke, and Equality: Christian Foundations of John Locke's Political Thought.* New York: Cambridge University Press, 2002.

———. "A Right to Do Wrong." *Ethics* 92 (1981): 21–39.

Ward, Lee. *John Locke and Modern Life.* New York: Cambridge University Press, 2010.

Weinreb, Lloyd L. *Natural Law and Justice.* Cambridge: Harvard University Press, 1987.

Weinrib, E. J. "Corrective Justice." *Iowa Law Review* 77 (1992): 403–25.

Wolfe, Christopher. *Natural Law Liberalism.* Cambridge University Press, 2006.

Wolterstorff, Nicholas. "An Engagement with Rorty." *Journal of Religious Ethics* 31, no. 1 (2003): 129–39.

Zuckert, Michael. *Natural Rights and the New Republicanism.* Princeton: Princeton University Press, 1994.

———. *Launching Liberalism: On Lockean Political Philosophy.* Lawrence: University Press of Kansas, 2002.

———. "The Fullness of Being: Thomas Aquinas and the Modern Critique of Natural Law." *Review of Politics* 69 (2007): 28–47.

———. "On Constitutional Welfare Liberalism: An Old-Liberal Perspective." In *Liberalism: Old and New.* Edited by Ellen Frankel Paul, Fred D. Miller, Jr. and Jeffrey Paul. Cambridge University Press, 2007.

INDEX

Anderson, Ryan T., 152n24
anti-foundationalist, 4, 22, 148
Aquinas, St. Thomas, 17, 23, 92–93, 97n, 112, 114, 117, 118n42, 119, 131–32, 149, 161; and classic natural right, 14; and Finnis, 9; and Grotius, 28; and Locke, 20–21, 24, 31, 33, 36; natural law theory, 99–109; and Spanish Thomists, 13, 25–26; and Zuckert, 18, 123
Aristotle, 18, 56, 67n, 119, 131; and actuality of capacity for reflection, 66; and Aquinas, 102–104, 105n, 108n109, 109; and the beginning of the *Politics*, 26–27; and Cicero, 99; and classic natural right, 14; and the death penalty, 156n32; and the definition of nature, 111; and humanity/unique selfhood distinction, 89; and human nature, 110; and induction, 116; and intellectual history, 161; and justice, 137–38; and the natural law tradition, 93, 96–98; and natural morality, 3; and New Natural Law theory, 114; and the second ordering fact, 90–92
Ashcraft, Richard, 47n108
autonomy, 83–85, 143. *See also* self-direction

Barber, Sotirios A., 57n3
Beccaria, Cesare, 159
Brake, Elizabeth, 152n25

Campbell, David E., 4n6
Cicero, 14, 23, 26, 112, 119, 131n21, 161; and Aquinas, 101–3, 106–7, 109; and Aristotle, 96–99; natural law theory, 92–95
communitarian, 17–18, 62, 130

concurrent univocal ownership, 43, 50. *See also* concurrent univocal property
concurrent univocal property, 39, 50, 52, 76
continuity-compatibility position, 5, 7–17, 18n50, 19–21, 25, 120, 124
Copernicus, Nicolaus, 161
Corvino, John, 148n13, 152n23
Crosson, Frederick, 96n35

death penalty, 142, 155, 157–59
Descartes, René, 64n, 89
dignity, human, 1, 9, 84, 86, 130
discontinuity-compatibility position, 21–23, 25, 131
discontinuity-incompatibility position, 14–16, 18, 20, 25
divine law, 28, 73
Divine ownership, 22, 32, 40, 42–43, 51–52, 54, 134, 138
Divine workmanship, 31, 35–38, 47, 49–50, 53, 75
Dunn, John, 24, 32n34, 36n64
Dworkin, Ronald, 18n50, 81n46

Essay Concerning Human Understanding, 34, 37–39, 42–43, 48–49, 54–55, 63n20, 67, 75, 77
eternal law, 100, 106–8, 150

Feinberg, Joel, 58
Filmer, Robert, 41, 44n96, 45
Finnis, John, 1, 5n, 8–9, 11–13, 16, 19, 57n4, 95n32, 113, 115n126, 115n128, 116n131, 120n2, 121–24, 130n19, 133
First Treatise on Government, 41, 44n96, 45–46

INDEX

Fortin, Ernest, 16–17, 19–20, 95n34, 96n, 109, 110n115, 122
foundationalist, 22

Gallagher, Maggie, 148n13, 152n24
George, Robert, 5n, 95n32, 113–15, 152n24
Gewirth, Alan, 57n4, 58n7, 84
Girgis, Sherif, 152n24
Glendon, Mary Ann, 4n7, 17, 57n1
Goerner, E. A., 110n116
Grisez, Germain, 1, 114
Grotius, Hugo, 25, 27–30, 32, 36, 112

Haakonssen, Knud, 28
Hart, H. L. A., 11
health care, 142–48, 151
Hobbes, Thomas, 2, 3, 15, 17–25, 29–30, 54, 57, 60n10, 67, 75, 84, 121–22, 124, 132, 158, 161; and Locke, 31–33
Hooker, Richard, 20, 24, 28, 31–32; and Grotius, 29; and Locke, 26–27
Horwitz, Robert, 36
human being, 51–52, 68, 70, 88–89, 108, 119, 134–36
humanity, 21, 51, 54, 76, 84–86, 88–91, 93–100, 103, 107–9, 116–17, 119, 128, 134; as legislator of natural law, 110–13; in Locke, 48–49
human nature, 27, 68, 91–92; and Aquinas, 101–3, 107–9; and Aristotle, 97, 99; and Cicero, 93–95; and Finnis, 9; as legislator of natural law, 110–13; and Locke, 55; and Maritain, 6–7; and New Natural Law theory, 115–17; 118–19, 131–32
human rights, 57, 60n11, 120n1, 126
human workmanship, 48–51, 78
Hutcheson, Francis, 130

induction, 108–9, 116–17
is-ought distinction, 59–60, 72, 114–15, 118

Jefferson, Thomas, 140
Jordan, Michael, 91

Kant, Immanuel, 84

labor, 70, 78–80
Las Casas, Bartolomé de, 25
Laslett, Peter, 33
Launching Liberalism, 18nn50–51, 24n2, 57n4, 58n5, 83n3, 120n3, 123, 139n

law of nations, 112–13
law of nature, 43, 47, 53, 90. *See* natural law
liberalism, 12–13, 18n50, 19, 32, 92, 122–3, 148, 160; and New Natural Law theory, 118
Locke, John, 1, 15, 18, 19–23, 24, 60n10, 63n20, 67, 69–70, 73, 76–79, 85, 90–91, 92n, 112, 117, 119, 121, 123–24, 132, 134, 138, 140, 157, 161; and Aquinas, 31, 33, 36; on concurrent univocal ownership, 40–44, 50; and the death penalty, 158–59; and discontinuity-compatibility position, 30–31; on Divine ownership, 31, 35, 44, 47; and executive power of the law of nature, 28; on God, 36–39, 42, 44, 48, 51, 128; and Grotius, 32, 36; and Hobbes, 31–33; and Hooker, 26–27; on humanity and human nature, 48–49, 55; and intellectual history, 25–31; on labor, 45, 50; on natural law, 30–37, 47, 52–55; on natural rights, 30–37, 46–47, 52–55, 57, 82; and "nesting" property, 51, 54; on property ownership, 46–47, 50; and Pufendorf, 29–30, 32; and right of revolution, 35; and right to life, 67; on the self, 48, 61–62; on self-consciousness and unique selfhood, 48–50; on self-ownership, 31–32, 35, 37, 44, 47, 50, 53, 56; on self-preservation, 75; and Spanish Thomists, 32–33; state of nature, 33, 52; and Tierney, 24
Loving v. Virginia, 150

Macedo, Stephen, 83n1, 152n23
Machiavelli, Niccolò, 161
MacIntyre, Alasdair, 4n8, 17, 18n50
Macpherson, C. B., 24, 32n40
man, 48–49, 67–68
Mansfield, Harvey, 24
Maritain, Jacques, 1–4, 7–10, 13–15, 17–18, 21, 130, 148, 150n17
Mill, J. S., 83–84, 121, 161
Moore, G. E., 58n6

naturalistic fallacy, 58–60, 95
natural law, 60, 73, 112, 120, 125–27, 129–31, 133–34, 136–39, 141: and Aquinas, 100–101, 106–9, 113, 123, 140; and Aristotle, 99, 101; Christian, 19, 22; and Cicero, 93–98, 99, 101; compatibility with natural rights, 3; and continuity-compatibility position, 121–22, 124; and the death pen-

alty, 156, 158, 160; and executive power of punishment, 28, 158; as foundation for natural rights, 6–7, 9, 13; and God, 27–29, 128; and Grotius, 27; and health care, 143, 145, 147; and Hobbes, 29, 54; and Hooker, 27; and incompatibility with natural rights, 16, 19–20; and intellectual history, 25, 160–62; as a law, 110–12; and the law of nations, 113; and Locke, 30–37, 47, 52–55, 158; medieval, 132; and New Natural Law theory, 95, 108, 113, 116–18; "old," 92, 99, 109, 119, 135; permissive, 10, 26, 31, 33, 51, 59; and Pufendorf, 30; relationship with natural rights, 2, 5, 8, 14, 16, 18, 20; as resistance doctrine, 35; and same-sex marriage, 149, 151; and second ordering fact, 91–93

Natural Law and Natural Rights, 8–9, 13n35, 16, 57n4, 114, 115n126, 115nn128–29, 116n131, 120n2, 121, 130n19, 141

natural morality, 3, 17, 22–23, 92, 119–20, 128, 131–33, 137, 140–42: and the death penalty, 155, 159–60; and health care, 147; and intellectual history, 160–62; and intersubjective two-sidedness, 136, 138; and same-sex marriage, 148–51, 153–55

natural right(s), 57, 83, 86, 88, 119–20, 123, 126–28, 133–34, 138, 141: and Aquinas, 9, 124; benefit, 142–45, 147, 154; classic, 14, 98, 110, 131–32; compatibility with natural law, 3; and continuity-compatibility position, 121–22, 124; and the death penalty, 155–56, 158–60; definition, 73; as derived from natural law, 6–7, 9, 13; and Grotius, 27–28; and health care, 142n; and Hobbes, 29, 54, 57; and human dignity, 9; incompatibility with natural law, 16, 19–20; and intellectual history, 12, 25, 160–62; language of, 8, 11, 17; to liberty, 77, 79, 81, 125, 128, 130, 135, 139, 142–45, 147, 154; to life, 74–77, 81, 143–44, 155–60; and Locke, 30–37, 46–47, 52–55, 57, 82; to marry, 150–51, 154; modern, 15; and natural morality, 92; and ordering facts, 73; order of priority, 81–82; and politics, 139; to property, 78–82, 144, 146; and Pufendorf, 30; relationship with natural law, 1–2, 5, 8, 14, 16, 18, 20; and self-direction, 85; and self-ownership, 32, 73; to self-preservation, 76, 78; and Spanish Thomists, 25–26; and true propositions of practical relevance, 130, 136, 139–40, 146–47, 157, 159; and the *UDHR*, 5

Natural Right and History, 14–15, 17n47, 54n134

Nederman, Cary, 12n31

New Natural Law, 1, 5, 113–15, 117–18, 130

Nicgorski, Walter, 94n28

Nicomachean Ethics, 90, 97, 99n50, 102, 105nn94–95, 114, 137, 156n31

Nozick, Robert, 79–80, 83n3

Nussbaum, Martha, 143n6

Oakley, Francis, 11–13

ordering fact, 72–74, 114, 117, 124–25, 127, 135–36, 138, 141, 148, 161; first, 23, 73–74, 78, 84–88, 145; second, 23, 90–93, 95, 109–10, 112, 119

ownership, 70, 78, 87: of actions, 49; concurrent univocal, 39–44, 50, 52, 76; Divine, 22, 31, 40, 42–44, 47, 51–52, 54, 134, 138; human, 42; and labor, 79; natural, 88; and "nesting property," 52; self-, 19–20, 22–23, 26, 31–32, 35–37, 40, 43, 47, 51–54, 67, 69, 71–76, 80–81, 86–87, 91, 124–26, 134–36, 139, 145, 151, 156

Pangle, Thomas, 24n2

person, 48–49, 51, 53

Plato, 3, 14, 89–91, 110, 131n21, 161

property: exclusive, 42, 45, 47–50, 69, 75; inclusive, 42, 44–45; "nesting," 50–52, 134; vs. possession, 47n109. *See also* ownership

Ptolemy, 161

Pufendorf, Samuel Von, 25, 29–30, 32

Putnam, Robert, 4n6

Questions Concerning the Law of Nature, 30, 33, 34n52, 36–40, 42, 44, 47, 49, 54, 92n, 128

Rawls, John, 3n5, 61n12, 118, 121, 126, 149, 161

Raz, Joseph, 83n1, 157n33

reason, 3–4, 93–98, 103–6, 108–9, 116, 119, 124, 129–30, 137, 148, 150; practical, 101, 104–5, 109, 115, 117; speculative, 101, 104, 107, 115

reflective capacity, 63, 68–70, 74, 86–88, 91, 109

Richards, David A. J., 149n16, 150n20, 154
rights: as claims, 58; human, 57, 60n11, 120, 126; negative / liberty vs. positive / benefit, 57, 151; proto-, 81n45; strict vs. loose, 59–60; talk, 60, 140, 148. *See also* natural right(s)
Rorty, Richard, 3n5

same-sex marriage, 4n6, 142, 148–55
Sandel, Michael, 17, 61n12, 61n15
Seagrave, S. Adam, 3n4, 93n16, 151n22, 152n24
Second Treatise on Government, 35, 38–39, 41, 43, 44–46, 48–50, 52–53, 138, 158
self, the, 17, 49, 51, 53, 63, 81, 85, 87; actual, 67–74, 76–77, 85–90, 92, 111, 135–136; in Locke, 48, 61–62; potential, 67–74, 77–80, 85–91, 135–36; and reflective capacity, 66n23; and self-consciousness, 61
self-consciousness, 23, 51, 55–56, 61, 67, 73–74, 76, 78, 81–82, 85–87, 89, 91–92, 95–96, 110–12, 124–27, 136, 151; as basic self-awareness, 62; and Cicero, 93; in Locke, 21, 48–49; and natural law, 109–12; and self-awareness, 62; and introspection, 65–66; and labor, 79–80; in Locke, 43, 49–50; and the natural right to property, 79–80; as reflective activity, 62–64, 66, 71, 77
self-direction, 83–86, 130, 133, 135
self-ownership, 19–20, 22–23, 32, 40, 51–52, 54, 67, 69, 71–72, 74–76, 80–81, 86–87, 91, 124–27, 130, 134–36, 139, 145, 151, 156; as foundational natural right, 73; and labor, 79; in Locke, 30–32, 35, 37, 44, 47, 50, 53, 56; and the natural right to property, 79; and self-direction, 83–85; and the Spanish Thomists, 26
self-preservation, 15, 33, 44, 74–76, 78, 93
Sigmund, Paul E., 24n2
Simmons, A. John, 35n60
Singer, Peter, 126n
Socrates, 14, 90, 105
Solzhenitsyn, Aleksandr, 133n
Spanish Thomists, 25–26, 59, 123, 132; and Grotius, 28; and Locke, 32–33
state of nature, 33, 52, 54n134, 75, 158–59
Strauss, Leo, 1–4, 14–16, 17n47, 18–21, 24, 32nn37–38, 54, 141, 148
Suarez, Francisco, 9, 17, 25, 27–28, 132; and Grotius, 29

substance, 48–50, 67–68, 85
Summa Theologica, 92n, 99–101, 104, 106, 108nn109–12
Sunstein, Cass, 157n33

Taylor, Charles, 17, 61nn12–14, 62, 63n19, 86n10, 88
Tierney, Brian, 3n4, 5n, 9–13, 32n36, 40, 42, 44–45, 59, 112n121, 120n2, 121–24, 132n, 133; on Grotius, 27–28; on Hobbes, 29; on Locke, 24, 31n33
true propositions of practical relevance, 129–31, 139–40, 146, 149, 151, 153
Tuck, Richard, 11, 13, 27–28; on Hobbes, 29
Tully, James, 31nn31–32, 32n35, 32n41, 36n62, 41–42, 44–45, 47, 49, 78
Two Treatises of Government, 34n55, 34n57, 37, 42, 49, 75. *See also First Treatise on Government*; *Second Treatise on Government*

unique selfhood, 50–52, 54–56, 117, 119, 128, 134–36; and Cicero, 93; in Locke, 21, 48–49; and natural law, 109–12; and second ordering fact, 84–86, 88–91; and workmanship, 53
Universal Declaration of Human Rights, 5, 8

Veatch, Henry, 114
virtue, 15, 94, 97, 102, 104–5, 131, 137–38
Vitoria, Francisco de, 25–26

Waldron, Jeremy, 24n2, 31n31, 125n
Ward, Lee, 24n2
Wolfe, Christopher, 5, 12, 120n2, 121–24, 133
Wolterstorff, Nicholas, 3n5
"workmanship argument," 31, 37–39, 42–44, 47, 52

Zuckert, Michael, 1n, 5n, 24n2, 26n4, 26n7, 30nn26–28, 32nn38–39, 33n49, 36n63, 37n65, 57nn2–4, 58n5, 81n45, 83n2, 112n120, 113n122, 118n134, 120n3, 137n, 139n, 142n4, 144n10; and critique of continuity-compatibility position, 123–24; and discontinuity-incompatibility position, 18–20; on Grotius, 27–28; and natural right to property, 78–79

www.ingramcontent.com/pod-product-compliance
Lightning Source LLC
Chambersburg PA
CBHW051359290426
44108CB00015B/2086